The Postmedia Effect

Also by Marc Edge

Pacific Press: The Unauthorized Story of Vancouver's Newspaper Monopoly (2001)

Red Line, Blue Line, Bottom Line (2004)

Asper Nation: Canada's Most Dangerous Media Company (2007)

Greatly Exaggerated: The Myth of the Death of Newspapers (2014)

The News We Deserve: The Transformation of Canada's Media Landscape (2016)

Re-Examining the UK Newspaper Industry (2023)

THE POSTMEDIA EFFECT

How Vulture Capitalism is Wrecking Our News

NEW STAR BOOKS LTD
No. 107–3477 Commercial St
Vancouver, BC V5N 4E8 CANADA
1574 Gulf Road, No. 1517
Point Roberts, WA 98281 USA
newstarbooks.com . info@newstarbooks.com

Copyright Marc Edge 2023. All rights reserved. No part of this work may be reproduced, stored in a retrieval system or transmitted, in any form or by any means, without the prior written consent of the publisher or a licence from Access Copyright. The publisher acknowledges the financial support of the Canada Council for the Arts, the British Columbia Arts Council, and the Government of Canada.
Nous reconnaissons l'appui financier du gouvernement du Canada.

Cataloguing information for this book is available from Library and Archives Canada, www.collectionscanada.gc.ca.
isbn: 978-1-55420-197-6

Cover design by Oliver McPartlin
Typeset by New Star Books
Printed and bound in Canada by Imprimerie Gauvin, Gatineau, QC
First printing April 2023

To Maggie May, who tried to fix Canada's news media.
Wake up Maggie, I think I've got something to say to you.

CONTENTS

Foreword   IX
Preface   XII
   1. A question of control   1
   2. The road to financialization   31
   3. The bailout campaign   53
   4. Project Ice   79
   5. A certain sameness   107
   6. Shaking down Big Tech   139
   7. A perfect marriage   167
   8. The tipping point   199
Endnotes   207
Bibliography   257
Index   265

FOREWORD
BY ALEXANDRA KITTY

Finding the truth in a sea of lies is a difficult undertaking, and requires skill, persistence, honesty, and intellectual independence. Without information, we have no idea of the true state of reality. Over the decades, civilians entrusted journalists to find out for them; unfortunately, the arrangement didn't work out as planned for one important reason: the mechanics of media ownership do not align with the mechanics of gathering news, and owners trump those who work for them. In a pre-Penny Press era, news outlets were brazenly partisan because lofty government patronage appointments were given if the outlet could malign opponents and exalt their sides effectively.

Eventually, the rewards for such manipulative arrangements didn't work out, and then journalistic objectivity became the replacement business model for attracting news audiences, and it was held as the Gold Standard for a few decades until social media supplanted legacy media: by allowing regular citizens the ability to communicate with the world without the journalist middleman, the discipline lost its way when it failed to adequately re-invent itself. Instead, the profession began to go back to its more partisan roots, and raw data and facts were eclipsed by opinion and outright propaganda.

For journalists, this slide back into the past began to decimate their credibility and clout, but for media owners who always saw their product as a widget to make money, they cracked down on their rank and file and found ways to turn a profit by hook or by crook: from selling prime real estate where their once majestic newsrooms occupied, churning out advertorials paid for by the very people and groups who were being extolled, to cajoling the governments they were meant to scrutinize and expose into giving media outlets tens of millions of dollars. The robber barons found increasingly dubious ways of funding their lifestyles, but at the expense of journalism itself.

Yet journalists still lament and blame the public for no longer buying the hype of the noble reporter. The lack of self-awareness is apparent as is the profession's inability to regain ground and trust. When news reports perfectly align with what works for the outlet's robber barons, those who are struggling or have different life requirements walk away, yet nothing has changed in the profession. No mea culpa, and no revolutionary break from those shackles.

Perhaps the most obvious example of this intellectual void is the journalistic output of Postmedia properties. Heavy on opinion, but light in factual reporting, much of what it offers is adherence to partisan worship. Here, there is no pretence of muckraking or turning over every rock.

When Toronto mayor John Tory abruptly resigned from office after admitting to an affair with one of his underlings, one *National Post* columnist made a shocking admission in his February 10, 2023 article:

> Chaos merchants like Tory's predecessor, Rob Ford, don't come along every day. But it did at least have the virtue of believability. If there was one thing we could be sure of about Tory, it's that City Hall journalists would get their Friday nights back.[1]

That journalists don't bother to work overtime looking for corruption because the current mayor looks respectable is telling. There is corruption and incompetence around the clock, and a vigilant journalist will push past the boundaries of time to expose it. Any j-school student who spends an hour at city hall will know from witnessing first-hand or hearing the gossip of various affairs and outright shenanigans, but here, the *Post* will never make any previous mention of Tory's antics that ran counter to his image of

---

1. Chris Selley, "John Tory's political career ends in the stupidest way imaginable," *National Post*, February 10, 2023. URL: https://nationalpost.com/opinion/chris-selley-john-torys-political-career-ends-in-the-stupidest-way-imaginable.

serious businessman with a long and seemingly enviable marriage. Yet the column made another troubling admission:

> Many other Canadian politicians must be lying awake at night looking at the ceiling, wondering if the Canadian media's traditional hands-off approach to their personal lives is still in effect.

Honey traps, nepotism, and conflicts of interest were *hands off* according to the *Post*. Reporting on a politician who recently was given strong mayor powers and ruled over Canada's largest city was supposed to be given a *pass*. The affair wasn't a mere lapse or even just an abuse of power: the timing of the revelation or even the identity of the former underling was never disclosed; so people would have no idea of the long-term consequences or the motives of the tryst. But that was okay to give sketchy information because it was to protect someone in power. The message was clear: nothing to see here, even if independent outlets gave more information days later.

Yet even then, the columnist thought it was Tory's fault that more wasn't swept under the rug:

> Had he simply honoured his "two terms and I'm gone" pledge, the Star might well never even have run the story.

In other words, journalists don't bother informing their citizens of skulduggery out of deference to authority. The *National Post* had just said the quiet part out loud.

It is difficult to imagine a news outlet with columnists who see nothing wrong with withholding vital information from the public and helping present a false image to news consumers, yet Postmedia makes it a habit, meaning that everything you think you know is a lie and a distortion. It is not deference or sophistication which self-censors the legacy press, but the self-interest of their corporate overlords.

The opaque and serpentine vortex where journalists, robber barons, and governments work together to ensure stagnant predictability is made simpler when journalists choose to be stenographers. These are not wild jungle cats hunting and gathering information, but docile and trained circus animals made to seem tough and ferocious to the audience, but will merely snarl and pounce on cue by their owners to hide the bigger show behind the curtains, such as who is footing the bill for the act and why.

Postmedia is a classic case of hedge fund rule: news properties are acquired to squeeze assets without investing in the future of the outlet, and when there are no more assets to squeeze, both the private and public sectors are enticed to buy their coverage, if not for self-aggrandization, then for fear-mongering against a rival. When those games don't bring in enough to satisfy those robber barons, then lobby the various levels of government to give them millions of dollars, even as audiences turn away. Postmedia is the poster child for these games, and those looking for real news, will not find it here.

What you are about to read is a meticulous and thorough audit of these machinations with the kind of research that Canadian journalists should do, but don't. The results of Marc Edge's on-target audit of Postmedia are sobering, devastating, shocking, surreal, and maddening, but his gift is in presenting the facts empirically, rationally, and objectively without bombast or carny. That there are no over-the-top accusations or sensationalist speculations shows how far and wide the problems have become. He is the definitive chronicler of Canada's journalistic travails: always detailed and exhaustive, but never to harm, but to help improve the journalistic product.

Take a deep breath, leave your illusions behind, and fasten your seatbelt as you go down the twisted rabbit hole known as Postmedia. It will be a wild and eye-opening ride.

PREFACE

This is the third book in what turns out to be a trilogy. It began in 2001 with *Pacific Press: The Unauthorized Story of Vancouver's Newspaper Monopoly*, which was an updated version of my doctoral thesis in the E.W. Scripps School of Journalism at Ohio University. It focused on the 1957 partnership between the *Vancouver Sun* and *Province*, but as an academic history it had to end at least a decade in the past, so I chose as an ending point the *Sun*'s move to morning publication in 1991.

Five years after *Pacific Press* was published, the Southam newspaper chain was being badly mismanaged by Canwest Global Communications, which was owned by Winnipeg's Asper family. New Star publisher Rolf Maurer approached me about writing a sequel, which appeared in 2007 as *Asper Nation: Canada's Most Dangerous Media Company*. It advanced the story sixteen years from where I had been forced to leave it in *Pacific Press*, and by dealing with recent events it qualified less as a traditional academic history than as a work of contemporary history or even journalism.

The Postmedia Effect advances the story of what Canada's largest newspaper chain has gone through by another sixteen years. In that time, its ownership has gone from good to bad to simply appalling. The Southam family, which owned the *Province* when Rolf and I started there as cub reporters in the 1970s, were responsible owners who put journalism first and made a point of granting local autonomy to their publishers. Rolf got out of the newspaper business in 1979, but I hung on for sixteen years, by sheer coincidence. I was lucky enough to get out before the Aspers took over Southam, and I did so in part because I knew that things were going to get bad when I saw Conrad Black coming down the road.

Black changed journalism in Canada in two main ways. First, with his founding of the *National Post* in 1998 following his hostile takeover of Southam two years earlier, he made overt polit-

XIII

ical partisanship by newspapers acceptable again for the first time since the Party Press era in the 1890s. His neo-conservative initiative has since been extended to the Southam dailies, first clumsily by Canwest, and in recent years more successfully by Postmedia. Partisanship would be fine in a pluralist media system as was seen in the 19th century when newspapers proliferated and there was at least one for every point of view. It is less defensible in such a concentrated newspaper industry as we have now.

The other way Black changed journalism in Canada was to squeeze it financially by cutting costs mercilessly in order to produce enormous profits, as will be described in Chapter 2. These two trends, which unfortunately continue, are his dark legacy.

Some might dismiss the entire subject of this book as moot because they expect newspapers to go extinct within a few years. The financial viability of newspapers has been a major avenue of my research for the past decade and was the subject of my 2014 book *Greatly Exaggerated: The Myth of the Death of Newspapers*. It showed that despite an historic economic downturn and technological revolution that saw newspapers in the U.S. lose about half of their revenues in just a few years, and those in Canada about a quarter, no publicly-traded newspaper company recorded an annual loss on an operating basis from 2006-13. This was a result of their ability to quickly downsize, unfortunately by mostly laying off journalists. I concluded that newspapers will survive because they are highly scalable and are successfully rearranging their business model to rely less on advertising and more on reader revenues.

My most recent book on this subject, *Re-examining the UK Newspaper Industry*, was published last year by Routledge and shows that newspapers there are doing the best they have in years despite, or perhaps because of, not receiving a government bailout. As a result, I continue to believe that newspapers will transition successfully to hybrid digital publications which will likely continue to include a print component. This line of research will also be expanded on in Chapter 2.

I would like to thank Alexandra Kitty for her wonderful Foreword. The seed of this book was actually planted in 2018 when she interviewed me for a book she was considering writing on Postmedia, but never did, no doubt for lack of time. I was surprised that she had time to write this Foreword, given that she has written at least a dozen books herself since 2005. Her books on journalism have been a well-kept secret in her own country, however, as they have usually been published in the UK, like 2018's *When Journalism Was a Thing*, or in the U.S., like 2005's *Outfoxed*. Given the crying need for informed media criticism in Canada, I wish she would concentrate more of her efforts here.

Jesse Brown first pointed out the problem in his 2014 article "Nobody's a Critic" for *The Walrus*. "The Canadian media is insular, heavily concentrated in Toronto, and more of a club than an industry," he noted.[1] At least he has done something to help address the problem with Canadaland, the news website he publishes. Lawrence Martin put it succinctly in a 2022 *Globe and Mail* column. "Despite its exponential growth in importance," he pointed out, "the media industry gets only a small fraction of the scrutiny that other powerful institutions do."[2]

> Big issues go largely unexamined in Canadian media. We rarely take a critical look at the unfettered rise of advocacy journalism, the impact of the disappearance of local newspapers or media ownership monopolies. There are precious few media columnists in this country. There is no overarching media institute to address the problems.[3]

I would like to thank Harrison Samphir and Cy Gonick of *Canadian Dimension* for allowing me to be a media columnist since 2021 for their long-publishing bastion of critical thought, in which capacity I have done much of the research for this book. I would like to thank Chris Russill, past editor of the *Canadian Journal of Communication*, for accepting my 2020 and 2021 articles which also feature prominently in this work. The same should be said of Philippe Ross, editor of the *Canadian Journal of Media Studies*, for accepting my 2016 and 2018 articles on Canadian newspapers. Special thanks go to Bruce Livesey, Mark Bourrie, J-P Turcotte, and Marshall Soules for reading my first draft and providing their feedback on it, along with Bryan Carney and Kim Kierans for passing along certain documents in their possession. I am especially grateful to the Saskatchewan Arts Council for awarding me a 2022 Access

Copyright Foundation Marian Hebb research grant, which aided my literature review enormously. I would also like to thank the staff at my local branch of the Vancouver Island Regional Library for indulging my incessant requests for inter-library loans, renewals, and overdue returns. Finally, thanks to Rolf Maurer for taking such an interest in this book that he served not only as its publisher but also as its editor, along with his assistant Melissa Swann for all her hard work in its production.

Ladysmith, B.C.
March, 2023

CHAPTER 1
A QUESTION OF CONTROL

Paul Godfrey seated himself to testify. The wiry 77-year-old newspaper company executive had been called to account by the federal government for the latest devastation his chain had wreaked on Canada's news media. Hearings in Ottawa had convened quickly in 2016 after the company Godfrey headed, which owned most of the country's largest newspapers, merged its newsrooms in four of Canada's six largest cities where it published both dailies, despite promising not to.

Godfrey's promise had been spread across all political levels, from mayors right up to new federal Liberal leader Justin Trudeau, after Postmedia Network bought 175 newspapers in 2014 from Sun Media, the country's second-largest chain.[1] The resulting monopolies in Vancouver, Calgary, Edmonton, and Ottawa had been controversial from the outset, but Godfrey quickly allayed fears over the increased concentration of media ownership. "I attended two of his private dinners in fine Alberta restaurants where he vowed to keep the newsrooms separate," recalled Margo Goodhand, who was then editor of Postmedia's *Edmonton Journal*. "We might even have to reinvest in the Sun newsrooms, he mused aloud in Calgary… They'd be competitive, distinct, and entirely independent, he said."[2]

The 2016 merger of newsrooms and the layoff of 90 journalists by Postmedia was just the latest disaster in the slow-moving train wreck that was the newspaper crisis. Following years of layoffs and a few closures following the 2008-09 recession, local journalism in Canada had taken a beating. The cutbacks to news reporting were worst at Postmedia newspapers, however, because it was 92 percent owned by U.S. hedge funds that were skimming off most of its earnings as interest payments on the massive debt they also held. MPs wanted to know what was going on.

Dressed in a blue suit and wearing reading glasses under his deeply-furrowed brow and combed-back, graying hair, Godfrey audaciously started with a sales pitch to the Heritage committee in his opening statement. "Come back and advertise in our newspapers and on our websites," he pleaded. "Ad budgets have been cut, and the cuts from the Government of Canada have disproportionately been to newspapers."[3] Television's share of the federal ad spend, he noted, had increased from 48 percent to 54 percent, while that devoted to online media, much of which was foreign-owned, had almost doubled. Print advertising had been cut in half to only 8.5 percent. The Heritage ministry was the worst offender, he told its standing committee, as while it had spent $6 million on advertising that year, none went to print. "If you're going to advertise, then you should give some consideration to Canadian publications."[4]

Liberal MP Adam Vaughan then began to grill Godfrey. They had crossed swords a few years earlier, when Vaughan was a Toronto city councillor and Godfrey was chair of the Ontario Lottery and Gaming Corporation with grandiose plans for a mega-casino on the downtown waterfront.[5] Vaughan had won that encounter, as Godfrey was fired by incoming premier Kathleen Wynne.[6]

"Postmedia's largest shareholder is a U.S. hedge fund named GoldenTree Asset Management," Vaughan pointed out to Godfrey. "Why would we fund a failing business model that's owned by U.S. interests?"[7]

"Your facts aren't correct," Godfey shot back. "The fact is that this company is controlled by Canadians."[8] It was a convenient fiction that Godfrey relied on, enabled by a loophole that lawyers had found in Canada's 25-percent limit on foreign ownership of newspapers. To accept the separation of ownership and control as meaningful, however, required an almost complete suspension of disbelief. The *Globe and Mail* had already reported in 2014 that Godfrey conferred with Postmedia's foreign owners frequently and that the hedge funds had pushed for the acquisition of Sun Media. "Paul doesn't make major moves without calling them first," it quoted an anonymous source close to the company as saying.[9]

Vaughan attempted a weak comeback, having obviously not done his homework. "That being said, why would we bail out a U.S.-indebted company?"[10] Godfrey took a bit of poetic licence to evade that one. "You're not bailing out a U.S. company," he replied. "You can be critical of GoldenTree Asset Management, but I'll tell you that you're barking up the wrong tree."[11]

Then Godfrey went on the offensive again, pointing out the recent closures of the *Guelph Mercury* and *Nanaimo Daily News* as proof of the newspaper industry's decline. "If it continues to follow the trend it's on, you won't be sitting here and talking about whether there should be subsidies or not," he told Vaughan. "You'll be talking about how we are going to continue to create a group of journalists producing content for Canadians... If you think that's not going to happen within the next three years, you're going to find that there will be a lot more closings."[12]

Godfrey repeated his threat later in the hearing. "I'm not trying to paint an overly bleak picture," he insisted in response to MP questions. "I'm painting the picture that's out there."[13]

> I will tell you that within three years, there'll be many more closures in some of your own communities because of the state of the newspapers. You're our elected representatives. I commend you for even having this meeting. If you decide to do nothing, that's your call. I'm not trying to paint an uglier picture than what it is. It's ugly and will get uglier, based on the trends that exist today.[14]

Little could observers have known just how ugly things would get when Godfrey and the newspaper lobby he assembled didn't get the bailout they wanted, and it wouldn't take three years. It would only take half that long for things to get very ugly indeed in Canada's newspaper industry.

More pressing to Godfrey, however, was a time bomb that was ticking inside Postmedia's finances. To defuse it would take some fancy footwork that would raise the company's foreign ownership even higher. Few realized just how close Postmedia was to imploding. Standard & Poor's had downgraded its credit rating to triple-C-plus from single-B-minus in late 2015, calling its capital structure "unsustainable" and warning that the company could struggle to refinance its high-interest debt.[15] Making things worse was the fact that most of Postmedia's debt was in U.S. dollars, and a falling loonie meant that payments on the bonds that Postmedia had issued in 2011 had since risen in Canadian dollars by more than 30 percent. "With the Canadian dollar falling the way it's falling," Godfrey told the Canadian Press, "that's almost like a noose around your neck."[16]

GoldenTree was also unhappy, having watched Postmedia's advertising revenues continue to drop and the price of its shares fall to only 6 cents, which made its 58 percent stake in the company worth only about $9 million.[17] The hedge fund had hired an investment bank to drum up interest in ownership of Postmedia, the *Globe and Mail* had reported that March, and it had approached a half dozen potential buyers.[18]

The *Globe's* incisive Streetwise business column didn't like the hedge fund's chances of offloading its investment in Postmedia, however, mostly due to its ticking debt bomb, a restructuring of which risked wiping out much of GoldenTree's investment. Its reporters pressed Godfrey on whether the company could continue to meet its interest obligations. "So far, we haven't missed a payment," he replied. "Hopefully we won't miss a payment." Streetwise saw little hope for Postmedia, contacting several potential investors who said they had been approached but were not interested. "Postmedia appears to have little value to salvage," it added, "and what does exist will take a lot of heavy lifting to unearth, sources said."[19]

Created from bankruptcy

The newspaper crisis had literally created Postmedia, which in 2010 rose from the ashes of bankrupt Canwest Global Communications after it was caught holding the bag when the 2008-09 recession dropped advertising revenues sharply worldwide. The bag held $4 million in debt on which Canwest could no longer make the payments. GoldenTree was actually betting on it going bankrupt, as it had been buying up Canwest debt on the bond market at pennies on the dollar, and it acquired more than enough to take the company over.

Canwest and its owning Asper family of Winnipeg had bought the historic Southam newspaper chain in 2000 as part of the brief but disastrous enthusiasm for "convergence" of media ownership between print and TV. To get in on the trend that swept the country's media at the millennium, Canwest went deeply into debt to add newspapers to the Global Television network it had owned since the mid-1970s.[20] The Aspers quickly went from riding high at the millennium to being out of business less than a decade later.

The newly-formed Postmedia Network took over its newspapers and began to make massive layoffs, for which hedge fund owners were notorious. It cut most of the editing positions at its newspapers across the country by centralizing their production at a strip mall in Hamilton. Postmedia then paid $316 million in 2014 for Sun Media, which was Canada's second-largest newspaper chain. That gave it the tabloid *Edmonton Sun* in addition to the broadsheet *Journal* it already owned in Alberta's capital, along with a *Sun* just to the south in Calgary, where it also published the dominant *Herald*. In Ottawa, a *Sun* similarly shone in the shadow of the *Citizen*. Postmedia's plan in those cities, Godfrey had assured all concerned, was strictly a mechanical combination similar to that operating for decades at its dailies in Vancouver, seeking $6-10 million a year in cost savings through efficiencies in administration and production, but keeping separate newsrooms.[21]

The only problem was that the federal Competition Bureau had neglected to make the promise a condition of allowing the purchase. Soon Postmedia's required savings grew to $50 million as its advertising revenues continued to fall. Now the same stories and bylines were appearing in both local newspapers while scores more journalists were laid off to cut costs.

The little chain that grew

The Sun tabloids were near and dear to Godfrey, who had piloted the growing Sun chain for most of the 1990s. He broke into the newspaper business in 1984 as publisher of its flagship *Toronto Sun* straight from a career in local politics, where he served as a North York alderman for almost a decade starting in 1964 before going on to serve five terms as chairman of the now-defunct Metro Toronto conurbation.

He quickly rose through the corporate ranks, becoming president and chief operating officer of Toronto Sun Publishing Group in 1991, which was then owned by Rogers Communications, and CEO a year later. "By 1999, he had led a management buyout of the Sun's newspaper assets, taken that company public and arranged its sale to Quebecor," noted the *Globe and Mail*. "The end result essentially tripled the company's value and put an estimated $28-million into Mr. Godfrey's pocket."[22]

The "little newspaper that grew" proved that colourful tabloids could find an audience in cities dominated by a larger broadsheet. Competing dailies had been folding for decades across North America as mass media alternatives exploded, but in Canada the success of tabloid Suns bucked that trend. In Vancouver, there was already a *Sun* and it was a broadsheet, but its *Province* partner converted to tabloid format in 1983 to keep the Sun chain out, and the makeover proved wildly successful, making it especially popular with younger readers. Both Vancouver dailies were already owned by Postmedia, and had been operating since 1957 in a partnership that was ruled an illegal monopoly but allowed to continue on the basis of "economic necessity."[23]

Foreign ownership

GoldenTree Asset Management's majority ownership of Postmedia should not have been allowed under Canadian law, which limited foreign ownership in this culturally-sensitive industry to 25 percent, but decades of legal challenge to such limits had badly eroded them. Sharp lawyers found a loophole that did an end run around the law by forming a publicly-traded company with two classes of shares. Foreign owners were given stock that varied in voting power, which supposedly kept their "control" of the company under the allowable limit, even though their ownership well exceeded it.

GoldenTree reached out to Godfrey, who had headed a rival bid to acquire the newspaper chain out of bankruptcy, to run its new Canadian operation. It needed someone with not only some serious newspaper acumen, but also plenty of friends in high places, and Godfrey was without doubt the best possible candidate. *Torontoist* described him in 2015 as "a consummate networker and backroom operator, especially in local Conservative circles," but added that "his track record has sometimes raised questions regarding whose interests he works for."[24] Phil Lind, a Rogers executive who helped hire Godfrey to run the Toronto Blue Jays baseball team it owned, wrote in his 2018 memoirs that "few are better political operatives than Paul."[25]

The *Globe and Mail* described Godfrey as a "consummate strategist" in a 2014 profile. "Mr. Godfrey begins planning his next moves early each day during solitary walks along Toronto's Bay Street. His Labrador retriever nudges him awake around 5:30 a.m. and they set out from his home at the Four Seasons Private Residences."[26]

He had left the newspaper business in 2000 after brokering the $983-million sale of Sun Media to Quebecor, which gutted it with 300 layoffs. He was chair of the Ontario Lottery and Gaming Corporation when Canwest lured him back as president and CEO of its flagship *National Post* in 2009. Godfrey was already 71 by the time GoldenTree came calling the following year, asking him to head the whole chain, but he couldn't say no. Not with what they offered him.

"I've been a workaholic all my life, and I'm not slowing down," he told *Toronto Life* when he was 73. "I work out three times a week, which keeps me energized... I start by running six kilometres, then I'll do lateral lifts with 12-pound weights while standing on one foot on a Bosu ball. I'm stronger now than I was in my 40s."[27]

Competition Bureau failure

Postmedia's 2014 purchase of Sun Media raised concentration of newspaper ownership in Canada to among the highest in the world. The Competition Bureau had been a huge failure in preventing it, seemingly waving the white flag at every opportunity to enforce the country's anti-trust laws. Its gyrations in allowing Postmedia's acquisition of Sun Media, however, proved the height of absurdity.

Its economic analysis laughably concluded that the tabloids acquired from Sun Media didn't compete for advertising with the company's broadsheets. It cited one paper by an economist which concluded that newspaper monopolies in Canada didn't result in higher prices despite decades of studies worldwide which showed they did.[28] That had all gone down on Stephen Harper's watch as Conservative prime minister, however, as had Postmedia's foreign ownership. Many hoped the new Liberal government elected in late 2015 would do something to clean up the mess that Americans were making of our news media.

Long-time Vancouver Centre MP Hedy Fry was doing her best to try. She had been outraged by the merging of newsrooms in her town. Fry quickly convened hearings in Ottawa that February of the standing committee she chaired of the Department of Canadian Heritage. "I know that our government has a strong will to deal with this now," said Fry, then 74. "The thing about politics is that the time comes one day when stuff is facing you so hard that you have to do something about it. That time has come."[29]

The hearings would eventually result in a report that recommended changes to media regulation in Canada in order to bring ownership concentration under control. Unbeknownst to most, however, a parallel process was already underway which would ensure that another narrative dominated. The Heritage committee was supposed to tour the country that summer to hear from Canadians, but after the money proved unavailable in its budget, the field work had been contracted out to a so-called "think tank" in a study funded partly by Heritage and partly with corporate money.

Postmedia "a cancer"

The *Toronto Star* was Postmedia's — and Godfrey's — harshest critic for their decimation of Canada's largest dailies. It had blasted Postmedia earlier in 2016 as nothing less than "a cancer on Canadian journalism." The malignancy was created by "quick-buck hedge funds in the U.S.," railed the *Star*. The acquisition of Sun Media was a "thinly disguised foreign takeover" that resulted in "a far greater concentration of news media ownership than exists in any other major economy."[30]

From what *Star* business reporter David Olive could tell, there couldn't be much life left in Postmedia, which was fortunate. "As long as the biggest newspaper publisher in the country clings to life," he quipped, "it is a blight on all the communities it underserves." Postmedia was in "such wretched condition," he insisted, that it was surely "not long for this world." Postmedia was "flirting with insolvency," according to Olive, since its earnings continued to plummet in lockstep with its advertising, which was increasingly migrating to the Internet.[31]

The company had been so laden with debt held by its hedge fund owners that it couldn't possibly keep up the payments much longer due to its falling revenues, according to Olive. "Postmedia has installed a time bomb on its balance sheet of $672 million in debt owed to the U.S. hedge funds," he pointed out, and much of the debt had to be paid in mere months. "It's very difficult to see where Postmedia will get the money to do this," Olive continued. "The interest payments have become downright asphyxiating."[32]

Of the $82 million in operating earnings that Postmedia would generate that fiscal year, fully $72 million would go to servicing its debt, meaning that its profits went mostly to its bondholders rather than its shareholders.

Olive had calculated for an article the year before that they had already extracted close to $340 million in interest payments from Postmedia in their first four years of ownership. "The real story is that a Postmedia, leveraged to the hilt, can still generate just enough cash to further enrich Postmedia's mostly US absentee owners," he wrote. "In the looking-glass world of financial engineering, you can profit handsomely from an asset of steadily declining value. That is, from picking the carcass clean."[33]

To keep its head above water while carrying such a crushing debt, Olive noted, Postmedia had already laid off more than half of its employees, "which means that countless news stories are no longer reported." There couldn't be much more left to cut. He pointed to rumours that Postmedia was on "a deliberate path to self-destruction," as a second bankruptcy might allow its hedge fund owners to "get their hands on a bankrupt Postmedia's real estate and other assets at fire-sale prices."[34]

Olive noted that Postmedia had been lobbying Ottawa for a relaxation of media ownership rules because "some of the deepest-pocketed bidders on a bankrupt Postmedia's assets are likely to be foreigners."[35] Little could Olive have guessed that not only would Postmedia keep hanging on for years, but that soon his own newspaper would be taken over by the same type of financial wizards.

Political partisanship

What rankled many wasn't so much the news that Postmedia was cutting from the pages of Canada's largest newspapers, but what it was replacing it with. Under Godfrey, who had been a long-time Conservative politician, the newspapers had seemingly turned into an unabashed mouthpiece for the Conservative Party.

Many of Postmedia's largest dailies carried full-page ads across their covers on the eve of the 2015 federal election headlined "Voting Liberal will cost you" or, depending on the riding, "Voting NDP or Liberal will cost you." Editors were ordered to endorse Conservative candidates, contrary to long-standing practice at the Southam newspapers. The *National Post's* editorial pages editor, Andrew Coyne, resigned after his column endorsing another party was killed, or "spiked" in newspaper parlance.[36] The blog Torontoist cruelly nominated Godfrey for its 2015 Supervillain of the year award over the embarrassing partisanship.

> His ham-fisted support of the Conservatives during the federal election campaign made a laughingstock of the country's largest newspaper for the Tories regardless of the opinions of local editorial staff... Reeking of desperation, the front page of the chain's papers bore a Tory attack ad during the final weekend of the campaign. Readers and employees were disgusted, while the competition... had a field day attacking Godfrey's disregard for freedom of the press.[37]

The outrage spread internationally, with the U.S.-based Poynter Institute calling it "the ugliest political episode in Canada's postwar era," adding: "The stain of this shameful moment in Canadian journalism will never wash completely clean."[38] British newspaper *The Guardian* pointed out that the political partisanship made a mockery of promises Postmedia had made to the Competition Bureau to uphold editorial diversity among its acquired Sun newspapers. "In seeking permission for the takeover, Postmedia assured the regulator that its newspapers would pursue independent editorial policies. Mere months later they were predictably backing Harper's Conservatives."[39]

Petroleum propaganda

And it wasn't just politics. Postmedia had been literally selling its support for Canada's controversial energy policies, according to documents unearthed by investigative online journalists. The Vancouver-based *Observer*, which would soon expand nationally, came across a 2014 corporate presentation in which Postmedia promised to promote whatever policies the Canadian Association of Oil Producers wanted.

"With images of pipelines in the background, the presentation went on to explain how it would link Postmedia's sponsored energy content with CAPP's 'thought leadership' and stimulate conversations on social media," noted the *Observer*.[40] To environmentalists, this helped to explain the growing amount of pro-oil propaganda appearing on the pages of Postmedia newspapers, whose opinion sections became a haven for climate change deniers. Academic studies found the bias palpable. "Postmedia has a record of publishing climate science rejectionists and pumping up the oil and gas industry on its comment pages," noted one.[41]

This kind of sponsored content, which was also known as branded content or native advertising, blurred the line between editorial and advertising, and research showed that most readers couldn't tell the difference. It was a growing revenue stream for websites and even some newspapers, however, and Postmedia wanted in on the bonanza.

Million-dollar bonuses

Then there was the rich pay package Godfrey commanded for transforming Canada's largest newspaper chain into an ever-larger foreign-owned vehicle for corporate and political propaganda. Postmedia had given Godfrey a $400,000 bonus in 2015 for stick-handling the Sun Media acquisition, plus other bonuses on top of his base salary of $950,000 that brought his annual compensation to $1.76 million, up from $1.42 million the year before.[42]

An analysis by PressProgress, a website of the Broadbent Institute, would show that top Postmedia executives received $3.9 million in 2016, which would rise by more than a third to $5.345 million the following year. It would also find that they received more than $20 million in compensation over a five-year period from 2013, including $8.2 million by Godfrey alone.[43]

Such largesse towards its executives stood in stark contrast to Postmedia's layoffs across the country and especially to a decision by its workers at the *Vancouver Sun* and *Province*, who took a voluntary 10-percent pay cut to save 21 jobs. Godfrey defended his pay in an interview with CTV News. "I'm an experienced executive, there are very few in the newspaper business," Godfrey said. "If I walked out the door tomorrow, where would they hire? They'd probably have to pay more."[44]

He told *Toronto Life* that the criticism of his pay was unfair. "The board knew my track record and asking price. Plus, there are not many people in Canada who can run a newspaper chain. Look around. The *Star* can't find a publisher or president. The job is hard and full of heartache."[45]

A change of ownership

Godfrey would need all of his high-finance acumen to solve Postmedia's ticking debt bomb, and in doing so he would pull such a fast one that it would take years to sink in that the newspaper chain had actually changed owners. "Few people noticed," noted the *New York Times* a few years later, "including some of the chain's employees."[46]

GoldenTree's founding partner Steven Shapiro had helped to finance both the management buyout of Sun Media led by Godfrey in 1996 and its sale to Quebecor three years later when he worked at CIBC, so he understood the company well. He normally filled GoldenTree's seat on Postmedia's board of directors, but he had taken 2016 off as a sabbatical year.[47] His replacement had resigned from the board that April, however, after it struck a special committee to review options to improve the company's "capital structure and liquidity."

Godfrey admitted that the move provided "another sort of wrinkle in things going forward. We don't know what their position is."[48] GoldenTree looked west, across the Manhattan skyline from its offices on Park Avenue, toward New Jersey, to some low-rent hedge funds on which it hoped to unload its stake in Postmedia.

The debt that GoldenTree had acquired prior to Canwest's bankruptcy came at bargain prices. The company's first-lien bank loans, which were secured by hard assets like real estate, sold on the bond market for about 30 cents on the dollar, according to the *Globe and Mail*. Its unsecured bonds, $450 million of which the desperate Aspers had issued at rates as high as 12.5 percent in an attempt to keep their company afloat, went for as little as 10 cents on the dollar as second-lien debt.[49]

The real genius piece of financial engineering, however, came when GoldenTree kept the debt it held on the books of the reconstituted company, meaning that any earnings Postmedia generated had to go toward paying it first every month. All it had to do was to keep the company alive long enough to collect on its loans. A bond paying 12.5 percent interest bought for 10 cents on the dollar, after all, provided a return of 125 percent a year.

Keeping Postmedia alive would not be easy, however. Publishers around the world were laying off staff almost continually just to stay afloat due to their plunging ad revenues. At Postmedia, however, the urgency to make layoffs was multiplied by the company's crushing debt. In the first four years of GoldenTree's ownership, Postmedia's revenues fell by more than a third.

A reporter for Bloomberg noted in April 2016 that the bond market price for Postmedia's US$222 million in second-lien debt had fallen to 14 cents on the dollar from 71 cents that January. "That price suggests the market is bracing for a debt restructuring that could force lenders ... to take substantial writedowns, convert the bonds to equity, or wipe their investment out altogether."[50] If the company had to declare bankruptcy again, a Liberal government might not look so kindly on it remaining so overwhelmingly in foreign hands.

Postmedia had recently been pressing its case for easing foreign ownership restrictions on newspapers, the *Toronto Star* reported, hiring an Ottawa lobbyist to push for changes to the rules. It also sent Godfrey and board chair Rod Phillips to the capital, according to the *Star*, to meet with a senior political adviser to the new prime minister to discuss "possible changes to long-standing cultural protections that bar majority control of media companies by foreigners."[51] Allowing even more foreign ownership of Canada's largest newspaper chain might be a hard sell in Ottawa, however, and would require a re-arrangement of Postmedia's ownership structure.

Postmedia's first-lien debt was held by Canso Investment Counsel, a suburban Toronto investment fund which had loaned it the money to buy Sun Media. Canso had extracted very favourable terms for the loan, including that it would be partly paid off whenever Postmedia came into any extra cash, such as from asset sales. Canso had been quietly buying up Postmedia debt and had accumulated about $100 million of it by the time the company went looking for financing of its 2014 Sun Media acquisition.

"It was not until Postmedia started talking to existing debt holders to see if they would buy more bonds that it became clear Canso owned at least half of the outstanding first-lien bonds," reported the *Globe and Mail*. "Canso then agreed to buy the whole $140-million of new debt. And Canso had leverage to ask for all of it — it owned so much that its consent would be needed to allow the financing."[52]

By June, Streetwise seemed to hold out even less hope for Postmedia, and none for GoldenTree. "It's become clear there's no white knight coming to save the day at debt-laden Postmedia." Media companies such as Torstar and Glacier had passed on the opportunity to buy into Postmedia, it reported, as had private equity funds. The fate of the country's largest newspaper chain, Streetwise predicted, would be decided in "a showdown between its two major creditors, a rough-and-tumble New York-based distressed debt investor and a 15-employee bond fund from the Toronto suburbs." It even predicted a winner, based on the fact that Canso's loan to Postmedia was a first-lien note while GoldenTree held second-lien debt. "Here's the spoiler alert on how any faceoff would end: The Canadians will win."[53]

Meet the new boss

Two months after his appearance in Ottawa before the Heritage committee hearings, Godrey announced a "plan of arrangement" which some described as a mini-bankruptcy. Postmedia's existing shareholders were wiped out and its $345 million in second-tier debt was exchanged for new shares in the company. In a complicated transaction, GoldenTree was replaced as the company's largest debtholder by Chatham Asset Management of Chatham, New Jersey. It paid $100 million for GoldenTree's bonds, then immediately forgave the debt in return for shares of Postmedia stock.

Chatham then made new loans to Postmedia of $115 million at 10.25 per cent, mostly so it could make a $78-million payment to Canso. Its Canadian lender then agreed to extend Postmedia's remaining first-lien debt of $225 million, which paid 8.25-percent interest, until 2021. Postmedia's debt burden thus fell from $648 million to a much more manageable $341 million, which at lower interest rates saved it $50 million a year in payments. News of the rearrangement immediately doubled Postmedia's share price on the Toronto Stock Exchange to 3 cents.

The manoeuvre raised Postmedia's foreign ownership level to a dizzying 98 percent. Chatham itself received 61 million new shares, which brought its holding in the company to 65 percent and gave it 32 percent of Postmedia's voting rights plus three seats on its board of directors. The *New York Times* would later note that the change in ownership "happened so quietly that Postmedia's own financial news site described it as a debt restructuring in a report that included a single mention of Chatham as 'one of the investors.'"[54]

Meet the new boss, not quite the same as the old boss. Under Chatham's ownership, the *Times* noted, the cuts would continue, with another 1,600 employees or 38 percent of its workforce shown the door over the next four years. The real change, however, would come as Postmedia "centralized editorial operations in a way that has made parts of its 106 newspapers into clones of one another."[55]

While the corporate restructuring received little mainstream media notice outside of Canada's business press, it was met with disbelief in alternative media. "The deal surely shreds the phony claim that Postmedia is a Canadian-controlled company," railed Paul Willcocks, a former publisher of the *Victoria Times Colonist*, on the Vancouver website The Tyee. "Who really believes, no matter how elaborate the share structure, that the corporation is Canadian-owned at this point?"[56]

Former *Vancouver Sun* and CBC television reporter Ian Gill described Postmedia as "essentially now just a debt service agency for an offshore hedge fund."[57] The constant cost-cutting required to pay its loans, Gill quipped, had helped reduce most of the country's largest newspapers to "a highly concentrated, nutrient-free, quivering intellectual Jell-O."[58]

The deal was lucrative for Godfrey, however, as the company's new owners insisted that he stay on even longer past normal retirement age to keep working his corporate magic. They offered him even more money — a $900,000 "retention" bonus if he stayed on to helm the sinking ship, plus another $1.4 million for his four top lieutenants. Unions that represented Postmedia workers demanded they return the bonuses.[59] "This is an absolute disgrace," said Martin O'Hanlon of CWA Canada, which billed itself as The Media Union.[60]

> The fact that it is even legal shows how broken our system is. Godfrey has all but destroyed a once-venerable newspaper chain. And it's not because newspapers aren't making money — they are. It's because he needs to feed profits to predatory hedge fund lenders who keep him in their pocket with these big bonuses.[61]

Postmedia workers also looked askance at the bonuses the company's executives were being paid while they were cutting more and more names from its payroll. After the company announced benefit cuts at its non-unionized newsrooms in early 2017, including to health benefits, pension plans, and parental leave, *National Post* editorial staff asked O'Hanlon and the CWA to help organize the newsroom's first union. "It's not that people aren't willing to sacrifice, especially to save the company," he told the *Globe and Mail*. "But when they see [Godfrey] and his guys padding their pockets, they're not willing to sacrifice."[62]

The union drive was framed by the *Globe* as a "hell-freezes-over moment" for the conservative daily. After the CWA signed up a majority of *Post* employees over the next six months, a close vote that fall was disputed and the issue landed with the Ontario Labour Relations Board.[63] It ruled the following spring that the ballot of eligible bargaining unit members failed by a vote of 31-32.

An investigation by the website Canadaland chronicled what it called "an overbearing response from management," which included charges of intimidation. It quoted one former Post journalist as saying that the newsroom became a "very toxic environment" leading up to the vote. "The paper's internal culture presented hurdles for the prospective union; though many reporters skew less stridently conservative than the paper's bombastic opinion section," Canadaland noted. "Even so, many workers felt the situation had deteriorated to the point that they needed protection as a group from the vagaries of Postmedia management."[64] *Frank* magazine published an e-mail to staff from columnist Terence Corcoran as an example of the pressure campaign. "Newspapers are losing revenues and no union can stop the declines and the need to make adjustments in the new business environment," he argued.[65]

Bonuses "justified"

Godfrey disagreed that the retention bonuses were inappropriate. "They did that so the executives would stay on during this whole restructuring process," he explained to BNN Bloomberg. "The executives did stay on through the restructuring process and developed the strategy going forward."[66]

One interviewer wanted to know how Godfrey would explain his bonus to Postmedia employees who were being denied cost-of-living wage increases as the company slashed a further 20 per cent from salaries. "I'd have told them that we did a global search for investors and only one company, Chatham Asset Management, stepped forward," he replied. "They handed over $100 million but first wanted assurances that key employees, me included, would stay. Did I feel awkward about the bonus? Yes. But how would staff feel if we shut down and there were no severance deals at all?"[67]

Even Conrad Black found the arrangement unseemly. "The bond holders control the company and are content to bleed it dry with the complicity of management," he tweeted. "Bankruptcy is next."[68] Godfrey found the criticism a bit rich coming from a man who went to prison for five years a decade earlier after being convicted on charges of fraud and obstruction of justice while piecing off his own newspaper company. "That is not true at all," Godfrey responded. "If it wasn't for these people who had bonds [and] converted them to equity, there'd be no Postmedia today."[69]

Black had bedeviled Godfrey before, arguing in a 2015 conference call of shareholders that Postmedia's only option was to spend its way out of decline by investing in stronger content. "Some of [Postmedia's] newspapers have deteriorated a long way from what I remember," he said as Postmedia shares closed at 80 cents. "Some of it you can't avoid. Some of it you can. But please build the quality, otherwise you're going to retreat right into your own end zone, if you'll pardon the sports metaphor."[70] Godfrey shrugged off Black's suggestion, but even he had to admit that the cuts his newspapers had endured were making them worse. "Are our papers as good as they used to be?" he asked in an interview with *Toronto Life*. "No, but they haven't become unacceptable."[71]

Bailing the company out

Godfrey had now achieved two of his three aims. He had withstood the inquisition of politicians in Ottawa and deftly disarmed Postmedia's debt time bomb, even if he had just kicked it down the road a few years. Now he turned his attention to his third objective, which was to find a more reliable source of income for Postmedia. "I've had a good run," he told *Toronto Life*, lapsing into a baseball analogy, "but I want one more extra-base hit, even if it comes in the bottom of the ninth with two out and two strikes."[72]

Actually, if Godfrey could pull this one off, it would be more like a grand slam home run. What he had in mind was for the Canadian government to underwrite the entire newspaper industry, including Postmedia. He had read a report in the *Globe and Mail* on a paper written by Richard Stursberg, a former head of CBC English, which proposed a new way of funding Canadian media with tax credits. The paper, which Stursberg wrote at the request of Rogers, proposed creating a new government agency that would provide tax credits to encourage the production of any Canadian content, including newspaper articles.

"Since journalism is important to civil society and local TV news and newspapers are increasingly unprofitable businesses," reported the *Globe*, "Stursberg argues they are as worthy of public support as Canadian film or TV. But the notion of government funding, no matter how independently administered and automatically triggered, makes most print journalists queasy."[73] Tax credits solved that problem, claimed Stursberg, who would expand on his argument in a 2019 book titled *The Tangled Garden*. "The tax-credit approach was best for news," it explained, as it would safeguard the independence of journalism "because it involved no judgments by politicians or bureaucrats. They were like any tax measure: If the costs qualified, the payment was automatic."[74]

Godfrey liked Stursberg's idea so much that he invited him to dinner with Postmedia's board of directors. "The board members were enthusiastic," recalled Stursberg. "After the dinner, Godfrey agreed to round up the other newspapers and see if they were prepared to finance a study on how tax credits might work for them."[75] Stursberg enlisted in aid of his project former *Toronto Star* publisher John Cruickshank and Stephen Armstrong, a long-time Ontario civil servant he described as a media economics expert.

The newspaper leaders soon met in Postmedia's boardroom to discuss the plan and were even joined by a senior official from Unifor, a union that represented many of their workers. "It was a strange gathering," recalled Stursberg. "Many of the publishers actively disliked each other. They *all* disliked Paul Godfrey, who they blamed for giving them a bad reputation in Ottawa."[76] [emphasis in original] Their reasons for disliking Godfrey were neatly summed up by one publisher, according to Stursberg. "First he instructs his papers to support Stephen Harper, and then every time he lays off some journalists, he gives himself a bonus. It makes us all look bad at the Prime Minister's Office."[77] The press barons liked Stursberg's idea, however, and even agreed to open their books so he could better craft his study.

The report of the Heritage committee on Media and Local Communities to which Godfrey testified wasn't expected until mid-2017, by which time the newspaper industry would have a comprehensive bailout plan to immediately propose. It would be put forward by its trade association News Media Canada, which had been formed earlier in 2016 through a merger of the Canadian Newspaper Association, which represented dailies, and the weekly newspaper group Canadian Community Newspapers Association.

Meanwhile, however, the think tank report on Canada's news media was released in early 2017, and it could not have done a better job of portraying the situation of newspapers as dire, even if it did play more than a little bit fast and loose with the facts. Produced by the Ottawa-based Public Policy Forum and authored by its new head Edward Greenspon, a former editor of the *Globe and Mail,* it provided a credible basis for the proposal that NMC was tasked to produce, so much so that the two groups began working together on the bailout plan.

The newspaper bosses were not impressed with Greenspon's policy recommendation of a government fund to support "civic function journalism," or coverage of democracy, according to Stursberg, much preferring his idea of tax credits. "They had two fundamental objections," noted Stursberg. "First, they objected to the idea of a fund that they would have to apply to. ... Second, they found the concept of 'civic journalism' too limiting."[78]

> They had whole sections of their publications that touched on everything from business and sport to culture and lifestyle. They offered book and movie reviews, financial advice, society gossip, profiles of famous personalities, obituaries, crossword puzzles, hockey scores, weather, horoscopes and on and on. The idea that they would be reduced to covering mayoralty races and library openings filled them with dread.[79]

Greenspon assured them that "the mandarins in Ottawa did not like the idea of tax credits," according to Stursberg, so the group decided to put forward both ideas when they met with senior government officials that spring. "If the mandarins really hated tax credits, then better the fund than nothing. As one of the publishers said to me, 'At the end of the day, if the money has to be delivered in a brown paper bag late on Sunday nights in the alley, we'll take it.'"[80]

Their April 2017 meeting in Ottawa with some of the country's most senior bureaucrats did not go well, according to Stursberg. "There was some grousing about fake news and the usual genuflections to the importance of serious journalism... It looked like a victory for civic journalism."[81] Greenspon kept sounding out the bureaucrats, Stursberg added, but his idea was going nowhere. "He continued to report that there was no sympathy for tax credits. The boffins at finance hated the tax credits that already existed and wanted nothing to do with extending them to newspapers."[82]

Heritage report

The Heritage committee's report on Media and Local Communities was finally released in June of 2017. Titled *Disruption: Change and Churning in Canada's Media Landscape*, it surveyed the sorry state of Canadian journalism, which it largely blamed on Postmedia. "We are now able to see, fully, the devastating impact of the 2014 Postmedia/Sun Media merger," it pointed out. "Postmedia now owns 15 of the 21 largest English language dailies in Canada and eight of the nine in the Western provinces."[83] Postmedia's massive layoffs of journalists, it added, had greatly diminished the diversity of voices in Canada and even challenged its democracy.

The report made many sensible recommendations, some of which were long overdue, like changes to charitable giving laws to allow tax-deductible donations to fund non-profit journalism, as was allowed in other countries. It also urged changes to the Competition Act, as had a 2006 Senate report on news media, only to be ignored by a newly installed Harper government. News media mergers and takeovers should be treated differently from those in other industries, both reports urged, by adding a diversity test as used in some other countries in order to prevent market dominance by any media owner.

The Fry report left vague any process that should be implemented for subsidizing local news, however, urging only that the Heritage minister "explore the existing structures to create a new funding model that is platform agnostic and would support Canadian journalistic content."[84] As for where the money should come from, however, the report had a very definite idea. It pointed to the vast revenues that Canada's monopoly cable companies were raking in for broadband Internet service provision, which generated profit margins of around 45 percent.

The cablecos were profiting richly from connecting Canadians to the Internet, which in the case of broadband was via the same cable that carried television programming. Bell, Rogers, Shaw and the very few other cable and satellite companies that dominated the industry had for years paid a 5 percent levy on their cable TV revenues, which was imposed to claw back a slice of their monopoly profits to fund Canadian content. The levy went into a Canadian Media Fund, which spent $371 million on Canadian television and digital projects in 2015-16. To fund Canadian news content, the Fry report recommended that the cable levy should be extended to this lucrative broadband provision, an idea which the cablecos had resisted fiercely for years.

The idea was shot down before it could even get off the ground, however. In a time-honoured tradition, the Fry report was leaked to the press and spun to advantage. The *Globe and Mail* reported that a broadband "tax" was its central proposal, which "would open up the government to accusations that it is once again raising taxes on consumers."[85] The article quoted Stursberg as calling the idea "not a viable or desirable option." Calls had been made for years to claw back some of the rich monopoly profits the cablecos made on Internet service provision, for which Canadians paid some of the highest rates in the world, but the telecom giants claimed the revenues were needed to fund the development of broadband and promised to pass on any such levy to customers. "Further taxing of ISPs would raise the cost of service and slow the deployment of high-speed networks," Stursberg told the *Globe and Mail*.[86]

The plan was quickly scotched by Trudeau when it was put to him by reporters in Montreal less than an hour after the report was released. "We're not going to be raising taxes on the middle class through an Internet broadband tax," he said. "That is not an idea we are taking on."[87] Fry attempted to set the record straight, noting that the recommendation had been mis-characterized to the prime minister, as it was not for a tax to be paid by consumers but instead for a levy imposed on ISPs. She sent him a copy of the report highlighting the areas in which he had been misinformed. "Obviously he hasn't read it," she told the *Hill Times*.[88]

The damage had already been done, however. Don Martin, the host of CTV's *Power Play* public affairs program, declared the idea "dead on arrival" in an interview with Fry, who protested that "it was a set-up."[89] *National Post* columnist Andrew Coyne saw the setback as only temporary.

Yes, the government may have rejected that particular proposal. But it is very much interested in bailing out the media, by which I mean particularly the company I work for, Postmedia — almost as interested as Postmedia is in being bailed out... So we must assume it is going to happen... and all of the elaborate exchange of courtesies that is now going on is simply to provide cover for a decision that has already been taken.[90]

Bailout proposal

Within hours, the newspaper industry weighed in with its proposal for a new journalism funding model, but it was hardly platform agnostic. The very next day after the Heritage report was delivered, News Media Canada proposed extending to daily newspapers the Canadian Periodical Fund, which already provided $75 million a year in subsidies to magazines and weekly newspapers, and boosting it to $350 million a year for five years. The proposed additional aid totaled $1.375 billion and would come mostly in the form of a labour tax credit of 35 percent for every journalist employed, to a maximum salary of $85,000. But the industry's proposal was rejected by Ottawa.

"Our approach will not be to bail out industry models that are no longer viable," then-Heritage Minister Mélanie Joly said that September in unveiling a new cultural policy for Canada. "Rather, we will focus our efforts on supporting innovation, experimentation and transition to digital."[91] Even more irksome to newspapers, the government's culture strategy included a $125-million deal with Facebook for a news "incubator" at Ryerson University and a $500-million investment from Netflix to produce content in Canada over the next five years. As far as publishers were concerned, these digital freeloaders should not only be paying their fair share of taxes in Canada, they should be paying for the news stories they carried on their platforms.

The ugliness Godfrey had promised followed within months. In a move that screamed "up yours" to Ottawa, the two largest chains in Canada traded 41 newspapers in late November 2017, mostly in Ontario, and closed 36 of them, laying off 290 workers and creating dozens more local monopolies. Postmedia received 22 titles from Torstar, including commuter tabloids in Winnipeg and Ottawa, and announced that they would all be closed except for the weekly *Exeter Times-Advocate*.

Torstar got back nineteen newspapers in the deal and closed fifteen of them, including the paid dailies *Barrie Examiner*, *Orillia Packet & Times*, and *Northumberland Today*. It announced, however, that it would continue to operate the paid dailies *St. Catharines Standard*, *Niagara Falls Review*, *Welland Tribune*, and *Peterborough Examiner* through its Metroland Media division. While the deal appeared lopsided in Torstar's favour since it ended up with four newspapers that were still publishing to only one for Postmedia, the real scorecard was the layoffs, which stood 244-46 in favour of Godfrey's team.

The strategy employed by Postmedia and Torstar in dealing with the Competition Bureau seemed to be one of surprise. They did not contact the bureau until a half hour before the deal was announced, when both companies' lawyers phoned it to convey the news and insist that the properties involved did not comprise assets large enough to trigger premerger notifications.

Postmedia issued a statement outlining the deal which ended: "The transaction is not subject to the merger notification provisions of the Competition Act and no regulatory clearance is required to close the transaction."[92] The reference was to a requirement in the Competition Act of advance notice of any merger involving assets or revenues exceeding $88 million. That wouldn't stop the regulator from investigating, however. "A few days later," the *Globe and Mail* would soon report, "the bureau asked to review the transaction agreement, which it received in early December."[93]

A new Black Monday

While Torstar issued a statement and refused further comment, Godfrey oddly did the opposite and made the media rounds. He freely admitted that the deal's catalyst had been Ottawa's rejection of NMC's bailout proposal. "It really picked up steam when the feds closed the door on any assistance for the industry," he told the *Globe and Mail* for its front-page story. "All these products are losing money. We have no choice but to concentrate our focus...

We feel that this is a necessity. We're talking about the survival of these [remaining] papers, and the survival of the industry."[94]

Globe and Mail columnist Elizabeth Renzetti called the trade and closures "breathtakingly cynical" for blatantly eliminating competition.[95] "It wasn't cynical at all," Godfrey told The Canadian Press. "It was life-saving. Some of those communities can't afford to have competing newspapers because there's just not enough ad revenue to support them. Eventually, they'd all fold, instead of just some of them."[96]

"This is a crisis situation," Godfrey told the *National Post* for a story buried deep inside its business section. Coverage in Postmedia newspapers accentuated the positive. "The firms say they remain committed to local news and are only closing papers in regions served by multiple publications," added the *Post*. "For example, Torstar bought Ontario's *Barrie Examiner* and owns the *Barrie Advance*; it will close the *Examiner* and continue to operate the *Advance*."[97]

What it didn't mention was that most of the remaining newspapers were weeklies and many of those closed were dailies, meaning that a lot less local news would now be reported, and less often. It also didn't mention the hardship being visited on the laid-off workers. "It means no job, I lose my truck and no Christmas for my kids," Jay Rice, a subcontractor for the *Barrie Examiner*, told CTV, adding that he only found out that he had lost his job when he showed up for work. Long-time reporter Cheryl Browne heard about the deal before she made it to the *Examiner* newsroom. "We were hoping for the best, but when we got here there was a sign on the door saying we were closed," she said, adding wryly: "The government didn't bail us out."[98]

At a wake for the *Orillia Packet & Times*, Joella Shaughnessy Sidhu teared up as she recalled her decades at the *Packet*, editing, taking pictures, and covering news stories from a plane crash to a royal tour. "It was my whole life," she told a *Globe and Mail* reporter. "I lived for nothing else."[99] Two community newspaper associations in Quebec issued a statement "denouncing a deal... effectively eliminating local newspapers and monopolizing withering advertising markets," and directly contradicted Godfrey by characterizing the industry as "thriving."[100]

The *Winnipeg Free Press*, one of the few major independent dailies left in Canada, observed that "the Canadian newspaper industry has a new Black Monday."[101] The reference was to the simultaneous 1980 "Black Wednesday" foldings of the *Winnipeg Tribune* and the *Ottawa Journal* which triggered the Royal Commission on Newspapers. Included in the latest closures was Winnipeg's free commuter daily *Metro*, which Torstar flipped to Postmedia. "I'm shocked," said James Turner, a journalism instructor at Red River College and a former *Metro* reporter. "I don't know how the economies worked, but it seemed like they were running an efficient ship. There were always ads in it, so it must have been making some money."[102]

In this real-life board game of Monopoly, Postmedia suddenly owned the *Metro* tabloids in Winnipeg and Ottawa, which competed with its morning *Sun* dailies there, so they were closed. *Metro* had come to Winnipeg in 2011 in the wave of commuter tabloids that swept the world in the dying years of the print advertising bubble. Most had faded away since the bubble burst, however. While once there were three commuter tabloids in Vancouver, for example, now there was only one with the closure of *24 Hours*, which Postmedia traded to Torstar but was closed since it competed with its *Metro* there. The death of *24 Hours* in Vancouver, which launched in 2005 and was the second most-read newspaper in Western Canada before Postmedia acquired it as part of its 2014 purchase of Sun Media, was almost a relief. It had been kept alive for more than a year as a zombie newspaper after its newsroom was closed by Postmedia, which continued to fill it with stories from its *Sun* and *Province* dailies.[103]

Unifor president Jerry Dias had a simple solution to the problem illustrated by the closures. "If the government wants to have a thriving industry, if they want to have freedom of expression, if they want to have journalistic integrity, then we're going to have to find a mechanism to deal with it," Dias told the Canadian Press. "You put money into journalism. That's what the issue is."[104]

The newspaper swap "effectively divided the province of Ontario into two zones of mutual exclusivity, or regional monopolies," noted Dwayne Winseck of the Canadian Media Concentration Research Project at Carleton University. "The upshot of this pattern is that several regional press groups have been consolidated across the country, each with a de-facto monopoly in their territory."[105] By closing the newspapers they acquired, Postmedia and Torstar would each face less competition in certain markets, noted Winseck, including the Kawarthas and the Niagara regions for Torstar, and Ottawa, London and the Kingston-Belleville region for Postmedia.

The closures and Postmedia's acquisition of Sun Media in 2014, Winseck added, increased its share of the Canadian newspaper market from 20 percent to 28 percent, as measured by revenues. The only question was whether the Competition Bureau would do anything about it. "The fundamental reorganization of the newspaper industry ... has proceeded over the years with hardly any notable intervention from the Competition Bureau."

> The Bureau's long and uninspired track-record of inaction stands as a monument to remind us of Canadian regulators' hesitance to interrupt media owners' prerogatives and so-called market forces. In the meantime, yet another media industry fundamental to democracy remains in distress, with no clear relief on the horizon.[106]

Media denials

In a bizarre turn, Postmedia executives insisted they were surprised when Torstar closed most of the papers it had traded for. The reason for their disclaimers was that under the Competition Act, executives of the companies faced up to 14 years in prison and $25 million in fines if convicted on criminal charges of conspiracy to reduce competition. That could include agreeing not to compete in certain geographic areas, conspiring to restrict the supply of a product, or fixing prices.

"The fact is collusion is just not legal so what we were very, very careful to do was not to speak to each other about what the end result was going to be," Godfrey told the Canadian Press. "Look, we have enough trouble running one newspaper chain and deciding what to do. What they do we always considered is their business."[107] In an in-studio interview with BNN Bloomberg, Godfrey kept emphasizing that one point. "First of all, we didn't know what they were going to do and they didn't know what we were going to do."[108] Godfrey again admitted that the companies made the deal because the federal government refused to bail them out despite two reports that urged assistance to the newspaper industry. "The door was slammed immediately, so what do you expect us to do? We're trying to keep this thing going."

> We waited around eighteen months waiting for the federal government to examine two committee reports, one done by the Public Policy Forum who recommended some aid. The Heritage committee also recommended ... a certain tax of Google and Facebook. The feds didn't do that so suddenly we had to do something.[109]

Godfrey admitted that the deal came at Postmedia's suggestion, but he kept making that one point repeatedly. "We asked Torstar if they were interested in doing this, but it was only today that I found out what they were going to do and they found out what we were going to do. We didn't know what each other were doing, so we did the deal."[110] Postmedia's chief operating officer Andrew MacLeod added denials of his own. "We didn't know what their plans were, and they didn't know the same for us," he told the *Globe and Mail* a day after the deal went down.[111] The company's second in command, who had joined Postmedia in 2014 from BlackBerry and was expected to soon succeed Godfrey as CEO, also told a *National Post* reporter that the companies had been "extraordinarily careful" not to share their plans for the properties.[112]

Godfrey doubled down on his denials the following week during an in-studio interview with CBC's *On the Money* program that was nominally about Quebec's announcement of $36.4 million in aid for newspapers in that province but soon focused on the Torstar swap. Godfrey admitted that the companies had been discussing the deal for a couple of years. "We didn't want to make the deal," he told host Peter Armstrong. "We didn't want to, either of us, I suppose, didn't want to enter a deal where you start to hurt community newspapers."[113]

> But when the federal government decided that they weren't going to proceed on reports they commissioned

themselves there was no choice but to talk to each other. Our staff numbers had dropped, so we figured we'd consolidate our footprint. We wanted to really zero in on London and Ottawa. They thought that was OK providing they could look at Niagara as being their footprint.[114]

Godfrey insisted, however, that neither party to the transaction knew that the other would close almost all of the newspapers it traded for. "We did not have any idea what they were going to do and they didn't have any idea," he said. "We understand the legal rules involving collusion and you can ask anybody from Torstar, you can ask anybody from Postmedia."[115] Pressed by Armstrong on whether Postmedia really didn't know what Torstar was going to do, Godfrey repeated his denial. "We didn't figure that at all. You only figure that if you knew something. We were more concerned with what we were going to do, and I'm sure they were concerned with what they were going to do. ... You don't share your game plans with your competitors."[116]

The words of the two Postmedia men would soon come back to bite them.

CHAPTER 2
THE ROAD TO FINANCIALIZATION

The worst thing that ever happened to newspapers was that they made so much money.

There was a very good reason that newspapers were so profitable. "A successful newspaper cannot help having higher profit margins than most other businesses because newspapers, to use economic jargon, are more 'vertically integrated' than most other businesses," explained newspaper stock analyst John Morton. "Almost everything else that adds value to the final product — news and advertising content — is created in-house [and] it also retails its manufactured product — the newspaper — directly to its customers."[1]

Some businesses were low-margin enterprises that depended on a high volume of sales to raise their profits, such as department stores, which had to source their wares from a range of suppliers, from manufacturers to wholesalers to distributors, each of which had to make a profit of its own. "Now consider a newspaper," wrote Morton. "The only materials it needs to acquire on an ongoing basis are newsprint, which it normally gets directly from the manufacturer, and newswire and feature services, which are minor cost items."[2] As a result of buying directly from suppliers and retailing directly to customers, newspapers were able to cut out the middlemen and keep the profits for themselves. "Newspapers earn most of the various profit margins that drive up the operating costs of most other businesses."[3]

Newspapers which began life in centuries past as small businesses often started by printers were at first highly political in nature, usually supporting one party or another in what became known as the Party Press. The earliest newspapers often did not include ads. The *London Gazette* established in 1666 initially refused them as "not properly the business of a Paper of Intelligence," but it was soon earning almost as much from paid notices as from copy sales.[4] The demand for ads was so high that entire publications filled with them began to be distributed for free, such as the *Public Advertiser*, which first appeared in 1726 and the *Daily Advertiser*, which emerged four years later.[5] By 1783, there were five dailies in London devoted entirely to advertising.[6] The onslaught of ads became a sore point in 1728 for coffee houses, which subscribed to numerous newspapers for patrons to read, according to one history. "The coffee house owners wanted news for their customers to read, but claimed that up to 50 percent of material in the papers was advertising. The coffee house proprietors threatened to start publishing their own news, but nothing came of it."[7]

The coffee house culture of 18th century London was a high point in communication history for the increased level of public participation it brought to politics, according to Jürgen Habermas, but it was a privilege restricted to white, land-owning males. This brief flowering of informed discussion on political issues was soon displaced, Habermas noted in his classic book *The Structural Transformation of the Public Sphere*, by a more commercial culture brought by advertising and other forms of mass persuasion.[8] The party press in the U.S. became commercialized in the 19th century as news increasingly became a commodity.[9] It wasn't until the 1890s, however, that publishers in Canada abandoned overtly partisan politics in their drive to maximize profits, often adopting a sensational American style of journalism to build audiences for advertisers.[10]

Traveling radio salesman Roy Thomson discovered how to make newspapers even more profitable. Thomson found out how much money newspapers made when he owned a radio station in the 1930s that shared a building with the *Timmins Daily Press*. He bought it, and dozens more across North America and Great Britain, applying a highly-profitable formula of strict cost controls. Thomson Newspapers became notorious for penny pinching, paying low salaries, issuing pencils individually, and requiring reporters to use scrap paper instead of providing them with notebooks. "My purpose is to run newspapers as a business," he told the 1962 Royal Commission on the Press in Britain, where he had recently bought the *Sunday Times*. "To make money."[11]

The only better way to make money was in television, according to Thomson, who famously described Scottish Television when he opened it in 1957 as "like having a licence to print your own money."[12] He was awarded the hereditary title Lord Thomson of Fleet in 1964, which passed on his death in 1976 to his son Kenneth and in 2005 to his grandson David, who was listed in 2019 as the wealthiest person in Canada with a net worth estimated at $37.8 billion. The Thomson family's media empire includes hundreds of specialized publishing companies and online databases, the global news service Thomson Reuters, the *Globe and Mail*, and a third of the Canadian Press news service.

Conrad Black updated Thomson's newspaper cost-cutting formula and by the millennium had built the world's third-largest newspaper empire.[13] Shut out of buying major dailies in Canada for decades due to his neo-conservative politics, Black bought the failing *Daily Telegraph* in London for a bargain price in 1985, then cut almost three quarters of its staff. From a loss of £8.9 million in 1986, it recorded a profit of £41.5 million in 1989. Black then broke a strike by *Telegraph* journalists by publishing with only management personnel, which he said exposed "one of the great myths of the industry: that journalists are essential to producing a newspaper."[14]

Black's lieutenant David Radler said that the secret to their minor Sterling Newspapers chain's success was "the three-man newsroom, and two of them sell ads."[15] When their Hollinger Inc. bought the Chicago Sun-Times in 1993, Radler doubled the paper's profit margin by cutting 20 percent of its staff, but he irked those who remained by cutting power to the building's escalator. Radler became known as the "human chain saw" for the cost-cutting technique he applied to each new publication he and Black acquired, usually in the U.S., where they built the second-largest chain in the country.

> I visit the office of each prospective property at night and count the desks.... That tells me how many people work there. If the place has, say 42 desks, I know I can put

that paper out with 30 people, and that means a dozen people will be leaving the payroll even though I haven't seen their faces yet.[16]

Big business

Advertising turned the newspapers that had started out as small businesses into very big businesses indeed. Nobody ever made much money selling newspapers, however. In fact, they were usually sold at a loss or given away free to attract more readers, who could in turn be sold to advertisers in what media economist Dallas Smythe called the "commodity audience."[17]

The economics of newspaper publishing were counter-intuitive, to say the least. Huge profits could be made by selling a product for less than its cost of production. At the height of the print advertising bubble in the late 20th century, newspapers routinely made 20 to 30 percent profit margins and in monopoly markets could often make 40 to 50 percent. Monopoly was where the money was, because not only could publishers raise advertising and circulation rates at will, they could also scrimp on the product to save on costs without fear of losing customers to the competition. You could thus make more money by selling a poor product than from offering quality merchandise. Increasingly publishers began to buy up or merge with their competition in pursuit of more lucrative monopolies.

When the Special Senate Committee on Mass Media chaired by Keith Davey was called to investigate a media monopoly in New Brunswick, it found the problem was spreading nationwide. By 1970, "genuine" newspaper competition existed in only five Canadian cities, its report noted, with the Southam, Thomson, and FP Publications chains controlling 44.7 percent of the country's daily newspaper circulation, compared with 25 percent in 1958.

> This tendency could ... lead to a situation whereby the news (which we must start thinking of as a public resource, like electricity) is controlled and manipulated by a small group of individuals and corporations whose view of What's Fit to Print may closely coincide with ... What's Good For Business... There is some evidence, in fact, which suggests we are in that boat already.[18]

The Davey committee forced Canada's newspaper companies to open their books, and called what it found astonishing. "An industry that is supposed to abhor secrets is sitting on one of the best-kept, least discussed secrets, one of the hottest scoops, in the entire field of Canadian business — their own balance sheets."[19] From 1958 to 1967, before-tax profits at Canadian newspapers ranged from 23.4 percent to 30.5 percent. After taxes, they were 12 to 17.5 percent, compared to 9 or 10 percent in other manufacturing and retailing industries. "Owning a newspaper, in other words, can be almost twice as profitable as owning a paper-box factory or a department store."[20]

Its report recommended a Press Ownership Review Board to approve newspaper sales or mergers whose basic guideline would be that "all transactions that increase concentration of ownership in the mass media are undesirable and contrary to the public interest — unless shown to be otherwise."[21] It never came about, which Davey lamented in his memoirs. "We had to conclude that we have in this country not the press we need, but rather the press we deserve," he wrote. "The sad fact is that the media must self-regulate because most Canadians are not prepared to demand the press they need."[22]

Self-regulation certainly didn't prevent what rocked the Canadian newspaper industry next. August 27, 1980 became known as "Black Wednesday" for the simultaneous closures of the *Ottawa Journal* by the Thomson chain and the *Winnipeg Tribune* by Southam, which resulted in two more local monopolies. A Royal Commission on Newspapers was called almost immediately by Prime Minister Pierre Trudeau, and it pointed out less than a year later what was obvious to everyone. "Newspaper competition, of the kind that used to be, is virtually dead in Canada," it noted. "This ought not to have been allowed to happen."[23]

Southam and Thomson by then controlled 58.3 percent of the nation's English-language daily newspaper circulation between them, the Royal Commission calculated, and it warned that the situation would only grow worse without a brake being applied to ownership concentration. A proposed Canada Newspaper Act designed to do so was never enacted, however, as the federal government changed from Liberal to Progressive Conservative. The inaction led to Canada having the most highly concentrated newspaper ownership in the world by the 1990s. "At the national level, no developed country has so concentrated a newspaper industry," concluded Peter Dunnett in his 1988 book *The World Newspaper Industry*. "In Canada the newspaper market is unusual in that it is still growing and could accommodate new entrants."[24]

After Black engineered a hostile takeover of Southam in 1996, his Hollinger chain owned 42 percent of Canadian newspapers, as measured by paid daily circulation.[25] What visited Canadian newspaper ownership next, however, qualified as nothing less than a full-scale catastrophe. Black was offered a seat in the House of Lords by British prime minister Tony Blair in 1999, as was the tradition for major UK newspaper publishers, but his appointment was blocked by Liberal prime minister Jean Chretien, who objected to the constant attacks on him from Black's new *National Post*. Black consequently renounced his Canadian citizenship, and under the rules limiting foreign ownership of newspapers in Canada, he was forced to sell the Southam chain he had schemed for years to acquire.

Foreign ownership

Most countries limited or prohibited foreign media ownership, according to a 1999 study, "at least partly out of fear that foreign owners would use those outlets to manipulate public opinion in times of national crisis."[26] Foreign ownership of Canadian newspapers was supposedly limited in two ways. The 1985 Investment Canada Act limited foreign ownership to 25 percent in "sensitive" areas, including book, periodical, and newspaper publishing. Section 19 of the Income Tax Act also limited to 25 percent foreign ownership of magazines and newspapers in which the cost of advertising could be claimed as a tax-deductible business expense.

The issue of foreign ownership of Canadian media had been raised by a 1961 Royal Commission on Publications, which recommended ending tax breaks for U.S. magazines, such as *Time* and *Reader's Digest*, which published Canadian editions that competed with domestic magazines such as *Maclean's*. Rapidly-expanding U.S. newspaper chains also began eyeing Canadian acquisitions by the mid-1960s, which prompted the Southam chain to prevail upon the then-Liberal government for newspapers to be included in the 1965 changes to the Income Tax Act that were designed to protect magazines.[27]

By 1990, however, the UK chain Trinity International still owned more than a dozen newspapers in Western Canada, according to the *Globe and Mail*, that had been "grandfathered" under the limit. *Reader's Digest* got around the rule, it added, by setting up a Canadian charitable foundation to own 75 per cent of its English and French editions in Canada. "The balance of the shares are held by a wholly owned subsidiary of the parent company, Reader's Digest Association Inc. of Pleasantville, N.Y.," noted the *Globe*. "It also owns 100 per cent of the lucrative record, book and direct-mail operations. But Reader's Digest has never used this corporate structure to buy other Canadian publications."[28] One Southam executive warned that if Trinity had found a way around the law, other foreign newspaper owners could do the same.

> The key to the arrangement is a company called Canwest Publishers Ltd., whose name appears on the masthead of papers in the MetroValley group. Canwest, which owns the "publishing rights" to the different titles, is 25 per cent owned by Trinity. The remaining shares are presumably owned by Canadians, making it eligible to meet Revenue Canada's Canadian ownership requirements.[29]

Canwest Global Communications, which owned the Global Television network, had been founded in 1974 by Winnipeg tax lawyer Izzy Asper, a former leader of the Manitoba Liberal Party. Asper skirted Australia's 15-percent foreign ownership limit on television stations after buying Network Ten there in 1992 by holding most of its shares as non-voting debentures, a tactic that the Australian government would eventually ban in 1997.[30] Black used the same structure after he joined a consortium that bought the Fairfax newspaper chain in Australia. He quit the country after a Senate inquiry was convened into an admission he made in his 1993 autobiography *A Life in Progress*. There, Black wrote that he had lobbied the Australian prime minister, who promised to push for raising the foreign ownership limit on newspapers "if he was re-elected and Fairfax political coverage was 'balanced.'"[31]

When Black quit Canada after Chretien tried to block his peerage, he passed the Southam chain on to Asper, who bought it as part of the millennium fad known as "convergence," according to which cross-media ownership was thought to be the way of the future. Some countries, such as the U.S., banned newspapers from owning television stations in order to protect media diversity. Canada had unfortunately left the door wide open for convergence, as a ban on cross-ownership brought in by the Pierre Trudeau government after the Royal Commission on Newspapers warned strongly against allowing it was dropped a few years later by the Progressive Conservatives of Brian Mulroney.

Convergence boom goes bust

Convergence brought fabulous prices for media companies during the dot-com boom, even digital startups with few revenues, under the assumption that online media were the way of the future. The signature convergence play went down in January 2000 when Time Warner, which owned the Time-Life magazine empire, Warner Brothers movie studios, and cable channels including HBO, MTV, and CNN, married dial-up pioneer America Online. The all-stock transaction created a company worth US$350 billion, of which AOL shareholders got 55 percent because its share value had been vastly inflated by the bubble that soon burst. It was the largest corporate merger in history, and likely the most disastrous. The AOL acronym was dropped from the corporate title in 2003 after AOL-Time Warner's share price fell by two thirds, and the division was sold by decade's end.

Enthusiasm for convergence briefly caught fire after the AOL-Time Warner deal, however, and the conflagration grew out of control in Canada. By the time 2000 ended, three major mergers and takeovers reshaped Canadian media.

First, telecom giant Bell Canada paid $2.3 billion for the CTV network and then partnered with the *Globe and Mail* to form a monstrosity first known as Bell Globemedia, which became CTVGlobemedia in 2006 after Bell's ownership stake was reduced to 15 percent. Then Canwest bought the Southam newspaper chain for $3.2 billion from Black, and finally Quebecor bought media conglomerate Groupe Vidéotron for $4.9 billion, adding the largest cable company in Québec and the TVA network to its Sun Media newspaper chain.

The convergence experiment lasted less than a decade, however, and its collapse left Canadian media in ruins. Canwest had taken on $4 billion in debt, which it could not service after the 2008-09 recession dropped advertising revenues worldwide. It declared bankruptcy in 2009 and was split into two companies at auction, with Postmedia buying its newspapers. The Thomson family asked out of the *Globe and Mail*'s partnership with CTV in 2010, citing fundamental differences between the newspaper business and television. Quebecor actually made a success of convergence in Quebec, but retreated from the national market in 2014 when it sold the Sun Media chain to Postmedia.

There to pick up the pieces were the highly-profitable cable companies, whose rates the CRTC had deregulated in the 1990s with the introduction of satellite television service by Bell, which supposedly created competition for cable. Rogers bought the Citytv network in 2007, Shaw acquired Global Television out of bankruptcy in 2010, and Bell reacquired control of CTV later that year.

The takeover of Canada's TV networks by the country's cable companies created a highly-concentrated telecom sector. Concentration of newspaper ownership was already sky-high and would get even higher with Postmedia's takeover of Sun Media. The problem behind Canada's stratospheric media ownership concentration was identified by the 2006 report of Senate committee hearings on news media as one of "regulatory neglect" on the part of both the CRTC and the Competition Bureau.[32] (see Chapter 4)

Picking up the pieces

The road from concentration to convergence led finally to financialization, where some of Canada's most prized media assets were scooped up out of the bargain bin by hedge funds.

According to economist Thomas Palley, financialization was a process whereby "markets, financial institutions, and financial elites gain greater influence over economic policy and economic outcomes."[33] Its principal impacts, he noted, were to elevate the significance of the financial sector relative to the real sector, transfer income from the real sector to the financial sector, increase income inequality, and contribute to wage stagnation.[34]

According to journalist Rana Foroohar in her 2016 book *Makers and Takers*, financialization was an "economic illness" which led to income inequality and declining investment in needed research and development.[35] "Financialization is undermining our economic growth, our social stability, and even our democracy," she warned.[36] The rise of finance had "led to the fall of American business," she added, because it has "come to rule — rather than fuel — the real economy."[37]

Along with neoliberalism and globalization, financialization transformed world economies starting in the 1980s. It especially transformed media industries, which became highly financialized. In her 2010 book *Journalism in Crisis: Corporate Media and Financialization*, Spanish scholar Núria Almiron characterized financialization as "the primacy of financial over industrial logics."[38] In a "truly alarming" development, she noted, "finance capital has become the real owner of the world's top news-media firms."[39] This came at a cost for their journalism as they instead became only about making a profit. "Media corporatization first and later their financialization have constituted a scenario that turns journalistic autonomy into an illusion."[40]

> Financialized multimedia communication groups are today more of a market power — with multimedia influences and convergent interests with financial groups — than guardians of liberty, creators of consensus, egalitarian democratizers, or subverters of the structures of authority.[41]

Vultures pick the bones

The term "hedge fund" was coined by *Fortune* magazine writer Carol J. Loomis in 1966 to describe the spectacular success of an investment fund run by former *Fortune* magazine writer Alfred Winslow Jones. He had returned his clients gains of 670 percent over the previous decade, Loomis noted, which was almost double the 358-percent return for the top-performing mutual fund. The method he used was buying under-valued stocks, but also short selling over-valued stocks, betting that they would go down in price and he could profit on the difference. By betting on price movements both up and down, Jones reduced, or "hedged," his market risk.[42]

Jones avoided the regulation of mutual funds by operating as a limited partnership with fewer than 100 investors. He took 20 percent of the profits for himself, but charged investors nothing unless he made them money. Within two years, the number of hedge funds soared from a handful to more than 100, but they really took off at the millennium, rising from about 300 in 1990 to almost 6,000 in 2001.[43]

Avoiding regulation allowed hedge funds to operate in secrecy and "do almost anything they want," noted legal scholar David Skeel. That included not just short selling but also the use of exotic financial instruments such as derivatives and credit default swaps. One of the favorite hedge fund investments was to buy bonds issued by companies in financial trouble. "The funds pay a small fraction of the debt's face value," noted Skeel, "betting it will be worth more if the company's fortunes turn."[44] If the company went bankrupt, debt holders would also be in line to take it over.

Many of the companies in financial trouble at the millennium were newspaper publishers, who were facing new competition from the Internet. Hedge funds began betting on their fortunes falling, which they did with the 2008-09 recession. From 2004 to 2014, hedge funds and closely-related private equity firms, which bought whole companies rather than their shares or debt, increased their holdings of U.S. newspapers sixfold, and by 2014 owned six of the ten largest chains.[45] Unlike traditional newspapers owners, such as founding families and even chains, hedge funds and private equity firms focused entirely on profits at the expense of journalism. "The large investment groups tend to employ a standard formula in managing their newspapers," noted academic Penelope Muse Abernathy, "aggressive cost cutting paired with revenue increases and financial restructuring, including bankruptcy."[46]

While all newspapers have had to make layoffs in the face of falling revenues due to the Internet, hedge fund and private equity owners cut staff at a rate double or more that of other owners. According to the U.S. Bureau of Labor Statistics, newspapers cut 24 percent of their workforces on average between 2012 and 2016.[47] Digital First Media, which was owned by the hedge fund Alden Global Capital, cut its headcount by 72 percent over a six-year period, according to a study by the NewsGuild union, from 1,766 in 2012 to 487 in 2018.[48] While hedge funds were highly secretive, media analyst Ken Doctor found that Digital First made a 2017 profit margin of 17 percent, with earnings of $159 million on revenues of $939 million.[49]

One of the most aggressive newspaper buyers was the GateHouse chain, which was owned by the hedge fund New Media Investments. According to Abernathy, it spent more than $1 billion on 200 newspaper acquisitions between 2013 and 2018 to build the second-largest U.S. chain.[50] Its buying spree culminated in August 2019 when it outbid Digital First and paid $1.4 billion for Gannett, the country's largest chain. It borrowed the entire amount and more from another hedge fund, so Gannett was laden with debt. If it went bankrupt, the hedge funds would be first in line with their debt to take it over and shed legal obligations, such as leases, pensions, taxes, and union contracts. The Journal Register chain, which was owned by Alden, actually declared bankruptcy twice, first in 2009 and again in 2012, before merging with the MediaNews Group the following year to form Digital First.[51]

Hedge funds come to Canada

The $300 million in Canwest debt that GoldenTree Asset Management had bought on the bond market helped it to acquire its newspaper division out of bankruptcy in 2010, in spite of Canada's 25-percent limit on foreign ownership.

GoldenTree's founding partner Steven Shapiro was a former bankruptcy attorney who had been a research analyst for the high-yield investment bank The Argosy Group in New York when it was taken over by CIBC in 1995.[52] He then worked on financing both the management buyout of Sun Media led by Paul Godfrey in 1996 and its sale to Quebecor three years later before helping to found GoldenTree in 2000, so he understood the Canadian newspaper industry well.

The hedge fund formula of weaponizing debt allowed Golden-Tree to attach itself to the new company it called Postmedia, living off the high-interest loans it had acquired for pennies on the dollar. Its parasitic plan required only that it keep the host alive, but as long as it was, it would be in a sickly state.

The fact that GoldenTree and Postmedia's other foreign hedge fund owners could not legally control the company would not stop them from running it. While they could together exercise no more than 25 percent of the company's votes, as owners they held outsized influence over its affairs. The Canadian shareholders, after all, included Godfrey and other Postmedia executives who were hired by the owners and received compensation, including stock options and bonuses, that was determined by them. "Regardless of the legal power of Canadian shareholders to run the corporation through their appointed Canadian directors, Postmedia Network was factually subject to the wishes of foreigners," noted Harry Glasbeek, a professor emeritus of Law at York University in his 2017 book *Class Privilege*.[53]

> Control and influence could be exercised by people who are legally considered bystanders when it comes to corporate decision-making. ...What was important was not their technical status but their functional ability to make the blob do what they wanted it to do. Control is what counts. As President Nixon is reputed to have said: "If you have them by the testicles, their hearts and minds will follow."[54]

Once Shapiro took a one-year sabbatical from GoldenTree for personal reasons in late 2015 and gave up his seat on Postmedia's board of directors, however, the relationship seemed to sour. GoldenTree and the other hedge funds had already sucked hundreds of million of dollars in interest payments out of Postmedia, but the outlook for newspapers was hardly improving, and to many the prognosis appeared terminal. Shapiro's partners thus sold their investment in his absence to New Jersey-based Chatham Asset Management in 2016 for $100 million as part of Postmedia's financial reorganization.

Playing tough

Chatham was a very different hedge fund from GoldenTree. By using some innovative methods, it returned its investors an average annual return of 9.6 percent, outperforming its competitors by almost half and earning it some major clients, including the New Jersey and California state pensions. "Even by hedge-fund standards, Chatham flies under the radar," noted *Fortune* in 2019. It was founded in 2003 by Anthony Melchiorre after he was laid off as head of at Morgan Stanley's junk-bond trading group in New York. "He built his stature as a temperamental money-maker at the white-shoe firm," added *Fortune*. "His behavior infuriated some senior executives, according to former colleagues."[55]

> Although not physically imposing, Melchiorre could be foul-mouthed and loud, and would berate fellow traders as he bopped around the trading floor in his stocking feet. "He's a street fighter," said Mike Rankowitz, his boss at Morgan Stanley. "There are people who don't like him. That's because they are losing to him."[56]

From the beginning, Chatham offered investors a fund to sell short not just stocks, but also debt in its Chatham Asset Partners Short Credit Fund. It dealt in credit default swaps, which allowed investors to offset their credit risk with that of another investor. The exotic financial instrument played a key role in the credit crisis that led to the 2008-09 recession, as they had been packaged by major investment houses such as Bear Stearns and Lehman Brothers into mortgage-backed securities as insurance against mortgage defaults, which became widespread.[57] Chatham's fund was "designed for investors wanting to take a directional view that default swap spreads will widen, or for investors with credit exposures wanting to hedge their portfolios," according to a spokesman. "By taking exposure to the index the fund is attractive to investors that do not have the expertise to negotiate derivatives documentation themselves."[58]

Melchiorre and Chatham soon built a "formidable reputation," noted *Fortune*. "A Chicago-area kid who studied economics at Northwestern and got an MBA from the University of Chicago, his high-toned education didn't reduce the intensity of the former high-school football star."[59] The business magazine did a deep dive into the firm's rough and sometimes questionable tactics. "Playing tough is the Chatham way," it noted, adding that the firm and its founder had developed "a reputation for hard-edged business."[60] One business owner claimed that Chatham artificially drove down the price of his company's bonds by almost 30 percent, ruining his debt-restructuring efforts so Chatham could take control of the company. When he sued, Chatham counter-sued, claiming he had used company money to pay a Las Vegas escort $4,000, which wound up on the front page of the *New York Post* under the headline "Frisky Business." Carl Grimstad got the last laugh, however, when he won an US$11 million damage award.[61]

Questions had swirled around Chatham for years, noted *Fortune*. "Traders have privately criticized what they see as lofty valuations of illiquid securities. At least one executive … has accused the New Jersey firm of market manipulation. Federal regulators have been asking questions, too."[62] One brokerage received complaints, according to *Fortune*, that some of its brokers "agreed to buy bonds from Chatham with the promise the hedge fund would repurchase them at higher prices, according to people with knowledge of the situation."[63] Questions were also asked about Postmedia's bonds, according to Fortune. "The strong price of the debt is difficult to explain, traders say."

> Its bonds rarely change hands. Yet its junior bonds offer yields comparable to more senior securities. The notes don't pay regular interest in cash, a sign of their inherent riskiness. At least five other traders who've looked at the bonds say their prices seem too good to be true.[64]

A similar story soon began to unfold at the U.S. chain McClatchy, which owned major dailies such as the *Miami Herald*, *Kansas City Star*, and *Sacramento Bee* but suffered under a heavy debt load. Chatham began to buy up its bonds, which soon began to rise in price. "Its bonds staged an improbable rally last year, charting a steady climb over 50% from 80 to 125 cents on the dollar," noted *Fortune*. "That made it one of the best performing bonds in the world at the time … 'That's just not how bond math works,' said [one portfolio manager]. 'Something other than fundamentals are playing a huge factor in those bonds.'"[65]

After McClatchy declared bankruptcy in 2020, Chatham won control of it at auction and added its 30 titles to a newspaper stable that already included Postmedia and *National Enquirer* publisher American Media.[66] Harvard University's online journalism website NiemanLab even raised the possibility of combining the chains. "Under different circumstances, merging Chatham's Postmedia and McClatchy would be a natural in any number of ways," wrote Joshua Benton. "But I imagine the national border between them, as well as Canada's appropriate concerns about foreign media ownership, would get in the way there under a Trudeau government."[67]

The secret to Chatham's success in taking control of McClatchy, according to Bloomberg, was credit default swaps. "Leading up to the deal, Chatham had been selling swaps insuring against a default by McClatchy," it reported. "So if the transaction were to be completed, it would be getting paid CDS premiums to guarantee against a default that could never technically happen."[68] After investors made almost $500 million by buying credit-default swaps on the publisher, reported the financial news service, Chatham "stacked the deck with a deal that's threatening to make those swaps all but worthless. The McClatchy situation is the latest trade that's drawing jeers from critics who say the $11 trillion CDS market has devolved into a haven for manipulation."[69]

> Chatham struck a deal with the newspaper publisher ... to refinance most of its $710 million of debt with two new loans... Because of a condition in the deal with Chatham that would move McClatchy's borrowings into a new wholly owned subsidiary, the impact was seismic for holders of the derivatives. In a matter of hours, the refinancing wiped out 70 percent of the market value of a five-year CDS on McClatchy. ... But for Chatham, the deal could bring a potential windfall. Leading up to the deal, Chatham had been selling swaps insuring against a default by McClatchy.[70]

Selling social justice short

Soon even the *Toronto Star*, which started life as a strike newspaper and was unique among Canadian dailies in being guided by its so-called Atkinson principles including social justice and the rights of working people, fell prey to private equity.

Its founding families proved particularly poor at navigating the unfamiliar terrain that newspapers were entering. A series of management blunders in the 2010's rocked Canada's largest and most liberal daily. Its parent company Torstar lost a reported $40 million in developing a tablet app that failed to attract subscribers and was finally ditched in 2017.[71] It then embarked on a national expansion by hiring 20 new staff for its Metro chain of free commuter tabloids, rebranding them *StarMetro* and boosting their bureaus in Vancouver, Edmonton, Calgary, and Halifax in a strategy that lasted less than two years before also being scrubbed.[72] Most embarrassing of all, Torstar's offices were raided by law enforcement officers after it made a highly questionably, and possibly even illegal deal with Postmedia (see Chapter 4).

Torstar's profits fell to $29.2 million in 2019 from $34.8 million the previous year. Its 2020 first quarter report showed a shockingly low profit of $2.5 million, down from $6.7 million in the same period a year earlier. The sudden freefall, combined with onset of the Covid-19 pandemic, perhaps panicked members of the five families that controlled debt-free Torstar into selling it for $51 million, which was less than the company's $69.5 million in cash.[73]

Even curiouser, the *Globe and Mail* reported the next day, was that new owner NordStar Capital, a private equity partnership created for the occasion, had borrowed $50 million to finance the acquisition from Canso, which had financed Postmedia's purchase of Sun Media. The connection prompted speculation that a merger was imminent, but NordStar insisted that the financing arrangements were "not, in anyway whatsoever, connected directly or indirectly with any other media company."[74]

A year later, NordStar more than recouped Torstar's purchase price by floating its VerticalScope digital subsidiary in an initial public offering of shares that raised $125 million and valued the company at almost $400 million. VerticalScope, which operated more than 1,200 websites on topics ranging from cars and photography to parenting and sailing, attracted 100 million users a month and had generated more than $60 million in revenue in its previous fiscal year.[75]

The private equity partnership didn't last, however, with Paul Rivett insisting on cost cuts and Jordan Bitove on preserving quality journalism. In 2022 the parties went to court to divide the company.[76] The split went to arbitration, and Bitove emerged with ownership of Torstar.[77]

Press prognosis

The subject of newspapers would be moot if they didn't have a future. If news would soon be delivered only online and printing presses would be shut down, why worry about what happens to newspapers? The answer was that in the race to dominate the future of online news, newspapers were starting in first place.

Many assumed their demise as a medium, however, such as journalism professor Philip Meyer, who predicted precisely in his 2004 book *The Vanishing Newspaper* that due to a lack of readers the last copy would be printed in March of 2043.[78] The predictions accelerated as the 2008-09 recession claimed several long-publishing dailies and drove some of the continent's largest chains into bankruptcy.

But the chains were all still profitable because their newspapers were still profitable. The only thing that took them down was debt. The bankrupt chains got new owners, often the hedge funds which held their debt, and the newspapers continued publishing. My 2014 book *Greatly Exaggerated: The Myth of the Death of Newspapers* concluded that newspapers would survive in some form because they were highly scalable and could cut their costs almost as fast as their revenues fell. As a result, none of the more than dozen publicly-traded chains in the U.S. and Canada, I found, showed an operating loss between 2006 and 2013.[79]

Subsequent research has confirmed the staying power of the press around the world. A 2015 study of U.S. newspapers examined financial data to confirm that the industry remained profitable. "The review of this proprietary financial benchmarking data strongly supports Edge's conclusion that newspapers stabilized their financial performance and scaled their businesses to the reduced levels of advertising revenue."[80] A 2017 study of Belgian newspapers found that their profit margins averaged 10.7 percent in 2014, but that consolidation had seen the number of newspaper owners fall from six in 1990 to only two in 2014.[81] A study of Swiss press groups that same year found them to be growing in both market share and profitability, with the leading chain recording profit margins of 19 percent for its national newspapers in 2015 and 15 percent for its regional dailies.[82]

My 2023 study of newspapers in the UK, where all companies must file annual financial statements with Companies House whether they are privately-owned or publicly-traded, showed that their profits are the best in years since many have adopted online subscription schemes. The profits of Rupert Murdoch's *Times* and *Sunday Times*, for example, doubled to £52.5 million in 2022. Murdoch reversed the falling fortunes of the *Times* newspapers in 2010 by introducing a hard paywall, although notably a similar subscription scheme at his tabloid *Sun* failed, presumably because few readers were willing to pay for its kind of content, which could be found elsewhere for free on the Internet. The only paid national newspaper to cease printing in the UK in recent decades has been the *Independent*, which did so in 2016 because its digital edition was profitable as a stand-alone publication. The online-only Independent's profits quadrupled to £5.4 million in 2021, while its profit margin was a comfortable 13.1 percent.[83]

Media effects

Scholars sought for decades to unlock the secrets of mass persuasion that had been so amply demonstrated by the power of propaganda in fomenting two world wars. Sociologists simply assumed that media had powerful effects on audiences, and used the analogy of a hypodermic needle to inject beliefs and attitudes. Psychologists could find no measurable effects, however, noting that beliefs and attitudes were ingrained at an early age through a process of socialization by family, friends, and others. Changing people's beliefs, they found, was actually very difficult, as cognitive dissonance proved a powerful force to overcome. Other theorists, such as Walter Lippmann, pointed out that the power of media was in its ability to influence our perceptions. The accepted paradigm of powerful media effects became limited effects in the 1940s, but in the 1960s the work of two Canadian scholars began to again reverse the trend.[84]

University of Toronto political economist Harold Innis studied staple industries, such as the fur trade, cod fishery, and mining. He was studying the forest industry in B.C. when he realized that it was tied into price networks through the pulp and paper it provided to print the continent's newspapers. He switched to the study of communication and soon realized that throughout history, from the hieroglyphics engraved on stone tablets in ancient Egypt to the scrolls of papyrus in ancient Rome, control of a society's dominant medium meant control of society itself.

Innis's 1,000-page book manuscript went unpublished after his death from cancer in 1952, but his work was carried on by U of T colleague Marshall McLuhan, an English literature professor who dazzled the world with his media insights in the 1960s.[85] Even more powerful than media messages was the medium itself, he realized, coining the phrase "the medium is the message." Electronic communication like radio and television conveyed messages differently than linear print, and as satellites began to orbit the earth McLuhan saw it soon connected as one "global village." McLuhan's ideas would elevate him posthumously as oracle of the Internet Age, and he was installed on the masthead of *Wired* magazine in 1996 as its "patron saint."[86]

Media innovations often had unexpected effects, however. Media depictions of crime and violence that were out of proportion with reality led viewers to perceive the world the way it was portrayed on television, which was dubbed the Mean World Syndrome. More televised violence made people more fearful and thus more willing to accept repressive political solutions to crime. Live satellite broadcasting from the world's hotspots led to the so-called CNN Effect that saw generals conduct wars in real time based on what they were watching on television. The rise of Fox News in the 1990s led to the Fox Effect, which was a significant rightward shift found in voting between where the channel was offered on cable systems and where it was unavailable.[87]

Hedge fund ownership of newspapers, as pioneered by Postmedia in 2010, has had a devastating effect on Canada's news media. It has accelerated the decline of the newspaper industry by skimming the revenues of by far its largest chain off the top every month through debt payments. The Postmedia Effect took down not only Canada's largest newspaper chain, but then its second-largest chain Sun Media in 2014, and it threatens to consume the entire industry. Similarly in the U.S., the rise of hedge fund ownership starting in 2010 by firms such as Alden Global Capital and New Media Investments has had a devastating effect on journalism even as it was attempting the difficult transition to a new medium.

American Prospect laid bare the "malign genius" of the business model in 2017, noting that while the digital transition is a huge challenge for newspapers, ownership by private equity predators has made it all but impossible. "It allows the absentee owner to drive a paper into the ground, but extract exorbitant profits along the way from management fees, dividends, and tax breaks. By the time the paper is a hollow shell, the private equity company can exit and move on, having more than made back its investment."[88] This strategy, which is known as "harvesting," is the opposite of a sustainable business model, noted Harvard economist Michael Porter.

> A stagnant industry's market position is harvested by raising prices and lowering quality, trusting that customers will continue to be attracted by the brand name rather than the substance for which the brand once stood. This is a non-renewable, take-the-money-and-run strategy. A given crop can be harvested only once.[89]

The result of the harvesting strategy in the newspaper industry has been so-called "news deserts," where scant local journalism can be found.[90] The landscape is populated by what former *Buffalo News* editor Margaret Sullivan calls "ghost newspapers," which are mostly empty shells printed for the benefit of elderly subscribers while young people get their news from smartphones. The loss of journalism expertise and local knowledge that has been jettisoned to keep the shell game going, noted Sullivan in her 2020 book *Ghosting the News*, would be useful to help make a successful online transition. "For the sake of democracy, in America and around the world, we need to save as much as possible of what remains, bringing the traditional strengths into the digital age."[91]

In Canada, the problem has been complicated by the willingness of government to subsidize failing businesses such as newspapers. According to a 2018 University of Calgary study, Ottawa and the four largest provinces spent about $29 billion a year on business subsidies through program spending, the tax system, government business enterprises, and direct investment. "Federal and provincial subsidies combined represented almost half of corporate income tax revenue," it noted. "About 70 per cent of spending on business subsidies is used to address market failures."[92] Government subsidies for business, the CBC noted the following year, were greater than Canada's defence budget.[93] "In his 2018 Fall Economic Report, Finance Minister Bill Morneau announced that corporations would receive $14 billion in new tax breaks," noted a pair of Canadian scholars. "In a time of record profits, Canadian corporations already receive billions in subsidies every year, not to mention massive corporate tax cuts and loopholes."[94]

The problem of Canada's corporate welfare system was identified in 1972 by then-NDP leader David Lewis, who launched an attack on what he called "corporate welfare bums" during that year's election campaign. His book published earlier that year decried the "tax concessions and loopholes for which large, often foreign-owned corporations benefit at the expense of the ordinary Canadian taxpayer. The latter is forced to carry a heavier tax burden because the corporations do not pay their share."[95]

Fifty years later, the problem has only gotten worse. Now it's not just foreign-owned corporations that are living off Canadian welfare, but foreign-owned hedge funds which are holding our news media hostage, and they have mobilized the vast arsenal of persuasion that is the nation's press in aid of their harvesting strategy. The Postmedia Effect is more than just the hollowing out of a country's largest and most influential newspapers. It is the weaponizing of that influence to continue feeding off the dying remains of our country's news media.

CHAPTER 3
THE BAILOUT CAMPAIGN

Edward Greenspon's new job as head of the Public Policy Forum think tank was a lot like his first career in journalism since both required lots of networking. Greenspon was nothing if not well connected, especially in the nation's capital, where he spent six years covering Ottawa for the *Globe and Mail*, rising to bureau chief. He was described by the *Hill Times* as a "consummate Ottawa insider" upon being recalled to Toronto in 1999 and installed as the *Globe*'s executive editor.[1] Greenspon' first foray into management was short-lived, however, when he ran into the buzz saw that was deputy editor Chrystia Freeland.

The new arrival from the *Financial Times* in London was just 30 when she joined the senior editorial ranks of the *Globe and Mail*. The *Canadian Jewish News* described Freeland and Greenspon as part of a "triumvirate of 'generals,'" along with editor Richard Addis, that formulated the *Globe*'s strategy in the newspaper war that broke out in Toronto at the millennium after Conrad Black began publishing his new *National Post*.[2] According to *Ottawa Citizen* reporter Chris Cobb, however, it soon became obvious to Greenspon that with Freeland's arrival he "was not going to be part of any triumvirate."[3]

Addis, a Brit who had also been imported from Fleet Street, instead relied more on Freeland for strategy in the circulation and promotion war. "Richard and Chrystia met every morning by themselves," Greenspon confessed to Cobb for his 2004 book *Ego and Ink*, which chronicled the conflict. "I wasn't part of those conversations."[4] Addis told Cobb that while he initially found Greenspon enthusiastic, bright, and energetic, he soon came to consider him a "very ambitious hustler, and that gets right up my nose ... It is not the way that anyone I know, with any style, operates."[5]

He was stupid in that he was too ambitious ... He didn't have the skills necessary at that time to repair the newspaper. He didn't have a clue how to do it ... He was very upset that Chrystia was coming in over his head ... but obviously he wasn't going to be allowed to run things as he had before.[6]

The setback was daunting for Greenspon, who had turned down the job of managing editor at the *National Post*. He soon beat a hasty retreat back to the *Globe*'s Ottawa bureau after a news editor was hired behind his back. "I had been stripped of all my power," he explained to Cobb. Greenspon later prevailed on *Globe and Mail* publisher Philip Crawley to be put in charge of the newspaper's website, which he leveraged into the top job after Addis left in 2002.

Cobb found the bespectacled Greenspon "a quintessential *Globe and Mail* man [who] had impressed colleagues as an intelligent, ambitious person with a clear sight of his professional targets and, through the cultivation of key individuals, an ability to exert quiet influence, and make his views known, in places high above his station."[7] A 2003 profile in the *Ryerson Review of Journalism* noted that "some colleagues call Greenspon a control freak. Others just say he sets extremely high standards for himself and for others."[8]

> According to Darrell Bricker, Greenspon's co-author of *Searching for Certainty: Inside the New Canadian Mindset*, published in 2001, Greenspon is an honours graduate of Guilt Trip U. "If he felt I didn't keep a commitment to do something, it was like talking to your old Jewish grandmother," he says. "He would make you feel terrible that you let him down." As Bricker puts it, Greenspon doesn't get angry; he gets disappointed.[9]

Not everyone had been impressed with their book, however. "Nothing is rotten in the state of Canada if you believe *Searching for Certainty*," wrote a reviewer for *Quill and Quire*. "The cliché-clogged text also fails to explain why so few Canadian companies have been able to achieve the global domination allegedly within their grasp and does not devote enough ink to the significant cadre of Canadians who are ill-equipped to survive, let alone strive for victory, in the new economy."[10]

Crawley fired Greenspon in 2009, explaining in a memo to staff that the newspaper needed "new skills and different styles of leadership."[11] Greenspon bounced around a bit after that, first heading a panel for the think tank Canadian International Council that produced a 2011 foreign policy review.[12] He then spent a few years working for Torstar, where he helped launch its Star Content Studios to churn out native advertising.[13] He had most recently been an editor-at-large for Bloomberg News. The considerable connections he made over the years, and even his family ties, would soon come in handy, however.

It was perhaps fitting that Greenspon would end up heading the PPF. After all, he had won its Hyman Solomon Award for Excellence in Public Policy Journalism in 2002, following which he was immediately elevated to the *Globe and Mail*'s top job. The PPF described Greenspon upon naming him its president and CEO in March 2016 as "one of Canada's most accomplished journalists," noting that he had "worked at the intersection of journalism, business and public policy for more than 30 years."[14]

Greenspon's first major project for the PPF began in mid-2016, shortly after he assumed its leadership. The Heritage committee then holding hearings into media and local communities was supposed to tour Canada that fall to see for itself the problem on the ground and hear from Canadians first-hand about the state of local news provision, but sufficient funds were not available in its budget. That function was instead farmed out to the PPF. "We're not, if you will, hired by the government," said Greenspon. "But we're doing this in co-operation with the government."[15]

State of the news

The PPF's review, according to the Canadian Press, revolved around three questions: "Does the deteriorating state of traditional media put at risk the civic function of journalism and thus the health of democracy? If so, are new digitally based news media filling the gap? If not, is there a role for public policy to help maintain a healthy flow of news and information, and how could it be done least intrusively?"[16] A half-dozen roundtables with "invited experts" were planned, as was polling designed to determine "how

Canadians view the news media and its role in democratic society." A concluding symposium was scheduled for the fall.[17]

CBC News obtained a report which showed that the PPF had a deadline of year's end to deliver its report, for which it was being paid $270,000, with the Heritage department and the Department of Innovation, Science and Economic Development each contributing $100,000.[18] Where the other $70,000 came from could be inferred from the resulting report's final page, which thanked its "partners." In addition to the government of Canada, it listed CN, the TD bank, Montreal-based property management company Ivanhoé Cambridge, Toronto private equity firm Clairvest, the Canadian Journalism Foundation, and the Atkinson, McConnell, and Max Bell foundations.[19]

Chatham House rules

Secrecy surrounded the PPF's roundtables, which were invitation-only and held under Chatham House rules, which extracted promises from participants not to attribute what was said during discussion. Former *Ottawa Citizen* editor Andrew Potter attended the first roundtable in June 2016, which was held in the nation's capital, and commented on it generally the next day. "The conversation was more interesting than I expected, there was a good mix of new voices and extremely familiar faces, and pretty clear lack of sentimentality about the direction the business has taken," he blogged. "A few policy ideas were batted around, but I can't say there was anything really new or surprising on offer. Certainly no one there thought they had a magic bullet to give to the government."[20]

Potter did disclose his own position on the questions, however. "My contribution to the debate yesterday (aside from calling Facebook 'the devil') was to recommend a great deal of wait and see," he wrote. "I'm increasingly of the view that we need to just let this process play itself out. The convulsion of news media is a decade old, and it probably has another decade or so to go."[21]

> What the government should do, above all, is avoid doing anything that hinder the ferocious process of creative destruction that needs to take place. Worse than doing nothing would be a system that "bakes in"

the status quo ... Otherwise, the government should do whatever it can to make sure there are as few obstacles as possible to the generation and testing of new business models or content strategies."[22]

One "lively" roundtable held in Regina that September, according to a report in the local *Leader Post*, was attended by "a couple of dozen media executives, academics, journalists and industry representatives" but achieved "little or no consensus about what the government should be doing about it, if anything."[23] CBC News obtained summaries of three of the roundtable sessions with the identities of participants blacked out and reported that they included "the big media firms, such as Postmedia, as well as ethnic and Indigenous newspapers, broadcasters such as the CBC, digital firms, academics and others."[24] It also revealed the most prominent suggestions brought forward in the closed-door sessions. "Tax changes, better copyright protection and fees imposed on Facebook and Google are among the solutions being touted to help rescue Canada's ailing news industry," it reported in early 2017. "But the internal documents show top players are pressing for federal policies that would extract money from big digital news carriers that produce little original Canadian content."[25]

> The documents also show a broad disdain for direct government subsidies to the news business; a general belief that market forces should prevail; and the hope that any new policies should help all Canadian content producers.... "No company wants a government bailout," says the Toronto summary. "However, tools are needed to provide more balance for news organizations to compete against the large digital companies."[26]

The CBC report also quoted from an interim PPF report to the Heritage department. "Hobbled by falling revenues, legacy costs and lumbering cultures, and desperately trying to make digital inroads, established media companies have reduced their emphasis on the hunting and gathering of original news in favour of processing of existing news," it read. "For their part, new entrants generally lack the capital, critical mass or capabilities to produce the sort of professionally based iterative journalism critical to holding public institutions to account."[27]

The Public Policy Forum's final report was thus eagerly anticipated when it was released in early 2017. *The Shattered Mirror*, a reference to Senator Keith Davey's 1970 report on Canada's mass media, *The Uncertain Mirror*, it contained a dozen recommendations for improving news provision, which included extending to digital media the tax rules that favoured other Canadian media when it came to advertising and subjecting foreign ad sales to Canadian taxes. It urged that Canada's copyright law be updated to strengthen protection for news organizations and charitable giving laws changed to allow them to become non-profit entities and thus receive tax deductible donations. It proposed federal funding of $100 million to start a Future of Journalism and Democracy Fund, with continuing funding of $300 to $400 million a year coming from a sales tax on foreign media selling digital subscriptions in Canada and from removing tax deductions on foreign digital advertising.

The proposed fund would be managed independently of the government and invest in digital news innovation and civic journalism, with a focus on start-ups, local outlets, and indigenous operations. It would also underwrite civic-function journalism, fund digital innovation, research the role of news in society, and provide legal advice. To help fill the local news gap, the report suggested establishing a non-profit arm of the Canadian Press news agency called CP-Local with a staff of 60 to 80 journalists covering courts, legislatures, and city halls at a cost of $810 million a year. It also recommended barring the CBC from selling online advertising, focusing it more on civic news, and making its content available to other media outlets for free.[28]

One thing *The Shattered Mirror* did not recommend were tax credits, which it called a "very blunt tool" that could be "easily removed or reduced if a government becomes unhappy with the media." Tax credits had several other disadvantages, according to the report. "They treat those with a good record in making the digital transition equally with those whose record is poor. Meanwhile, their treatment of for-profit and non-profit news organizations is unequal."[29] The report noted "a great apprehension among early-stage digital news operators that tax credits would favour established for-profit companies that have lobbying power and lock in their position over potentially more innovative newcomers."[30] Tax credits, it added, were also "difficult to police for leakage."

> Money is highly fungible and, once credits are received, companies could apply them in many different ways, even if they are specifically for labour or digital technology. They could even be applied to a company's bottom line, to the benefit of shareholders and executives. From a fiscal point of view, tax credits have a tendency to grow indiscriminately, as businesses adjust their operations to fall within the ambit of the tax credit.[31]

The Shattered Mirror warned that with bad news for the industry piling up, the news media's "march to the precipice appears to be picking up speed. This slide may not produce the kind of crisis point that stops policymakers in their tracks, as the implosion of the auto industry in 2008-09 did, but the pace is unrelenting and the downward slope ever steeper."[32] The *Globe and Mail* noted that News Media Canada, the lobby group representing the country's newspaper industry, "quickly distanced itself from the report," stating that its recommendations would not do much to help build sustainable new business models.

"What I don't see is the money going to news outlets that are currently covering their communities, building out digital platforms and adapting to the new business realities," said NMC chair Bob Cox, publisher of the *Winnipeg Free Press*, who had been night editor at the *Globe and Mail* under Greenspon. "This is the bedrock of civic-function journalism in Canada and the best bet for ensuring its survival is to support it directly rather than pouring all resources into early-stage news operations and research on news and democracy."[33]

Reaction to *The Shattered Mirror* was otherwise mixed, noted iPolitics, with the Canadian Association of Journalists supporting several of its proposals but taking "no immediate position" on the rest.[34] The CAJ called incentives for advertising in Canadian online media and non-profit journalism "no-brainers."[35] The media union

CWA Canada similarly welcomed the report's call for non-profit news media to qualify for charitable status "in order to encourage local, non-profit ownership of newspapers rather than the destructive, predatory hedge fund disaster that is Postmedia." In a strongly-worded press release, however, the union representing 6,000 media workers urged stronger action. "This alone won't break up the Postmedia monopoly," warned union president Martin O'Hanlon. "We also need the government to introduce legislation or regulations to limit concentration of media ownership and prevent destructive leveraged purchases of important national companies."[36]

Out on the west coast, Rafe Mair, a retired talk show host and former provincial cabinet minister, smelled horse manure. "It's clear that The Shattered Mirror has nothing to do with democracy and good journalism and everything to do with bailing out an industry that's facing obsolescence," he wrote in his book *Politically Incorrect*, which was published shortly after his 2017 death. "So, do we just let them go broke?"[37]

> If they do, history teaches us that while there will be pain aplenty at the beginning, the void will be filled. But keeping them alive with government subsidies is a slippery slope to disaster. Instead of a news industry in thrall to big business generally and the fossil fuel industry specifically, they will no more wish to offend the government than they now do the fossil fuel industry.[38]

National Post columnist Andrew Coyne called the report "irreproachably responsible, admirably high-minded, and profoundly wrong" in also arguing for nature to instead take its course. "This is not a case of market failure, but of industry failure," he wrote. "Most of the industry's problems are self-inflicted, a series of bad choices in response to admittedly massive changes. But even if that were not the case, there is nothing whatever to prevent readers from paying for what we produce, if they so chose. They are simply choosing not to do so."[39]

The *Globe and Mail* noted that the report seized on 2016's moral panic of "fake news" to amplify its call for government action. "If Canadian news outlets get the massive federal bailout that a new think-tank report is calling for, they might want to send a thank-you note to Donald Trump," it said. "Mr. Trump's unexpected election, and the explosion of fake news that some have suggested helped vault him into the White House, hover like a smiling Satan over the report."[40]

> Fake news is not, so far, much of a problem in Canada, which may prompt readers to wonder why it is mentioned 39 times in the 108-page report. But some domestic publishers may be crossing their fingers in hopes that its appearance down south proves enough of a pretext for a government-led solution to their own financial woes.[41]

Scholarly criticism

Scholars who studied media economics in Canada similarly noted that *The Shattered Mirror* exaggerated the plight of newspapers and the threat of foreign Internet giants with selective data, exaggeration, and glaring omissions. It also glossed over some fundamental problems afflicting the newspaper industry, they pointed out, preferring to blame its woes instead on Google and Facebook. One critic called it "the funhouse mirror" for its exaggerations and found the report notable for what it didn't include. "The PPF report is silent on the problem of U.S. hedge funds owning Canada's largest newspaper company," he wrote, and "gives the Competition Bureau a pass, noting only that it was 'caught by surprise' by Postmedia's broken promises."[42] *The Shattered Mirror* promoted what this media critic called "the Big Lie that has surrounded newspapers for years — that they are losing money and thus dying."

> It repeats the canard that industry dominant Postmedia Network is bleeding red ink by mentioning that the company lost $352 million in its fiscal year ended last August 31. That's only if you deduct a $267 million "impairment" charge that reflects the reduced value of Postmedia's business on paper, plus a raft of other extraordinary expenses such as the $42 million cost of severing staff. Otherwise, on a cash-in/cash-out basis, Postmedia recorded operating earnings of $82 million on revenues of $877 million for a profit margin of 9.3 percent.[43]

Most questionable of all, according to this critic, was the report's prediction that newspaper sales would fall to only two per 100 households by 2025, down from 18 in 2015 and 49 in 1995. To support its contention, *The Shattered Mirror* produced a graph (Figure 1) which simply showed the current downward trend continuing unabated. "So ardently does the PPF promote the newspaper death myth," he noted, "that the heading for this section screams 'THE END MAY BE IN SIGHT.'"[44]

FIGURE 1

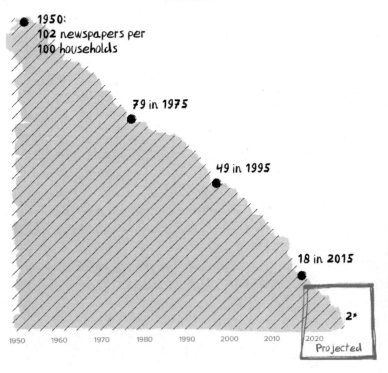

The graph was almost identical to one in a 2015 paper posted on the website of Winnipeg media consultant Ken Goldstein, the critic noted, who was singled out in the acknowledgements as having been "particularly patient in helping us understand industry numbers."[45] A former vice-president of Canwest, Goldstein warned that "there will be few, if any, printed daily newspapers" left in Canada by 2025.[46] The paper, which did not disclose its genesis, purpose, or funding, simply extended circulation trends downward in a graph similar to that in *The Shattered Mirror*, except that instead of only 2 percent, it forecast that newspaper penetration would fall to 5–10 percent of households by 2025. "To the extent that the trend lines are realistic, we do not believe that a viable print business model exists for most general interest daily newspapers once paid circulation drops below 10 percent."[47]

The Shattered Mirror further perpetuated the newspaper death myth, according to this critic, by noting completely without context that six Canadian dailies had closed, merged or changed publication frequency in 2016. Of them, however, only the *Guelph Mercury* was by any measure a major newspaper, ranking about 50th among Canada's 90-odd paid dailies then publishing with an average weekday circulation of about 9,400, which was down 25 percent in less than two years. Torstar closed the paper in favour of its twice-weekly *Guelph Tribune*, which it bought in 2004 from the Southam chain then owned by Canwest and was circulated free to about 40,000 homes.[48]

The other five former dailies were all small-town newspapers in Western Canada, only one of which was actually closed, with the others all moving to weekly publication. The other closed daily was the *Nanaimo Daily News*, which had a circulation of about 4,000. It had been bought from Glacier Media a year earlier, along with the weekly *Harbour City Star*, by Black Press, which already owned the twice-weekly *Nanaimo News Bulletin*. The purchase was part of a series of deals Black Press made with Glacier that gave it every community newspaper on Vancouver Island, which has about the population of New Brunswick. It soon closed the *Harbour City Star* and later closed the *Daily News* after it claimed it was "unable to develop a sustainable business model that would offset the high cost base of the *Nanaimo Daily News* in relation to its low paid-circulation base."[49]

The two B.C. chains were playing a real-life game of Monopoly right under the somnambulant nose of the Competition Bureau, buying, selling, and even trading newspapers back and forth, then closing competing titles to gain more lucrative monopolies.[50] This was context that might have reflected poorly on business practices in the Canadian newspaper industry, however, and was not mentioned in *The Shattered Mirror*.

The report also presented data from the Local News Research Project at Ryerson University, where Greenspon's wife, Janice Neil, was then head of the journalism school. The project began about the same time as *The Shattered Mirror* and was headed by Velma Rogers Research Chair April Lindgren, who did not hold a graduate degree. A Local News Map showed that 169 "news outlets" had closed since 2008, but its data were gathered online using "crowd-sourcing," so anyone could post on it. Studies of crowd-sourcing found it yielded low-quality results due to its openness, as "malicious" respondents could intentionally give wrong answers.[51] Reliability may also have been an issue for a study commenced in 2016 which asked respondents to provide data dating back to 2008. Lindgren and her team noted the project's impact in a 2020 academic journal article. "At a time when funders are increasingly demanding evidence that research dollars are well spent ... map data were incorporated into news and social media content that helped push the news industry's problems onto the government's policy-making agenda."[52]

The Shattered Mirror then stated without attribution: "Since 2010, there have been 225 weekly and 27 daily newspapers lost to closure or merger in more than 210 federal ridings."[53] The figure for dailies was correct, due mostly to changes in B.C. and the ongoing extinction of free commuter tabloids. The figure for weeklies, however, like findings of the Local News Map, flew in the face of News Media Canada data which showed that the number of community newspapers had stayed remarkably stable.

TABLE 1: Community newspapers in Canada

	TITLES	CIRCULATION
2017	1,032	18,802,329
2016	1,060	19,454,115
2015	1,083	20,973,352
2014	1,040	20,577,994
2013	1,019	19,612,930
2012	1,029	19,736,168
2011	1,042	19,312,842

Source: Canadian Community Newspaper Association/News Media Canada

Report "cherry-picks" evidence

Dwayne Winseck of Carleton University was another scholar who took issue with data presented by *The Shattered Mirror*. "The case that the authors of *The Shattered Mirror* make about the severity of the crisis of journalism is impressive at first blush," wrote Winseck in an 11,000-word blog entry. "Ultimately, however, it is neither convincing nor credible."[54]

Circulation trends for daily newspapers, according to Winseck, were "not the catastrophe that *The Shattered Mirror* makes them out to be." Sales per household, he noted, were increasingly less relevant as the number of households soared because people increasingly lived alone. The report thus exaggerated the decline of newspapers, claimed Winseck, because it had "selectively chosen a measure that paints the worst-case scenario."[55]

The Shattered Mirror's claim that between 12,000 and 14,000 journalism jobs had been lost since the 1990s, noted Winseck, was also flawed because it relied on headlines and union data that "do a great job chronicling jobs lost but a poor one at keeping track of those gained." Statistics Canada data, he pointed out, "depicts a wholly different picture," showing that the number of full-time journalists in Canada actually increased from about 10,000 in 1987 to 11,631 in 2015. "Once again consistent with a pattern, the authors ignore this data completely."[56]

Winseck saw in *The Shattered Mirror* a "willful refusal" to deal with media industry structures, which were "wholly ignored" in the report. "These examples are not innocent," he charged. "They are part of a process of 'threat inflation' with the aim of buttressing the case for the policy recommendations on offer." While exaggerating some threats, such as the online advertising dominance of digital giants Facebook and Google, the report downplayed one major problem, noted Winseck. "*The Shattered Mirror* also gives short shrift to the idea that media concentration and the structure of the communication and media industries might be a significant factor giving rise to the woes besetting the news media."[57]

According to Winseck, it was "folly to willingly turn a blind eye to high levels of media concentration and the peculiar structure of the media industries in Canada" because they "have had devastating impacts." He also pointed out that the country's largest media companies were making profits about four times the average of other Canadian industries. "These observations are at odds with the story of doom and gloom [that] permeates *The Shattered Mirror*."[58]

Winseck noted that the report's refusal to engage with media concentration was not surprising given that many of those involved in producing the report "have not just sat back and taken arm chair academic views on these matters but have been leading cheerleaders for the processes of consolidation." He declined to identify the cheerleaders, instead urging readers to do their own research. "The industrious reader need only consult the list of acknowledgements to sort out who is who and draw their own conclusions. Given all this, that media concentration wasn't on the agenda is not surprising."[59]

Joining the newspaper lobby

The Shattered Mirror at least earned Greenspon a new client, one with more media clout than he could have ever dreamed of. He was soon part of the newspaper lobby, working with Stursberg and News Media Canada, the newspaper industry trade association, which hoped to reap a government bailout thanks in part to Greenspon's report. A draft version of NMC's $1.375-billion bailout proposal that went out to stakeholders for comment that spring was printed on PPF letterhead and carried its logo at the top alongside that of NMC, though the final version oddly made no mention of Greenspon's group. Perhaps it wouldn't have looked good if the Public Policy Forum were seen to be promoting an issue on which it had so recently produced a government-funded and supposedly independent report.

NMC was careful, however, to acknowledge in its press release announcing its proposed Canadian Journalism Fund that the PPF had "brought together the industry, unions and digital only publications in both French and English to forge this proposal."[60] The bailout proposal's rejection by the federal government a few months later wasn't the end of the matter. It only meant more work for Greenspon.

Making government work better

The Public Policy Forum had been founded by former career public servant Arthur Kroeger, who retired in 1992 after having run six government departments during a 34-year career in Ottawa. "He set up shop in his dining room and called old contacts in business, labor and government," noted *Canadian Business*. "Kroeger established a blue-ribbon panel to develop ideas for making government work better."[61] *Financial Post* business editor Terence Corcoran attended the PPF's 30th annual awards dinner in 2017, which nominally celebrated "extraordinary Canadians" at home and abroad. At 150 tables multiplied by $6,800 each, Corcoran calculated, it also produced "at least $1 million in new funds the PPF can use to generate endless papers and reports providing ideological backing for Trudeau-style economic interventionism."[62]

Corcoran derided the gathering as a "Liberal hug-fest filled with deep-eyed handshakes and armgrabbing congratulatory gestures."[63] That year's gala was the first presided over by Greenspon, who quickly passed the baton to Justin Trudeau, who served as master of ceremonies. "In others words, welcome to Canada's undrained national policy swamp."[64]

> How many policy operations would be able to snag the prime minister to act as feel-good Friars-Club host for an evening of self-indulgent, self-congratulatory monologues on the greatness of Canada as a diverse, caring nation that is masterfully governed by the bureaucrats, politicians and plugged-in corporate and private collaborators assembled in the room?[65]

The Public Policy Forum billed itself as "an independent, non-governmental organization dedicated to improving the quality of government in Canada," added Corcoran. "But there was nothing independent about Thursday's event."[66] The kicker came when Trudeau presented an award to Canadian-born but London-based Dominic Barton, a managing partner at McKinsey & Company. The global management consulting firm was notorious for the tactics it counselled companies on, most notably downsizing and offshoring. It helped turn Enron from an oil and gas production company into an electrical commodities trader and, according to a 2013 history of the secretive firm, may have been "the single greatest legitimizer of mass layoffs than anyone, anywhere, at any time in modern history."[67]

McKinsey was also complicit in the 2008 financial crisis, according to the 2022 book *When McKinsey Comes to Town*, by promoting the securitization of mortgage assets and encouraging banks to load their balance sheets with this "toxic" debt. Its most shameful project, however, may have been working with drug companies such as Purdue Pharma and Johnson & Johnson to "turbocharge" their opioid sales by using data analysis to target physicians more likely to prescribe them. McKinsey ended up paying more than $600 million to settle claims against it by U.S. state governments resulting from the opioid crisis, which brought an estimated 500,000 overdose deaths between 1999 and 2020.[68]

The firm's dark past made many wonder if Canada's growing dependency on McKinsey to help run the federal government was such a good idea.[69] The misgivings grew after a 2023 Radio-Canada investigation found that the Liberal government had spent $66 million on sole-sourced McKinsey contracts since coming to power in 2015, a thirty-fold increase from the previous government.[70]

The connections between McKinsey, the Public Policy Forum, and Trudeau's ruling Liberal Party were certainly disturbing to Corcoran. "By amazing coincidence, Barton is also the head of Trudeau's Advisory Council on Economic Growth," he noted. "So there on stage was the prime minister introducing one of his own top policy advisers to receive an award as a great Canadian, with PPF's Greenspon warmly offering a congratulatory handshake and arm tug."[71] The award to Barton, Corcoran concluded, "consolidated the PPF as a Liberal policy front. That's not new ground for the PPF, but it has rarely been as dramatically confirmed."[72]

Go-to think tanks

The PPF was hardly a powerhouse among think tanks, however, placing only 35th in the Canada and Mexico category of the 2017 *Global Go-To Think Tank Index Report* rankings produced at the University of Pennsylvania.[73] A 2014 study found that it placed 13th out of 25 Canadian think tanks on Twitter with 3,952 followers, compared to 16,100 for the leading Fraser Institute.[74] By 2022, as the social media platform exploded in popularity and political influence, those numbers increased to 14,600 and 32,700, respectively.

The PPF served more as a boutique shop for clients with policy needs congruent with the Liberal agenda. There were exactly 100 think tanks counted in Canada by the Think Tanks and Civil Societies Program at Penn in 2017, compared to 1,872 in the U.S. The largest was the Vancouver-based Fraser Institute, which ranked 21st in the world, followed by the Institute for Research on Public Policy, which published the magazine *Policy Options*.[75]

Think tanks were the brainchild of Austrian economist Friedrich Hayek, whose 1944 book *The Road to Serfdom* warned of the dangers of government intervention in the economy and whose deregulationist writings inspired the neoconservative movement.[76] Hayek urged the creation of public policy institutes, as they preferred to be known, to win the "war of ideas" with those who instead favoured Keynesian policies of economic interventionism. Hayek helped found two of the original free-market think tanks, the Mont Pélerin Society in Switzerland in 1947 and the Institute for Economic Affairs in London in 1955.[77] A 2016 study found that think tanks in the U.S. had "held an extremely influential position in the policymaking process for at least fifty years."[78]

While the first emerged during the Progressive Era, noted James McGann, "it was not until the 1960s that think tanks took on their higher profile as actors in the policymaking process."[79] McGann saw three types of think tank: academic think tanks emphasized scholarly objectivity and the scientific credentials of their staff; contract think tanks balanced objectivity with the policy preferences of their clients; and advocacy think tanks adhered to strong values and often took positions on policy issues. "A great deal of funding is now project specific," noted McGann, "creating the potential for a wealthy partisan donor to determine a think tank's research agenda."[80] Think tanks had recently become "less grounded in rationality," he added, with many experts behaving as advocates. "Some think tanks became more concerned with visibility — raising funds and media attention — in the late twentieth century, thus accentuating their loss of impartiality."[81]

In her 2000 book *Slanting the Story*, Trudy Lieberman claimed that think tanks used "a variety of aggressive strategies" to influence media coverage of political and economic issues, which often led to "misleading and one-sided reporting that has given the electorate a distorted view of many important issues."[82] Think tanks turned the tables on consumer groups by portraying them as special interests, she added, and by de-legitimizing with accusations of bias the sources journalists once relied on for comment, such as academics and public interest advocates, replaced them as idea generators. By offering their own solutions and attacking policies they opposed, according to Lieberman, think tanks enjoyed spectacular media success. "They have become masters at cultivating the press."[83]

The Fraser Institute was established in 1974 after an NDP government was first elected in B.C. One of its first advisors was Hayek, then 75, and its initial funding of $100,000 came from executives of the forestry giant MacMillan Bloedel.[84] A 2004 study found that the Fraser Institute's annual funding had grown to $6.6 million, with contributions from large Canadian foundations such as the Max Bell Foundation and the Weston Foundation. The Donner Canadian Foundation, which was affiliated with the New York-based Donner Foundation, contributed almost a half million dollars to the Fraser Institute in 2002, noted Donald Gutstein.[85]

The media connection

In Canada, there was a close relationship between think tanks, journalists, and media owners. David Asper was a Fraser Institute trustee when his family's Canwest Global Communications bought the Southam newspaper chain in 2000; he resigned in 2003 when he was named chairman of the *National Post*. A reporter who visited the think tank's headquarters later that year, however, noted that it housed a David Asper Centre for the Study of Law and Markets.[86] His brother Leonard, who went on to head Canwest, was a trustee of the Toronto-based C.D. Howe Institute, which the *Globe and Mail* noted was "credited with influential arguments in the early 1990s that led to public support for deficit-cutting."[87] University of Western Ontario political scientist Donald Abelson noted of the C.D. Howe Institute that "few think tanks in Canada have attracted more attention in the media."[88]

Fraser Institute alumni soon made their way onto the editorial boards of Canwest newspapers, including Fazil Mihlar at the *Vancouver Sun*, Danielle Smith at the *Calgary Herald*, and John Robson at the *Ottawa Citizen*.[89] Mihlar, who was named editorial pages editor of the *Sun*, was a former policy analyst for the Fraser Institute. Smith, a former Fraser Institute intern who also co-hosted the television program *Global Sunday*, entered provincial politics in 2009 and became United Conservative Party leader and premier of Alberta in 2022. Gutstein undertook a thorough investigation of Canadian think tanks for his 2009 book *Not a Conspiracy Theory* and concluded that "democratic debate has been hijacked by corporate propaganda."[90]

> Wealthy businessmen created conservative think-tanks which dominate public policy discussions, but are never identified as agents of corporate power. Because of the media's unwillingness to "follow the money," Canadians and Americans know little about these developments. Business has captured the upper hand thanks to a coordinated, well-funded, prolonged effort.[91]

Because their self-interest would be obvious to all, Gutstein noted, business elites required support from "academics and professionals who tacitly assume the same goal as business: take the risk out of democracy by assisting in the management of public opinion in the interests of business."[92] The goal, he added, was to achieve hegemonic control, which Italian writer Antonio Gramsci described in the 1930s as "the organization of consent."

According to Gramsci, ruling elites perpetuate control not by force but hegemonically through cultural organizations such as schools, mass media, and the church. By controlling the agendas of these organizations, they create a "false consciousness" through which their preferred values and political choices become seen by the wider public as normal and natural. Control over the media is seen as key to exercising this type of "soft" power so that ruling elites need use legal means only as a last resort.

According to Gutstein, think tanks played an important role in exercising hegemonic control over Canadians. "This role in the propaganda system is filled by think-tanks and research institutes like the Howe and Fraser institutes, the Public Policy Forum and the Institute for Research on Public Policy."[93] Big business provided about $25 million a year to think tanks in Canada, according to Gutstein, "so they can hire and commission sympathetic academics to produce studies and reports compatible with the business agenda and market the reports through books, conferences, and media."[94]

Gutstein built on the work of Australian sociologist Alex Carey, who explained in his 1995 book *Taking the Risk Out of Democracy* how business manipulates public opinion to accept policies they would never vote for, such as tax cuts for the rich, fewer consumer rights, and weaker environmental regulations. Carey identified three key political developments in the 20th century: the growth of democracy; the growth of corporate power; and the growth of corporate propaganda "as a means of protecting corporate power against democracy."[95] He distinguished between "grassroots" propaganda, which was occasionally required to mobilize public opinion in support of war, and "treetops" propaganda, which emerged in the 1970s and was aimed at elites such as lawmakers and journalists, who were better able to directly influence the policy agenda.

The purpose of treetops propaganda, according to Gutstein, was "to set the terms of debate, to determine the kinds of questions that will dominate public discussion; to set the political agenda in ways that are favourable to corporate interests. If treetops propaganda is successful, grassroots efforts become less necessary."[96] Carey pointed to the rise in the mid-1970s of U.S. think tanks such as the Cato Institute, which with corporate funding published vast amounts of research promoting small government and free-market solutions to economic and social problems and were influential in reviving conservatism in the 1980s under Ronald Reagan.[97]

Walter Lippmann, a progressive American journalist and a founding editor of *The New Republic* magazine, exposed the power of propaganda in his 1922 book *Public Opinion*, drawn from his experience as part of the U.S. government's information effort in World War I. This landmark propaganda campaign quickly reversed public sentiment from isolationism to intervention in Europe and helped demonstrate the power of the press to whip up war fever.

The insights into propaganda provided by *Public Opinion* helped found the new post-war practice of public relations, as it showed how easily people's perceptions could be altered by distorted information. Lippmann's study of Freud's early theories of social psychology convinced him that groups respond not to ideas but instead to powerful symbols and images. The problem, according to Lippmann, was that the world was far too vast and distant for people to experience directly, so they instead had to rely on accounts of it carried in the mass media. The information people received from the media, however, was insufficient to provide an accurate picture of reality because it was often slanted by journalists to serve various purposes. The resulting distortions, Lippmann claimed, were incapable of informing citizens sufficiently to allow for an informed public opinion, or any real democracy.[98]

French philosopher Jacques Ellul noted in his 1965 book *Propaganda* that the most effective form of persuasion relied on the use of selective truths rather than outright lies. "Propaganda must be based on some truth that can be said in a few words and is able to linger in the collective consciousness."[99] Lies could also be effective, however, as proved by the Nazis. "Hitler's propaganda was able to make the lie a precise and systematic instrument," noted Ellul, "but this was not just a falsification of some figure or fact."[100] Hitler pioneered the "Big Lie" technique of propaganda, which he described in his 1925 book *Mein Kampf* as promoting a falsehood so "colossal" that no one would believe that others "could have the impudence to distort the truth so infamously."[101]

Propaganda scholars Garth Jowett and Victoria O'Donnell defined the dark arts as "the deliberate, systematic attempt to shape perceptions, manipulate cognitions, and direct behavior to achieve a response that furthers the desired intent of the propagandist." They developed a ten-step method of analysis which required scrutinizing an entire propaganda campaign, not just individual reports or messages, starting with its target audience.[102] In his 2002 book *The Idea of Propaganda*, Stanley Cunningham listed among its weapons "self-serving reports; lies, distortions, fabrications, and exaggerations; disinformation, selective disclosures and censorship ... rumours and gossip."[103]

By these measures, *The Shattered Mirror* was a masterpiece. It was a triumph of selective presentation that was rife with distortions, fabrications, exaggerations, and even censorship. *The Shattered Mirror* was the very definition of a self-serving report if it was intended to serve not the public but instead the newspaper industry. It even engaged in blatant censorship, as some of the biggest problems afflicting Canada's local news media, such as ownership concentration and foreign ownership, were never mentioned or summarily dismissed.

The newspaper lobby

Soon News Media Canada and the Public Policy Forum were joined in their campaign to promote government assistance for Canada's news media by Unifor, a union representing 12,000 Canadian journalists and media workers. The coalition was hardly a secret, having been noted on the website iPolitics in mid-2017 by Carleton University journalism instructor Paul Adams, a former CBC and Globe and Mail journalist. "Since the report came out, PPF has maintained a working group, including representatives from big media chains, media unions and luminaries like former CBC vice-president Richard Stursberg."[104]

The newspaper lobbying campaign announced itself in a *Globe and Mail* op-ed published that September. "Last April, on the heels of The Shattered Mirror report on news, democracy and truth in Canada," it noted, "the Public Policy Forum brought together about 40 news organizations and unions to propose solutions that would support employment of reporters and investment in innovation without sacrificing media independence or shutting out new competitors."[105]

The coalition hoped that Heritage minister Mélanie Joly would offer the lifeline they sought for Canada's newspapers. "A broke press isn't much of a free press," wrote leaders of News Media Canada, the Public Policy Forum, and Unifor in the *Globe and Mail*. "Others contend it's best to wait for news organizations to go bankrupt and then pick up the pieces. But once in bankruptcy court, it is the debt holders and not the public interest that is served, as we saw in 2010 when Postmedia emerged out of bankruptcy court with bondholders as owners and an unbearable burden of debt."[106]

They pointed out that the federal government had recently allocated $100 million to support local television news, and asked why the same sort of assistance could not be given to newspapers. "Suddenly, more local television reporters are working stories on more broadcasts across Canada. But why just television? Why not newspapers or digital-only publications? It's the reporting of news that's important, not the platform on which it resides."[107]

Unifor was a new kind of "general" trade union, having been formed in 2013 from a merger of the Canadian Auto Workers and the Communications, Energy and Paperworkers. With a membership of more than 300,000, it was the largest private sector union in Canada. While many unions supported and even campaigned for the NDP, Unifor openly targeted the Conservative Party, spending an estimated $1.8 million in advertising to help defeat it during the 2015 federal election campaign.[108]

Such political partisanship made some of Unifor's journalist members uneasy, but the union's president not only shrugged off the criticism but stepped up the activism by joining the industry campaign for a federal bailout in order to save jobs. "Some say the companies seeking assistance are doomed in any case," noted the *Globe and Mail* op-ed which carried the byline of Unifor president Jerry Dias alongside those of Cox and Greenspon. "That may be true, but established news companies and startups should be given five years to prove they can make a go of it."[109]

Their bailout proposal's rejection later that month was hardly the end of their campaign for government subsidies. In fact, it was just the beginning of massive pressure the newspaper lobby would put on the government. First, Greenspon picked up the pieces of their bailout plan's rejection in an article for *Policy Options* that was published less than a week after Joly's speech.

> The minister doesn't want to bail out the private sector news industry models that are no longer viable ... Joly also doesn't want to level the tax field by charging foreign sellers of digital services the same HST that domestic players are forced to pay. She doesn't want to place financial demands on platform companies like Facebook, Google and Netflix beyond voluntary contributions. She doesn't want to be seen to be encroaching on journalistic independence.[110]

That would soon change as the newspaper lobby's campaign built up steam. "As of now, the government seems to not share the sense of urgency felt by journalists and media owners about the continuing deterioration of journalism in Canada," wrote Greenspon. "But the economic and political situations may well change over the next year."[111] He noted a recent report by Moody's Investor Service which found that Postmedia had an "unsustainable capital structure," and predicted that its finances may be "insufficient to support its operations" over the next year. "A reading of the tea leaves also suggests the patience of billionaire families like the Thomsons (*The Globe and Mail*) and the Desmarais (*La Presse*) to underwrite losses in their news operations may be wearing thin."[112]

It was the most Canadian of polite ultimatums. "The possibility exists for a meeting of minds between the government and the news industry," concluded Greenspon. In reading through the government's new Creative Canada Policy Framework posted online, he saw some hope for a bailout yet. "It is a good thing more thinking time has been allowed around the policy framework," he wrote. "Despite Joly's rejectionist words on aid to media companies, the background documents accompanying her speech indicate she's not necessarily done with the news file ... Apparently, there's more to come in 2018."[113]

Indeed there was. As the new year dawned, one media critic urged government action to stanch the bleeding in local news by strengthening media policy to help protect journalism from the depredations of Darwinian capitalism and encourage the growth of digital media. "Whether our government has the foresight needed for this kind of bold action should become clear in 2018."[114] By the time the year was over, things would look very different for the newspaper industry in Canada.

CHAPTER 4
PROJECT ICE

The last week of November 2017 should have been a fruitful one for John Hammill, with Christmas advertising pouring in to fill the pages of newspapers for which he sold ads in the small Ontario communities of Orillia, Barrie, Collingwood, Bradford, and Innisfil.

Hammill had just started his second year as regional advertising director for Postmedia's six daily and eight weekly newspapers in its Northern Ontario region, having been promoted from publisher of its daily *Orillia Packet & Times*. "I'm excited about the Postmedia digital marketing solutions we now have available to offer our business partners," Hammill said in a *Packet & Times* article announcing his promotion. "Whether it's a website build, SEO (search engine optimization), SEM (search engine marketing), or Facebook campaigns, Postmedia has us positioned to be the one-stop shop for all marketing needs."[1]

The 44-year-old Lakehead University business graduate loved living in Orillia, the so-called "Sunshine City" in lake country 90 minutes north of Toronto. That's where he met his wife Laura, and together they were raising three kids in the town of 30,000, where the average house price was a relative bargain at $380,000. Hammill continued to be based out of the *Packet & Times* office in his new position, which allowed him to keep his home in Orillia. He volunteered in minor baseball and hockey and also served on the new Orillia Sports Council. The Ontario Winter Games would see 3,200 participants descend on Orillia that coming March to compete in sports from curling, skiing and figure skating to fencing, five-pin bowling and kickboxing. "I love the sports amenities, parks, etc. here as they are all fantastic," he said when Lakehead established a branch campus there. "The baseball/softball community is huge here and playing/coaching has been a blast over the years. There are lots of active service clubs such as Kiwanis, Lions and my Rotary Club that really do make a difference in and around the community."[2]

Hammill's workweek ended abruptly that Monday morning, however, after he heard the announcement about the blockbuster Postmedia-Torstar trade along with everybody else, with the chains swapping 41 titles and closing 36 of them. Within ten minutes, he received a letter from Postmedia's Human Resources department informing him that the company had sold the newspapers he worked for, and that the new owner would "not require your services."

He deduced that the companies had co-ordinated the closures, since he had been fired by Postmedia although Torstar was the new owner. "I didn't actually have too much of a problem with the swap then," Hammill later told the Vancouver-based website *The Tyee*. "I understand business."[3]

A civic institution

At 147, the *Packet & Times* was almost as old as Orillia itself. "A bust of its founder stands in the library," noted the *Globe and Mail*. "It appears, thinly disguised as the *Newspacket*, in humorist Stephen Leacock's fictional portrait of Orillia, *Sunshine Sketches of a Little Town*."[4] The newspaper, added the visiting *Globe* reporter, was closed "with a snap of the fingers" as the cruel consequence of a corporate transaction, then one final insult was added. "The *Packet* didn't get a chance to put out a final issue bidding farewell to the community it served for all those years."[5]

One resident started an online petition to restore the newspaper's Internet archives, which disappeared with the daily. "After the short-sighted decision," protested Mitchell Sleeman, "the town was surprised and saddened to learn that the archives of the historical newspaper — dating back to 1870 — were no longer publicly available online."[6]

While he didn't question the trade, Hammill did question the decision to close five papers for which he worked, since from what he could tell from the financial documents to which he had access as a manager, the group was doing well. In Orillia, Postmedia closed the *Packet & Times* while Torstar continued to operate the weekly *Advance*, which didn't make much sense to Hammill. "The biggest shocker was that in the Orillia market we were clearly the lead product," he told *The Tyee* by telephone. "As far as local ROP [run-of-press] advertising it was certainly my impression that the *Barrie Examiner* had the lead there, too."[7]

But it was the paid dailies, which were also stronger journalistically, that were shut down in favour of their free weekly competitors. "If you compared our Thursday to their Thursday, for instance, we had a lot more ads," Hammill said. "We owned the real estate market, we owned the new-builder market. We were the lead in every piece of business other than inserts."

Still, Hammill understood the transaction was just business and felt no need to go public with his doubts until he saw Postmedia CEO Paul Godfrey's interview on BNN Bloomberg, in which he claimed he had no idea that Torstar would close the newspapers it acquired from Postmedia. "That's when I spoke up," Hammill told *The Tyee*.

> "I must have seen the interview a dozen times," Hammill recalled, and each time he got angrier. So he contacted the Competition Bureau and shared his suspicious separation agreement. Although several others had come forward, he was told he was the only one willing to go on the record with his name.[8]

Directly contradicting what Godfrey claimed about all the closed newspapers losing money, Hammill told the bureau that they were instead making money, which was enough for it to start an investigation. The closed *Collingwood Enterprise Bulletin* was doing "really good," he said, while the *Barrie Examiner* was "doing okay," and he was surprised they had been closed.[9]

Hammill wasn't about to wait for the bureaucrats in Ottawa to bail him out, however, as he had a family to support. He had enough experience in the newspaper business to know that there was still a market for advertising in small communities such as his. Maybe it wouldn't be in print newspapers, but he knew that he could sell ads.

Hammill contacted Sault Ste. Marie-based Village Media, which published a string of online publications including SooToday.com, GuelphToday.com, BarrieToday.com, ElliotLakeToday.com, and TimminsToday.com. Together with several other laid-off *Packet & Times* workers, Hammill and Village Media founded OrilliaMatters.com, which went live in early 2018, not six weeks after their newspaper was closed. "We believe that locally-driven news is essential to communities," said Village Media CEO Jeff Elgie. "That's why we've started or helped launch more than 10 digital news sites in communities just like Orillia within the past few years — communities that in some cases were also told their local newspaper didn't factor into someone else's bottom line."[10]

Village Media hired ten former Postmedia employees, Hammill told the Tyee after Postmedia closed six more Ontario papers in 2018 and announced layoffs designed to cut its staff by another 10 per cent. "But there's still former Postmedia people that don't have jobs, so I feel for them. It's not my goal to have Postmedia go out of business. I have friends who are still there. They've got poor management. Maybe they should get rid of the guy at the top and get somebody in there who actually knows what he's doing."[11]

The disruption to local communities where Postmedia closed dailies was not just in news provision, he told Lakehead's online Alumni Spotlight. "Orillia had a daily newspaper for over 50 years and that daily news coverage ceased with the closure of the *Packet and Times*. Advertisers and readers were accustomed to the daily news cycle and that was pulled out from under them with no notice."[12]

A sorry record

Few held out hope that the Competition Bureau would step in to halt the trade between Postmedia and Torstar or the newspaper closures that followed. After all, it had taken no action when similar dealings went down a few years earlier in B.C., where the regional chains Black Press and Glacier Media had traded and closed dozens of titles, which accounted for a majority of the paid daily newspaper closures in Canada between 2010 and 2016.

Of the thirteen paid dailies that were closed, merged, or changed publication frequency during that period, including the *Nanaimo*

Daily News, nine were published in B.C. and owned by Black Press (six) or Glacier Media (three).[13] The two chains also closed numerous community newspapers they acquired from each other, with Black Press accumulating titles on Vancouver Island, where it soon owned them all, and Glacier Media adding newspapers in the Vancouver suburbs. "It is by now a familiar script," noted *B.C. Business* magazine in 2015. "Through horse-trading, Glacier Media or Black Press . . . become the sole owners of a community's weeklies. And then one of those papers shuts down."[14]

When Glacier closed the weekly *Westender* community newspaper in Vancouver at the end of 2017, which it had acquired from Black Press in a city where it already owned the thrice-weekly *Courier*, it brought to 24 the number of newspapers lost to closure or merger following their exchange of 33 titles.[15]

The Competition Bureau had also taken no action after Postmedia acquired Sun Media in 2014, effectively merging the country's two largest newspaper chains. Its ruling in that case was a watershed moment for newspaper competition in Canada. The deal itself was unprecedented. "This doesn't just alter Canada's print-media landscape," observed the *Globe and Mail*, "it takes a bulldozer to it." Postmedia, it added, had "thrown down the gauntlet to Canadian regulators, and forced the country to have a conversation that it has long avoided: How much are we willing to compromise the principles of a diverse and competitive press in the name of keeping it alive?"[16]

The *Toronto Star* noted that Postmedia's sudden newspaper dominance wasn't raising the concern it should have. "If the deal is approved by the federal Competition Bureau, one company will own almost all the significant daily papers in English Canada — with the exceptions of the *Star*, the *Globe and Mail*, *Winnipeg Free Press* and *Halifax Chronicle Herald*," it pointed out. "In most cities, the choice for newspaper readers will be between Postmedia — and Postmedia."[17]

The newly-enlarged chain, however, pushed hard for the deal to be approved. John Ivison argued in a column published in Postmedia papers across the country that his employer should be allowed to take over its largest competitor without regulatory interference due to the dire economic situation facing the industry. "Newspaper owners aren't bluffing this time," he wrote. "They are fighting to survive."[18]

> Everyone knows this — they see it before their eyes as their papers shrink in size, personnel and ambition. Against this gloomy backdrop, it seems unlikely that the regulator or the federal government will be motivated to intervene and block a deal that offers ballast to an industry buffeted by choppy waters.[19]

The Bureau investigated the transaction for five months and somehow concluded that the Sun newspapers Postmedia acquired in Calgary, Edmonton, Ottawa, and Toronto didn't compete with its broadsheets in those markets. "Extensive documentary and empirical evidence demonstrated that the parties are not close rivals from the perspective of readers," its ruling noted, "a finding that was supported by the views of market participants and by an analysis of the demographic characteristics of the parties' respective audiences."[20]

The tabloid newspapers acquired by Postmedia, the Bureau pointed out, appealed to different types of readers. "Furthermore, the evidence showed the presence of free local daily newspapers in the relevant markets to be an important competitive constraint."[21] Often derided as McPapers for their lack of news content, commuter tabloids would be the next to go, as the chains traded and closed them to eliminate competition for ever-scarcer ads. The Bureau said it took into consideration that the market for newspapers was declining, which limited the dominance any publisher could exercise. "Key metrics for the newspaper markets demonstrate that the print newspapers in these markets are facing a steady and continuing decline in readership and advertising," it ruled. "As a result, market conditions exert downward pressure on the parties' ability to exercise market power."[22]

Besides, Godfrey had promised that Postmedia would keep the newspapers, and their newsrooms, separate. "We intend to keep Sun Media's large daily newspapers in those markets where we overlap," he told the *Toronto Sun* when the deal was announced in 2014. "Their readers and their advertisers in many cases are different from those of Postmedia." The *Sun* reporter paraphrased

Godfrey's promise. "Sun Media will continue to operate independently with its own newsrooms and opinions, he said."[23]

He repeated the pledge after the Competition Bureau approved Postmedia's purchase in 2015. "Mr. Godfrey said Postmedia plans to follow the model it uses in Vancouver in its three new dual-newspaper cities," reported the *Globe and Mail*, "looking for efficiencies through combined finance, human resources, IT and production departments, but maintaining separate newsrooms and keeping both publications open."[24] By the time the Sun Media takeover was completed a few weeks later, however, the promise had already been softened. Postmedia's senior vice-president of content, Lou Clancy, backtracked by saying that some writers might be shared between the chains, but that the "Suns and Postmedia broadsheets would compete with each other."[25]

An economic law

Part of the problem was that the Competition Bureau was empowered to examine only economic factors, which in the case of newspapers meant advertising and not news. Its governing Competition Act was "not intended nor designed to deal with the important question of 'diversity of voices,'" the Bureau noted in a 2003 summary of its work in media industries prepared for a Senate inquiry into news media.[26]

The inquiry's subsequent report was harshly critical of both the Competition Bureau and, in broadcasting, the Canadian Radio-television and Telecommunications Commission for what it called their "neglect" of news media. "One challenge is the complete absence of a review mechanism to consider the public interest in news media mergers," it noted. "The result has been extremely high levels of news media concentration in particular cities or regions."[27]

Concentration of ownership, the report found, had "reached levels that few other countries would consider acceptable."[28] Canada was "unique among developed countries," it added, in not having a forum where mergers of news media organizations could be openly addressed. In addition to advertising, the Senate report argued that the Competition Bureau should also be able to consider the impact of a media merger or acquisition on the information needs of Canadians. It recommended adding a new section to the Competition Act to deal with the problem and suggested automatic review if any news media owner gained a market share of 35 percent or more.

As the Competition Bureau was unlikely to have the expertise to deal with the public interest in media mergers, it recommended that an expert panel review them. "The Competition Bureau's operating procedures may be well suited to analysing most markets for goods and services in Canada," it concluded, "but not the news media market."[29]

Press freedom provisions in the Charter of Rights and Freedoms, on which publishers had traditionally relied in claiming exemption from regulation, should only go so far, the senators reasoned. "The media's right to be free from government interference does not extend ... to a conclusion that proprietors should be allowed to own an excessive proportion of media holdings in a particular market, let alone the national market."[30]

Bad timing doomed the Senate report's recommendations, however, as a deregulationist Conservative government under Stephen Harper had been elected earlier in 2006 and would spend almost a decade in power, or just long enough to preside over Postmedia's foreign ownership and its takeover of Sun Media.

Another problem with the Competition Act was that it required the Bureau to allow any merger or acquisition which provided efficiencies of operation that outweighed any detriment to the public. "Even where there is a finding that a merger would likely substantially lessen or prevent competition," noted the Bureau in its 2003 review, "the Competition Act specifically directs that the merger be allowed to proceed if it would also likely result in gains in efficiency that are greater than and offset the effects of the lessening or preventing of competition."[31]

The loophole was similar to one employed by the Canadian Radio-television and Telecommunications Commission, which allowed networks acquiring licenced broadcasters to basically bribe their way into monopolies by making compensatory "public benefits" payments, which went mostly to Cancon but increasingly found their way into journalism schools.[32]

A hazardous precedent

The relevant section of the Competition Act had lain dormant for almost 30 years, however, until a Supreme Court of Canada ruling in the case of a hazardous waste merger in northern B.C. came down just as the Competition Bureau was investigating the Postmedia's takeover of Sun Media. The ruling provided an ill-timed precedent that disempowered the Competition Bureau. It was the court's first merger decision under the Competition Act since 1997, when it coincidentally also ruled on a newspaper case, and the first time it had ever considered the efficiencies defence.

The case involved Tervita Industries Ltd., which specialized in hazardous waste removal for oil and gas companies and took over its only regional competitor in 2011. After evidence showed that the acquisition would prevent an expected 10-percent drop in hazardous waste remediation costs in the region due to competition, the Competition Bureau ordered it to unwind the transaction or divest its newly-acquired landfill operations, but Tervita appealed its ruling all the way to the Supreme Court of Canada.

While the Supreme Court agreed that "there was sufficient other evidence upon which it could find a substantial prevention of competition as a result of the merger," it allowed the appeal because the Competition Bureau had failed to calculate the merger's anti-competitive effects. The efficiencies defence required the Competition Bureau to put a number on the lessening of competition, the court ruled, just as Tervita had done in quantifying the savings it expected to achieve from the merger, even if the savings accepted by the court amounted to only the equivalent of half the salary of one junior back-office employee. "Effects that can be quantified should be quantified, even as estimates, provided such estimates are grounded in evidence that can be challenged and weighed," the court ruled. "If effects are realistically measurable, failure to at least estimate the quantification of those effects will not result in the effects being assessed on a qualitative basis."[33]

The ruling's effect on merger and acquisitions law in Canada was profound. "This is a strange result, given that the [Competition Bureau] Commissioner's expert found that the merger would prevent a price decrease of at least 10 percent," noted *The Litiga-*

tor magazine. "The anti-competitive effects from such a prevention of competition must surely be more than one-half of one person's salary."[34]

The consensus was that the ruling would put the Competition Bureau at a major disadvantage going forward. "The SCC's decision will increase the burden on the Competition Bureau to challenge efficiency claims, as it now must spend significant time and effort to quantify the anti-competitive effects of such transactions," noted one analysis. "This will likely result in an approach that reinforces the role of efficiencies in merger reviews, which will benefit merger parties."[35]

One law firm observed that the SCC had imposed a "significant hurdle" for the Competition Bureau to overcome once the merging parties had established even modest efficiencies.[36]

The ruling changed Canadian competition law, and with the Sun Media acquisition in the docket, it came at the worst possible time for newspaper ownership concentration. It put Canadian merger law "far out in front of the wave" of integrating economic principles into merger law, noted one analysis by economists. "Tervita thus injected even more economics and econometrics into merger law."[37]

The injection was timely since the Competition Bureau was then headed for the first time by an economist. John Pecman soon joked in a speech to lawyers that he was "pleased that this ruling has clearly made that the only possible point of view" since people "have a natural tendency to see economists as the rock stars of competition law enforcement."[38] Despite its new leadership by an economist, in an era when quantitative economics dominated the field, the Competition Bureau somehow failed to quantify the public detriment of several daily newspaper monopolies.

Failure upon failure

The failure was even more troubling since the Competition Act had been intended in 1985 to make anti-trust law enforcement easier. The new Act "literally rewrote the book on competition law in Canada," according to one legal scholar, "particularly with regard to merger control and the review of the activities of dominant firms."[39] It replaced criminal procedures for the review of mergers and monopolies with civil ones, created a new administrative branch (the Competition Bureau) to investigate and rule on competition cases, and a quasi-judicial body (a Competition Tribunal) to adjudicate disputes. By lowering the bar for conviction from criminal law's proof beyond a reasonable doubt to the civil test of proof on a balance of probabilities, it was hoped that the Competition Act would provide a more effective anti-monopoly enforcement mechanism. Section 96 of the Competition Act, or its efficiencies defence, was "unique among competition/antitrust statutes around the world," according to one legal scholar.[40]

It was adopted because the then-Conservative government of Brian Mulroney "had high hopes that it would play a significant role in facilitating efficient restructuring in Canada," which in the end went largely unrealized.[41]

> Efficiencies do not have to be passed on to consumers. This approach occupies the middle ground between the approach of jurisdictions such as the E.U. ... and the approach of the U.S. Department of Justice, which appears to require efficiency gains to be so great that prices will not rise as a result of the merger.[42]

The previous anti-trust regulator, the Restrictive Trade Practices Commission, had failed to secure a conviction in any monopoly case it prosecuted since it had been established in 1952 due to the high burden of proof on it under the criminal test. It almost did in New Brunswick, where it actually won a conviction at trial against the Irving Oil family in 1972 after it acquired all five of the daily newspapers in that province. The tight control of New Brunswick's media by the Irvings had led the 1970 Senate report on Mass Media to describe the province as a "journalistic disaster area."[43] The RTPC obtained a court order that the Irvings divest one of their acquired newspapers, and each was fined $150,000, but the conviction was overturned on appeal and the Supreme Court of Canada upheld that ruling in 1977.[44] It even increased the burden of proof required for a conviction by ruling that the RTPC had to prove not only a lessening of competition but also a present detriment to the public, not a hypothetical future detriment. The court also, noted one legal analyst, "refused to infer public detriment from the one hundred percent market share of the accused."[45]

Criminal charges laid

The RTPC also laid criminal charges of conspiracy and monopoly against the Southam and Thomson chains after they simultaneously closed dailies in Winnipeg and Ottawa in 1980, which led to the Royal Commission on Newspapers.

During a raid on Southam's offices, one executive was seen tearing up a memo that estimated the increased profits for each chain without competition in those markets. Another crudely-shredded document retrieved from the wastebasket of a Southam vice-president contained the evidence investigators were looking for to prove collusion. It read: "They get out of Ottawa. They get out of Montreal. They get out of Vancouver. They get control in Winnipeg."[46]

Despite the damning evidence, Thomson claimed at their 1983 Supreme Court of Ontario trial that monopoly was a valid business goal and not necessarily detrimental to the public. "In a free enterprise system," the company argued, "it is legitimate for someone to try to put oneself in a monopoly position." The court agreed, concluding that the closures constituted "good business sense, not an illegal conspiracy."[47]

The acquittal was followed within a few years by passage of the Competition Act. The Competition Bureau it created soon got its first chance to prevent additional press ownership concentration when Southam began to buy up most of the community newspapers in the Vancouver area in the late 1980s to add to its monopoly on dailies there.

The 1957 merger between the *Vancouver Sun* and Southam's *Daily Province* had been contentious enough, prompting RTPC hearings in Ottawa and Vancouver. The merger which created Pacific Press was ruled an illegal monopoly but was allowed to stand as an "economic necessity" after the owners argued that one of their papers would eventually fold under the prevailing natural monopoly theory of newspapers.[48]

The monopoly should have been lucrative, but the powerful Pacific Press unions went on strike for months at a time to extract higher wages and job guarantees, which prompted the growth of a vigorous community press. Southam acquired the *Vancouver Sun* and thus full ownership of Pacific Press as part of the 1980 "Black Wednesday" dealings with Thomson, and soon set about buying up the area's community newspapers in order to cement its monopoly there. It owned most of them by 1990, including two of Canada's largest in the *Vancouver Courier* and the *North Shore News*.

The new Competition Bureau ordered Southam to sell both, and also the *Real Estate Weekly* chain of eighteen zoned editions it had acquired, because their common ownership lessened competition substantially for newspaper advertising in the Vancouver area. Southam refused, so hearings were held in Vancouver by a Competition Tribunal which found a monopoly only in North Vancouver and ordered the company in 1992 to sell either the *North Shore News* or the *Real Estate Weekly* chain. Southam appealed the ruling all the way to the Supreme Court of Canada, which upheld it in 1997.[49]

The Competition Bureau had an easier time negotiating with printing giant Transcontinental after it bought 74 Quebec community newspapers from Sun Media in late 2013.[50] They reached a consent agreement the following year under which Transcontinental would seek a buyer for 34 of the publications which competed.[51] It managed to sell only fourteen, however, of which three continued publishing in print and eleven online. It then closed the other 20, integrating them with its other community papers in the same regions and laying off about 80 workers. "The Bureau has done everything in its power to test the market to determine if there was a possible alternative to Transcontinental owning all the papers," Pecman said. "Unfortunately, in some cases like this one, where many newspapers are in financial distress owing to the ongoing transformation of the community newspaper industry, the market dictates that there are limited alternatives."[52]

This spotty record of anti-trust enforcement in the newspaper industry did not inspire much hope that the Competition Bureau would intervene in the Postmedia-Torstar trade and closures, but the whistleblower evidence provided by Hammill could not be ignored in such a high-profile case.

There were also several key differences between the trade and closures in Ontario and the ones in B.C., which the Competition Bureau had reviewed for more than two months before allowing them to proceed. The western transactions were not made all at once, but in a series of deals over a period of years. Most of the closures were announced piecemeal as well, often long after the trade or purchase. Most of the newspapers weren't closed outright but were merged with other newspapers or had their publication frequency reduced from daily to weekly or semi-weekly.

The most important difference, however, was the whistleblower evidence from Hammill. Without it, the Competition Bureau might not have even bothered investigating. Once it did, the evidence it found proved damning indeed. It would take months, however, for details to emerge, then many months more for the bureau to announce a decision.

The Local Journalism Initiative

In the meantime, however, the new year of 2018 finally brought some good news for the chains. At least, most would consider $50 million good news. That was the amount promised in February's federal budget to assist local journalism by improving news coverage in under-served communities.

Under the five-year program, publications could apply for funding to hire reporters in what was called the Local Journalism Initiative. The budget also promised that the government would investigate longer-term ways to fund news gathering, including "new models that enable private giving and philanthropic support" for non-profit journalism and local news. "This could include new ways for Canadian newspapers to innovate and be recognized to receive charitable status for not-for-profit provision of journalism, reflecting the public interest that they serve."[53]

It wasn't enough for the chains, however. News Media Canada criticized it as a "Band-Aid solution" that wouldn't do much to help dig its member newspapers out of the hole they were in. "It's not what we would have hoped for," said CEO John Hinds. "Ten million dollars over five years really isn't going to address the problem. That's really the cost of running one newsroom of a mid-size daily newspaper in Canada."[54]

News Media Canada chair Bob Cox complained in his *Winnipeg Free Press* column that the funding was less than one per cent of what Ottawa gave the CBC annually and amounted to only about $6,667 a year for each of the 1,500 newspapers across the country. "The money will not prevent more newspapers from closing and will not bring back any of the estimated 16,500 journalism jobs that have been lost across the country during the past 10 years," he wrote. "In the coming months and years, more and more Canadian communities will lose their local newspaper."[55]

Godfrey called it "very disappointing" and "a body blow to journalism in Canada," before again defaulting to threat mode. "It will mean the continuing of lost jobs in journalism. It will mean potentially closures of some newspapers."[56] He told the *Globe and Mail* that the government money was hardly worth the effort Postmedia had put into getting it. "This is most disappointing, and somewhat insulting when you consider all the time we've wasted making appearances in front of commissions they've set up."[57] He followed with an even more direct threat. "Continuing to ignore us means more job cuts, more closures and more anguish."[58]

Godfrey also dismissed the government's promise to explore the idea of granting charitable status to news outlets. "There are so many charities around," he said. "Who would you rather give to, SickKids Hospital or Postmedia and Torstar?"[59] He was even more candid during a television appearance in studio on the CBC. "It doesn't help us at all," a fast-talking and visibly upset Godfrey told *On the Money* host Peter Armstrong. "This is a token that is not even really a meaningful thing. This is really an insult to the entire industry ... Because of this there will be more cuts and more closures because this government does not want to help the industry."[60]

Godfrey claimed that the reason for such a small amount of funding was because the government didn't like the criticism it had received from some larger publications. "I really believe a decision was made to say look we'd rather have no newspapers than critical newspapers." He then repeated his warning. "Because of this there will be more cuts and more closures because this government does not want to help the industry," he said. "We're going to have to make more cuts in order to survive and that will mean poor journalism."[61]

One academic concluded that Ottawa had given up newspapers for dead. "They've decided they're not interested in saving the newspaper industry ... they're going to let it die and they're putting in place the structures to pick up the pieces," said Carleton University journalism professor Paul Adams. "They're looking past the existing industry to establish some kind of policy framework to cope with the day after."[62]

Others expressed relief that the government had not bailed out newspapers. "If you gave $5 million to Postmedia or the *Star*, that would be gone by lunch," Erin Millar, co-founder of the online start-up Discourse Media, told the *Columbia Journalism Review*. "So at least it's not a bailout."[63]

National Post columnist Andrew Coyne, however, saw it as the thin edge of the wedge. "It's only $50 million? For starters, yes. This is a big, indeed unprecedented step. Had the government weighed in with a boatload of cash all at once, it might have put people off. But the beachhead having successfully been established, does anyone really think it will stop there?"[64]

Admittedly, $50 million was a far cry from the $1.375 billion that MNC had asked Ottawa to add to the Canadian Periodical Fund in extending it to daily newspapers for five years. The method for dispensing the cash was also a bit arcane, with seven nonprofit news organizations, including News Media Canada, tasked with taking applications from media outlets and an independent panel of judges awarding one-year, renewable grants.

The result was soon 168 new reporting positions in more than 140 newsrooms across the country, however, most of which went to News Media Canada member newspapers. The stories that LJI reporters wrote for their host publications were made available to other news outlets through the Canadian Press under a Creative Commons license. Postmedia got a dozen of the 93 reporting positions that went to newspapers in the first round of awards announced at the end of 2019, compared to only twelve for digital media.[65]

News Media Canada was still not satisfied, and along with its partners Unifor and the PPF it would mount a relentless campaign throughout 2018 to push for a full bailout. As a result, things would look a lot different for Postmedia and the rest of the newspaper industry by the time 2018 ended. Soon the government would give in, and when it did, it began to open a can of worms that would quickly turn into something more like Pandora's Box.

Damning allegations

Behind the scenes, however, the chains were in legal trouble as 2018 dawned. The deal Postmedia had done with Torstar the previous fall, trading 41 newspapers and closing 36 of them, began to attract increasing interest from the Competition Bureau, although the story would not break until spring, when the *Globe and Mail* obtained court documents filed by the Competition Bureau which made some damning allegations.

Submitted in pursuit of search warrants, they described how lawyers for both companies had been working on Competition Bureau official Pierre-Yves Guay to call the investigation off. "A lawyer for Torstar e-mailed Mr. Guay to request a phone call with both companies' lawyers," according the documents.

> Mr. Guay replied by e-mail that this would be "highly inappropriate" and scheduled separate calls instead the next day. During those calls, "all counsel expressed a general sense of surprise and disappointment" about the criminal investigation, according to Mr. Guay. The bureau declined subsequent requests for calls and meetings with both the mergers and the cartels directorates.[66]

On January 11, according to the court documents, a lawyer for Torstar e-mailed Guay to ask that the bureau not search its offices because "Torstar would suffer significant reputational damage if search and seizure warrants were executed," to which Guay did not respond.[67] Postmedia then made an e-mail submission to Pecman the following month, the court documents added, arguing that the deal should be reviewed only under the civil merger provisions of the Competition Act, and not its criminal conspiracy provisions.

A conviction on charges of conspiracy under the Act could bring fines of up to $25 million for the companies and prison sentences of up to fourteen years for their executives. While the Competition Act had changed Canada's anti-trust legislation from a criminal law to a mostly a civil process, it did retain criminal charges in its Section 45 for cases in which competitors agreed to "fix, maintain, increase or control" prices, or conspired to "fix, maintain, control, prevent, lessen or eliminate the production or supply" of a product.[68]

While the court documents dealt mostly with obstruction by Torstar, they also set out Postmedia's side of the story. "Postmedia stated that its rationale for the deal was 'to generate positive cash flows from a group of failing community newspapers' by consolidating its flyer distribution services in certain areas," according to the *Globe and Mail*. "It also argued that print ad revenue was being leeched away by digital media competitors and argued that 'print and digital advertising ... belong in the same relevant product market' and that the deal created significant efficiencies."[69]

Postmedia's e-mail pointed to defences it could put forward, but they only applied to the merger provisions and not to the conspiracy section. "The merger provisions allow companies to adopt [a] 'failing firm' defence if a merger involves assets that are failing or have failed," noted the *Globe and Mail*. "A merger is also defensible if it creates efficiencies that 'outweigh and offset its likely anti-competitive effects.'"[70] Finally, the e-mail addressed the definition of a competitive market.

> In such a case, the bureau has to define the market ... that could be affected by a merger. In this case, while both companies have acknowledged that the deal lessened competition in certain regional print advertising markets, they also operate in an industry in transition that is competing not just with other print media, but also in the larger digital advertising economy, where competition remains robust.[71]

Companies "entered into a conspiracy"

The documents submitted to the Ontario Superior Court of Justice in early March 2018 claimed that Hammill's evidence indicated "prior negotiation, agreement or arrangement" between the companies related to the closings. As a result, investigators said they believed the companies had "entered into a conspiracy" because their agreement specified which employees would be terminated when the transaction closed. "The deal also included a non-compete agreement," reported the *Globe and Mail*, "specifying that the companies would not operate print or digital news operations or flyer distribution businesses in some areas for five years and would not operate digital news publications or daily free commuter papers in some areas for two years."[72]

A transitional services agreement stipulated that each company was to continue distributing advertising flyers, but only for newspapers that were to remain open. The documents also pointed to press statements made by Postmedia executives that both companies were unaware of the other's plans to close the papers as "inconsistent with actions taken by Postmedia and Torstar and with the terms and conditions set out in the transaction documents."[73]

After search warrants were granted, uniformed Competition Bureau officers raided the offices of both Torstar and Postmedia in mid-March, along with those of Torstar's Metroland chain in Mississauga and its *Hamilton Spectator*.[74] "It's nice to see the Competition Bureau finally barking, but it's hard to imagine there will be much bite," said Martin O'Hanlon, an official with CWA Canada, the union representing newsroom employees. "The damage has been done, the papers are dead, and they're not likely to be resurrected. But hopefully the bureau will surprise us and do something, including action to end these swap-and-close deals that have been disastrous for so many communities."[75]

The search of Metroland's headquarters found documents which referred to the deal as Project Lebron, presumably after the basketball star, but on Postmedia's end it was code-named Project Ice. The *Globe and Mail* not only broke the story on its front page, but it ran a long, scolding analysis under the headline "Torstar, Postmedia and the arrogance of the deal" that dissected Postmedia's denials. "Given the pattern of facts laid out by the Competition Bureau," it concluded, "the best course of action may have seemed to be: Do one thing, say another, and bet that no one ever found out."[76] The *Globe* seemed to delight in flaying its two main rivals.

> One would think that in a climate of deep concern about the health of journalism ... two companies that engage

in that business might have better assessed all the risks involved in shuttering small community newspapers, depriving citizens of local news and throwing reporters out of work. And that leads us to wonder, what, exactly, is going on in the boardrooms of these two companies.[77]

It suggested that Postmedia had "a Pecker problem," referring to one of its hedge fund overseers. "Perhaps the moral centre of Postmedia's board of directors is now David Pecker, the CEO of American Media Inc. (AMI), publisher of the National Enquirer." Pecker had been installed on Postmedia's board at the behest of Chatham Asset Management in 2016 after the New Jersey hedge fund replaced GoldenTree Asset Management as its majority shareholder.[78]

AMI, which also published magazines such as *Men's Journal* and *Us Weekly*, was another distressed media property in which Chatham had invested by buying up its debt. Its association with AMI soon brought worldwide headlines and no shortage of embarrassment during that year's U.S. presidential election. Pecker had used his notorious supermarket tabloid to back Donald Trump's campaign, the *Globe and Mail* noted, with an "endless series of false pro-Trump stories on the cover of the *Enquirer*."[79]

A scandal erupted, however, when it was revealed that the Enquirer had paid former Playboy model Karen McDougal $150,000 for her story about an affair with Trump, but had killed the story instead of publishing it. The scandal culminated in August 2018 when Michael Cohen, Trump's personal lawyer, was sentenced to three years in prison on criminal charges in connection with the affair, including campaign finance violations, tax fraud, and bank fraud.

Pecker was granted immunity in exchange for providing prosecutors with information about Cohen's involvement in payments to two women who had affairs with Trump that amounted to illegal campaign contributions, including information about the sitting president's knowledge of the deals.[80] Cohen in turn implicated AMI in the payments, which led to calls from Canadian journalists for Pecker to resign from Postmedia's board of directors, which he did at the end of that month.[81]

Where is our money?

The rebuke didn't deter the newspaper lobby from ratcheting up its campaign for increased government assistance. John Honderich, the chair of Torstar's board of directors, soon authored a column titled "Where is Ottawa's help for Canada's newspapers?" that listed 25 defunct dailies and 112 closed community newspapers for a total of 137 titles that had ceased publication in the previous decade. The list included more than a dozen newspapers Torstar itself had just killed off and almost two dozen more it sent Postmedia to be closed, along with two dozen B.C. newspapers similarly swapped and closed by Black Press and Glacier Media.

Honderich demanded to know where the money was that Ottawa had promised to assist Canadian journalism. "One or two exploratory talks have been held but there has yet to be even a request for proposals," he groused. "Maybe next year, we are told."[82] Honderich was only doubling down on a column he had written earlier that year even as Torstar was trying to stave off a raid on its corporate offices. "Canada is facing a crisis of quality journalism," he wrote in the *Star* and other Torstar titles, making no mention of his company's culpability in the crimes he would list. "Reporters are being laid off in droves, many smaller communities are now 'news deserts' with no local newspaper, and the amount of serious investigative journalism is declining sharply."[83]

While the Trudeau government seemed to share the concerns of newspaper publishers at the beginning of its mandate in 2015, Honderich noted, its response to the myriad recommendations made by the Heritage ministry report and the PPF's *Shattered Mirror* in 2017 had been "studied indifference."[84] To make matters worse, in announcing her government's decisions, Heritage Minister Mélanie Joly emphasized her government wasn't interested in bailing out "industry models that are no longer viable."

> Left starkly unclear was where quality journalism would then originate. And newspaper executives, myself included, were left asking: if this is what the Trudeau government really thinks, then why did we go through this lengthy process.[85]

Not only did the *Star* push for a bailout in its opinion columns, its news coverage was also enlisted in an attempt to help persuade Ottawa to assist the newspaper industry. A lengthy feature out of its Ottawa bureau in advance of the 2018 budget statement started with National Media Council chair Bob Cox helping to deliver editions of his *Winnipeg Free Press* that were late due to printing problems. "For Cox, the experience of meeting subscribers keen to get their morning read was a welcome reminder that local news is valued," wrote *Star* bureau chief Bruce Campion-Smith. "But the delivery of local news in Canada is threatened by more than a balky printing press."[86]

The article recounted the litany of newspaper industry woes, including a "precipitous decline in ad revenues, the shift to digital, and the domineering online presence of Facebook and Google," and also repeated the *Shattered Mirror*'s claim that 225 weekly newspapers had closed or merged since 2010. It predicted that the upcoming budget would adopt his group's suggestion of using the Canadian Periodical Fund to assist Canada's dailies, and quoted Cox as hoping for it to be tripled to $225 million a year, which was a lot less than the original ask of $350 million. It repeated Honderich's complaints of "studied indifference," added the thoughts of Unifor's Howard Law and Carleton's Paul Adams, and quoted Cox at length. "The simple fact is that most community journalism is being done by newspapers," he said. "They are the base of the news ecosystem in most cities and towns ... sometimes they are the only player."

Joly's rejection of News Media Canada's proposed bailout the previous fall obviously still upset Cox, but Campion-Smith proved unable to get an interview with the minister, settling for an e-mail exchange with a spokesman instead. "It just infuriates me when I hear her say that they won't support business models that are no longer viable because every single media business model is not viable, with the exception of Google and Facebook," Cox said. "The magazine industry wouldn't exist if it wasn't propped up by the federal government."[87]

Campion-Smith's one-sided article was too much for *National Post* columnist Andrew Coyne. "Nowhere in its nearly 1,300 words would you find any hint of a suggestion that anyone, anywhere outside of government, bore any reservations about the government getting into bed with the newspapers," he wrote. "The publishers have become increasingly shameless in advancing their self-interested cause, not just in the usual luncheon speeches or lobbying sessions, but more and more in the pages of their own papers."[88]

> Of all the voices that might argue for government support of newspapers, the very last should be those of the newspapers themselves, least of all in their own pages. This is not just craven, or in bad taste, or an obvious conflict of interest. It is crossing a line that should never be crossed. Consider. Here we have publishers issuing demands for cash to the government, in the run-up to an election, via the reporters they employ ... Call it blackmail, call it bribery, call it something in between, but it stinks.[89]

Its disappointment at the measly $10 million a year in federal funding only drove the newspaper publishers to step up the pressure campaign. In June, Postmedia announced it was shutting down community newspapers in Camrose and Strathmore, Alberta, along with titles in Kapuskasing, Ingersoll, Norwich, and Petrolia, Ontario, with the loss of sixteen jobs. In a cost-cutting move, it also stopped printing community newspapers it said were unprofitable in Portage la Prairie, Manitoba, and Kirkland Lake and Pembroke, Ontario, which would continue to publish online, while its weekly in High River, Alberta, would be reduced to biweekly publication.[90]

News Media Canada also hired lobbyist and Liberal insider Isabel Metcalfe, a former ministerial assistant, speechwriter, and federal candidate, to make its case in Ottawa. Subscription news service Blacklock's Reporter obtained documents which showed a "lobbying blitz" conducted on behalf of News Media Canada following the government's 2017 decision not to subsidize news media, in which Metcalfe held 79 meetings with senior officials, including in the Prime Minister's Office.[91] Metcalfe was influential indeed, having been named the second-most powerful of almost 800 Ottawa lobbyists in 2014 by *Maclean's*.[92]

News Media Canada and Postmedia had lobbied politicians and bureaucrats for years with limited effectiveness, with Godfrey himself trekking to the capital for no fewer than 41 meetings between 2012 and 2018.[93] The *Hill Times* reported in 2016 that News Media Canada's precursor organization Newspapers Canada had filed fourteen communication reports with the federal lobbyists registry in only a few months during the PPF's *Shattered Mirror* study and the Heritage committee hearings. The meetings with bureaucrats, mostly communications and media relations staff, according to CEO John Hinds, were aimed at "getting our message out ... that we're not dead, we're not a dinosaur."[94]

It was time to bring out the big guns in the form of Metcalfe and her firm Public Affairs Counsel, whose blitz finally broke through. Records obtained by Blacklock's under the Access to Information Act showed that she was able to deliver News Media Canada's message directly to Ottawa's corridors of power.

> Lobbyist Registry records show Metcalfe met then-Minister Joly and her successor, Heritage Minister Pablo Rodriguez, among twelve separate sessions with department staff. Metcalfe also lobbied thirteen deputy and assistant deputy ministers; had five meetings with the Prime Minister's Office; and lobbied the Department of Finance eight times including repeated meetings with Ben Chin, then-Chief of Staff to Finance Minister Bill Morneau.[95]

The Local News & Democracy Project

The Public Policy Forum also did its part, commencing a Local News & Democracy Project in early 2018 to "dive deeper into the state of local and community news media." With the support of six non-government partners, the project would "examine how, exactly, journalistic coverage of communities across Canada has changed over the past decade."[96] In conjunction with the London-based consulting firm Nordicity, it conducted a three-month content analysis of almost 815,000 print news articles on civic affairs in 20 communities across Canada. The PPF's website listed its partners — the Atkinson Foundation, Community Foundations of Canada, CWA Canada, the McConnell Foundation, Unifor, and the Vancouver Foundation — and linked to the project's publications, articles it placed in Canadian news media, and media appearances by its head Edward Greenspon.

Its report "Democracy Divided" which was published in August and co-authored by Greenspon and UBC assistant professor Taylor Owen, who also worked together on *The Shattered Mirror*, dealt with the growing threat of Google and Facebook. The Harvard website NiemanLab, however, found its assumptions "a little far-fetched" when it came to the supposed need for regulation. "Greenspon and Owen start with assumptions like 'there is a necessary role for policy; self-regulation is insufficient on its own' and 'elected representatives have a responsibility to ensure the public sphere does not become polluted with disinformation and hate by setting rules, not by serving as regulators.'"[97]

The PPF then published two studies on the same day in September that showed the continuing decline of journalism in Canada. The first, titled "Mind the Gaps: Quantifying the Decline of News Coverage in Canada," found that the number of articles generated by community newspapers in Canada had declined by almost half over the previous decade. News coverage of local municipal councils and other democratic institutions fell by more than one-third. The decline was consistent across the board in almost all of the 20 communities, the study found, regardless of population or whether papers were downsized or closed. "It's down whether you lost your paper, you didn't lose your paper, whether you're big, small or medium-sized, whether you're French or English," Greenspon told the Canadian Press. "There's a consistent trend line down, down, down."[98]

The second report showed that some news organizations moved to non-profit business models to adapt to a dramatic decline in advertising revenues. Montreal's *La Presse* newspaper, it noted, had announced earlier in 2018 that it would convert to a non-profit. The report used the analogy of community ownership of a football team in its title "What the Saskatchewan Roughriders Can Teach Canadian Journalism." Rather than one controlling shareholder, the Canadian Football League franchise was owned by many local shareholders, the report noted, suggesting that community ownership may prove to a viable business model for the newspaper industry. "People want news that is close to their community and reflects their community," Greenspon told the *Globe and Mail*. "And that's the key in the Saskatchewan Roughrider model."[99]

Bailout breakthrough

The newspaper lobby's campaign obviously had an effect, as Ottawa soon buckled under and bucked up. In his annual economic statement that November, Finance Minister Bill Morneau announced that the 2019 federal budget would include $595 million in tax credits to subsidize reporting, subscriptions to digital news services, and charitable donations to non-profit news media. Details of the plan would not be released until the budget was tabled the following spring, but Morneau announced in Parliament that the funding would start flowing with $45 million in 2019 and increase to $165 million in 2023.

The largest portion of the assistance would come in the form of labour tax credits to assist "trusted" news organizations. Eligibility for the wage subsidy would be determined by the Canada Revenue Agency based on advice from an "independent" panel of industry members that would consider which jobs and which news media outlets would be worthy of funding. A new category of charity would also be created to enable news media outlets to apply for non-profit status and thus issue tax-deductible receipts in exchange for donations. Subscribers to digital publications would also be allowed a 15 percent tax credit, to be capped at $75 a year.[100]

Conservatives criticized the measures as bound to make journalists and media owners beholden to the state. "The media should be independent from the government," said Carleton MP Pierre Poilievre. "We should not have a situation where the government picks a panel that then decides who gets to report the news. That is very dangerous."[101] Poilievre called the subsidies a giant "slush fund," according to the *Washington Post*, that was aimed at buying the support of journalists for the re-election of Trudeau's Liberals.[102] Torstar columnist Thomas Walkom warned that the federal government was "tiptoeing into a minefield," with the bailout. "Unless carefully directed," he wrote, "these subsidies won't necessarily encourage chains to spend more on news."[103]

Media critic John Miller saw the bailout as an affront to journalism's professional integrity and predicted that it would not achieve its stated objectives. "I wish I could say that [it] will accomplish even one of its stated goals," he wrote on his blog. "It won't. Not the innovate part. Not the new business model part. Not the public service part. And not the survival part."[104]

Coyne was even more direct, as usual. "The effect will be to inevitably and irrevocably politicize the press," he wrote. "The money the government is giving us is not going to solve our problems. It is only going to ensure we put off confronting them. Before long we will be back for more."[105] The worst part, he warned, would be the infighting between media members over the pile of loot the government had just showered them with. "To hell with it," he spat. "To hell with all of it. No newspaper publisher should have anything to do with this plan. And no journalist worthy of the name should go anywhere near that accursed panel."[106]

> This, at a time of maximum suspicion among much of the public about our credibility, or our good faith. You wonder what went on in all those closed-doors meetings? What undertakings were given? What threats were made? Relax. It's probably nothing. No, really. You can take our word for it.[107]

Doing a victory lap

The bailout brought jubilation from the newspaper lobby, however, especially from Godfrey, who called it "a turning point in the plight of newspapers in Canada" so significant that it even warranted the donning of track shoes. "I tip my hat to the prime minister and the finance minister," he said. "They deserve a lot of credit. Everyone in journalism should be doing a victory lap around their building right now."[108]

Less than a week later, Postmedia released information to shareholders in advance of its annual general meeting which showed that Godfrey's annual compensation for the fiscal year topped $5 million. In addition to his $1.2 million salary as CEO, Godfrey was awarded $1.2 million in bonuses, $2.4 million in stock options, and other compensation that brought his total remuneration to $5.04 million. Andrew MacLeod, who had been promoted a year earlier to president and chief operating officer, received $2.2 million, or more than double his compensation the previous year, while the total for Postmedia's top five executives came to more than $10 million.

Coming so soon after announcement of the bailout, the optics were appalling. "Godfrey's $5 million compensation reflects the costs, including salary, of about 65 reporters," noted Tim Bousquet, publisher of the online-only Halifax Examiner, which was so small that it would be ineligible for support. "But sure, let's give Postmedia public money because the company is struggling."[109]

Early in 2019, Postmedia announced that Godfrey, who was about to turn 80, would step back from management and serve out the remaining two years of his contract as executive chair of its board. As expected, it named MacLeod to replace him as CEO.

The bailout did not mean total victory for Godfrey's leadership of Postmedia, however, as the Competition Bureau investigation was still ongoing. "We remain confident that this will ultimately result in an exoneration," MacLeod said. "It's a considerable burden on the company. But we respect the right, obviously, of the Competition Bureau to go through its process."[110] It was a process that had already gone on for more than a year, however, with hardly a peep to emerge from the investigation since the March searches.

CHAPTER 5
A CERTAIN SAMENESS

As a media junkie, Margaret Ormrod gave as good as she got. The social justice warrior delighted in countering conservatives online, especially the political pundits who dominated the media where she lived in Alberta. The two-way nature of Web 2.0 in the age of Twitter and Facebook enabled Ormrod to act as nothing less than a citizen pundit. While once she would have been confined to writing a letter to the editor and hoping it might be printed, now the Edmonton office manager could instantly respond to any article she found online, tweeting out a link to it under her handle MaggieMay along her own sharp commentary. Ormrod's biting Irish wit and finely-honed sense of outrage soon attracted more than 9,000 followers to her @CailinasEirinn account on Twitter, where like many Canadians she increasingly led a double life online.

Many of the links that showed up in her Twitter feed were to news stories published in newspapers and posted on their websites for all to read. Despite the emergence of an online-only news media, legacy media's coverage and commentary continued to wield an enormous influence over public discourse. Newspaper publishers promoted their articles and columns by tweeting them out and posting them on Facebook, where they often paid for prominent positioning.

It wasn't easy being a liberal in a province that had elected Conservative governments for 44 straight years, often with nary an Opposition member, but the impossible finally happened in 2015 when the NDP was elected despite Postmedia ordering all four of its dailies to again endorse the Conservatives. It just showed that old media's power was receding in the Internet age, where anyone could be a citizen journalist, or like Maggie a citizen pundit.

Ormrod had especially enjoyed reading the *Edmonton Journal* for its progressive stance, which provided some needed balance to the rabid right-wing worldview of the tabloid *Sun*. That was before Postmedia merged their newsrooms in 2016, however, despite promising not to. Postmedia cut its Alberta staff savagely that day, laying off 35 in Edmonton and 25 in Calgary. "The quality of the *Journal*, *Herald* and *Suns*, already in decline, fell precipitously," noted Ian Gill, who quoted *Edmonton Journal* editor Margo Goodhand as describing her city's newspapers as being in "tremendously awful shape."[1] Soon even Goodhand was gone after Postmedia put the province's four dailies under the management of its *Calgary Herald* editor.

Ormrod found herself increasingly isolated politically throughout 2019. Not only was she now reading the same content in both Edmonton newspapers, but it seemed that both were getting more and more conservative, constantly attacking the federal government of Justin Trudeau, which she supported. She went online to research the sorry state of Canada's news media, and what she found prompted her to take action. "Over the past 12 months, I watched in dismay as Postmedia presented an extremely biased view of the Liberal Party of Canada, and unabashed support for the Conservative Party of Canada and the United Conservative Party in Alberta," she wrote to a media critic.[2]

Ormrod came to the conclusion that media ownership reform was essential to preserving any semblance of Canadian democracy and that breaking up Postmedia would be a good place to start. It owned eight of the nine largest newspapers in the three westernmost provinces, including both dailies in Edmonton, Calgary, and Vancouver, along with the two largest in Saskatchewan, the *Regina Leader-Post* and the Saskatoon *StarPhoenix*.

Even worse, the federal government was now subsidizing the all-devouring chain with a $595-million bailout on top of the $50-million Local Journalism Initiative it had announced earlier.

It just didn't seem right to Ormrod that taxpayer money should be showered on newspapers that were 98 percent owned by U.S. hedge funds which were sucking them dry to make loan payments to themselves. If only there was some way of persuading the hedge funds to hand over the news media hostages they were holding all across Canada.

A media petition

Then an idea occurred to Ormrod, who ran the suburban St. Albert office of her accountant husband Dennis. Anyone could submit a petition to Parliament if it first gained the support of five Canadian citizens or residents and the authorization of an MP. If it then got at least 500 signatures in the allotted time, it would be presented to the House of Commons by its authorizing MP and the government was required by law to table a response.[3] It didn't guarantee action, but it was a good way to express dissatisfaction.

There was probably only one thing that hedge funds understood, and that was money, Ormrod reasoned. If they were deemed ineligible as foreign owners for the bailout money Ottawa was dispensing, perhaps that would encourage them to sell the newspapers back to Canadians. Having read that suggestion on a website, she decided to incorporate it into her petition.[4]

She carefully followed the instructions for writing it, starting with a few whereases. "Canada's largest newspaper chain is owned mostly by U.S. hedge funds which did a legal end run around our foreign ownership limits," her petition started. "They were then allowed to take over our second-largest chain. Postmedia Network thus owns 15 of Canada's 21 largest dailies, including eight of the nine largest in our three westernmost provinces."[5] Ormrod knew that demanding another inquiry would be futile, but she wanted to point out just how many commissions had pointed out the growing problem of ever-tighter press ownership and had fruitlessly urged successive governments to deal with it.

> Federal inquiries going back 50 years warned Canadians about the dangers of growing media ownership concentration, including Reports of the Special Senate Committee on Mass Media (1970), the Royal Commission on Newspapers (1981), the Senate Committee on News Media (2006), and the Heritage Committee on Media and Local Communities (2017). All these reports urged measures to check concentration and then newspaper-television "convergence," but few were taken. By 2010, convergence left our news media in ruins. We are now bailing out big media.[6]

The petition concluded: "We, the undersigned, citizens of Canada, call upon the House of Commons in Parliament assembled to use our tax dollars to foster a more pluralistic Canadian news media by providing subsidies only to Canadian-owned publications."[7] All Ormrod needed now was for an MP to authorize her petition before it could be posted online for signatures. Her local representative Michael Cooper was a Conservative, however, and was unlikely to support anything proposed by a Liberal rabble-rouser like Ormrod. "I have written to MPs in the past and found it took more than three months to receive a reply," she complained.[8]

It soon occurred to her just who in Parliament might be willing to help her take on Big Media, however. Vancouver Centre MP Hedy Fry had just spent more than a year studying the problem only to see most of her report's suggestions for media reform ignored and newspaper publishers instead simply handed a $595-million bailout. Fry readily agreed to authorize Ormrod's petition, and it was finally posted online in March 2020.

Now all Ormrod needed for her petition to be presented to Parliament was the required number of signatures, but with her legion of Twitter followers and their dissatisfaction with Canada's news media, that wouldn't be difficult. "I need 500 signatures within 30 days," she announced in a tweet.[9]

The signatures piled up quickly, along with tweets of support. "Signed," replied a Twitter user named Janet Greaves the same day. "I think our reporters in the field need to shape up too."[10] One of Canada's most notorious online personalities even signed her petition.[11] "You have my unwavering support," wrote Ed the Sock, the Toronto cable TV puppet legend created in the 1980s by Steven Joel Kerzner. "Our media has been put on one plate and carved up to give US companies the power to influence the conversations about our future that we need to have w/o US interference."[12]

Ormrod's petition gained more than 1,000 signatures the first day it was online. "This is empowering," replied a Twitter user who took the name Disinfect Democracy. "Fighting for a free press beats the hell out of sitting around & fretting over not having one:)."[13] By the end of the 30 days, Ormrod's petition had gained 4,147 signatures and it was presented to Parliament in June, although

Fry had to do so by video from her home in Vancouver because of the Covid-19 pandemic.[14] All they could do now was wait for the government's response, which under the Standing Orders of the House of Commons had to be presented to Parliament within 45 calendar days.[15]

Turning hard right

The dissatisfaction Ormrod felt with the news media she consumed was shared not only by most of her Twitter followers, but by many other Canadians as well. Surveys were beginning to show that public trust in journalism was falling fast. A report by the Reuters Institute found that while 55 percent of Canadians surveyed trusted "most news, most of the time" in 2016, that number had fallen by a fifth to only 44 percent in 2020.[16]

The global communications firm Edelman, which had studied trust among Canadians for more than 20 years, began to find public confidence in Canada's news media ebbing away. From 71 percent of Canadians who said they trusted the news media in 2019, when the bailout began, the number would fall by almost half three years later.[17] An Abacus survey in 2022 confirmed the trend, finding that 44 percent of Canadians believed that much of the information they received from news media was false.[18]

There was good reason for such skepticism, especially when it came to Postmedia. Under the leadership of Andrew MacLeod, who replaced Godfrey as CEO at the start of 2019, the former Southam newspapers would become more partisan than even under Conrad Black or the Aspers. The *National Post* had been conceived as a conservative publication by Black in 1998 and it openly sought from the outset to "unite the right" of Canada's fractured conservative parties in an attempt to displace the ruling Liberals. The *Post* burst from the womb attacking with fervour the Liberal prime minister of the day, Jean Chretien, and it continued that tradition with Justin Trudeau.

The *Sun* newspapers, which Godfrey had headed for a decade and then added to Postmedia, had also always been conservative, but the former Southam dailies like the *Ottawa Citizen*, *Montreal Gazette*, and *Vancouver Sun*, had traditionally been more liberal.

Even more importantly, they had been fiercely independent under the chain's policy of granting local autonomy to publishers. In order to allow the newspapers to better reflect their communities, the Southams had always been hands-off owners. That was why the Aspers encountered so much resistance at the millennium when they tried to centralize editorial control in order to push their agenda of free-market economics, eliminating the CBC, and supporting Israel.[19] Where the Aspers failed in moving the Southam dailies to the right, however, Godfrey and MacLeod would succeed.

Postmedia's partisanship for the Conservative Party became blatant during the 2015 federal election when it ordered its editors to endorse for re-election the decade-old government of Stephen Harper. "Before you ask, this was a decision made by the owners of the paper," *Edmonton Journal* columnist Paula Simons revealed on Twitter. "As is their traditional prerogative."[20]

Postmedia had also ordered its four Alberta dailies to endorse the Conservatives during a provincial election earlier that year. "The owners of the *Journal* made that call," Goodhand admitted at the time. "Editorials are always expected to reflect the opinions of the owner/publisher."[21] Godfrey defended the corporate control over election endorsements. "Since God made babies, I think [they] were always made that way," he told the *Globe and Mail*, "and if anyone thinks otherwise, I think they were dreaming in Technicolor."[22]

That prompted John Honderich to respond in the *Toronto Star*. "Really, Mr. Godfrey?" wrote the Torstar chair. "You might want to examine the policies of other newspaper chains that tell an entirely different bedtime story."[23] Honderich noted that Southam "went to great lengths to emphasize individual publishers in each city were responsible for all editorial content, including election endorsements." So had the erstwhile Thomson chain, which once included the *Globe and Mail*, *Ottawa Journal*, *Vancouver Sun*, and *Montreal Star*. "The reason, of course, was self-evident," explained Honderich. "What was important or relevant to readers in Vancouver might not be so in Montreal, Ottawa or Windsor ... Newspapers are an essential informing part of the democratic process and their first responsibility must be to the local readers they serve."[24]

Postmedia's political engineering grew bolder just two days before the federal election, when its editions across the country came wrapped in full-page ads warning that "Voting Liberal will cost you." The stunt was met with a barrage of criticism. "This was crossing the Rubicon," wrote Geoff Olson in the *Vancouver Courier*. "Whoring out front pages across the country just days before an election was a low unworthy even of media mogul Rupert Murdoch and his boss, Satan."[25] Godfrey pointed out that advertising was how newspapers made money. "Anybody, the Liberals could have done it, the NDP could have done it, as long as they pay the going rate," he told the *Globe and Mail*. "Newspapers have to seek whatever revenues they can get."[26]

Canceling columns

Godfrey hit the trifecta on election day when *National Post* columnist Andrew Coyne resigned as the newspaper's editor of editorials and comments after his column endorsing a party other than the Conservatives was spiked. "As far as we're concerned, if you're the editor, you support the editorial position of the newspaper," Godfrey told the *Globe and Mail*.[27] It wasn't the first Postmedia opinion piece to be pulled for not toeing the company line, even that year.

A column by author Margaret Atwood that asked some hard questions about the Conservative prime minister had been pulled down from the *National Post* website that August before re-appearing in an edited fashion. "Why is Harper still coyly hiding the two-million-dollar donors to his party leadership race?" asked Atwood initially. "Don't we have a right to know who put him in there? Who's he working for, them or us?" That passage was reportedly deleted from the final version, along with other criticism of Harper.[28]

A Postmedia executive claimed that Atwood's column had been pulled because it had not been fact-checked. "Senior editorial leadership at Postmedia also had not concluded whether the column was aligned with the values of the National Post and its readers," *National Post* senior vice-president Gerry Nott explained in an e-mail to a *Star* reporter.[29]

A troubling trend

Postmedia's partisanship would only increase. *Maclean's* reported as an election was called for the fall of 2019 that "recent changes in the Postmedia group suggest a troubling trend is possible." It had appointed a chain-wide editor that June to oversee federal and provincial political reporting and commentary in all of Postmedia's newspapers, noted the magazine, adding that it "may be something to start worrying about."[30]

Kevin Libin had been editorials editor at the *National Post*, but before that he had been a founding editor of the ultra-conservative Calgary-based magazine *Western Standard*. "His new appointment means a single voice — and an ideological one — will now oversee or directly run political coverage in a fleet of papers," noted *Maclean's*, "many of which are not conservative papers at all, beginning in an election year."[31]

The move was the latest in an "inexorable push to centralization" by Postmedia, it added, with its political coverage now run out of Toronto and editing of all of the chain's newspapers moved to a central desk in Hamilton. Libin's appointment to oversee political coverage was especially worrying. "With oversight now centralized in a single editor, it's hard to know how much autonomy each paper's editor-in-chief would have over politics coverage, or how much political range readers can expect from Postmedia papers." *Maclean's* interviewed sources inside the chain and discovered that the move was part of a broader shift within Postmedia.

> More than one Postmedia journalist contacted for this story recalls being told by a senior staffer there was an impetus to tilt conservative in order to appeal to audiences that management felt were underserved by other media. One noted that even before Libin's appointment there seemed to be less space for reported stories that did not hew to a certain political world view.[32]

Maclean's lamented the "degradation of a news media that has generally avoided the U.S.-style partisan model," and fretted about the blurring of political reporting and commentary under an ideologue editor. "Newspapers have always taken editorial positions on political issues, but those are typically kept separate from their reporting function." It also asked whether such partisanship was appropriate under government funding. "Should a project with an explicitly partisan mandate for news coverage receive money earmarked for journalism? What are the optics for a Liberal government if it doesn't, when one member of the panel deciding that is the head of Unifor, a union explicitly campaigning against the Conservatives?"[33]

The Inside Story

Canadaland soon followed with what it called "The Inside Story of Postmedia's Right Turn." Its investigation traced the origins of the chain's political course change to October 2018, near the end of Godfrey's leadership. It was "the start of something unprecedented." Former *National Post* media reporter Sean Craig reported that several editors at the newspaper had been summoned to a meeting at company headquarters in Toronto where they were told that the *Post* "had to become more reliable in its conservative politics."[34] Their reaction was nothing short of dismay. "According to three sources familiar with the meeting, company president Andrew MacLeod told them that their paper ... was insufficiently conservative."[35]

Craig interviewed more than 40 current and former Postmedia employees for his investigation, none of whom would be quoted on the record for fear of reprisal. His article, which at more than 6,000 words was unusually long for an online publication, reported that management had "given a directive for all of its papers to shift to the political right, in an unprecedented, centralized fashion."[36] Libin's appointment in mid-2019 brought the first "full-blown change," according to Craig. "His mandate is straightforward: to make the papers more 'reliably' conservative. Fifteen current employees confirmed this was their understanding of his new role, and that it had been communicated to them by management or a superior." One prominent writer Craig spoke to "expressed concerns that Libin's views on climate change could pose a threat to objective coverage of issues such as carbon pricing across the chain." The planned hard right turn would be taken first at the *National Post*, according to Craig's sources, and then imposed on the former Southam dailies. "It is planned that the rest of the chain's broadsheets will follow suit, adopting a more consistent conservative outlook and a punchier political voice under Libin's guidance."[37]

> Many employees fear current plans to double down on what management calls "reliable conservative voices" will eradicate the local perspectives and political independence of some of Canada's oldest and most important newspapers ... In some large Canadian cities, Postmedia runs the only local daily newspaper (or in the case of Montreal, the only English-language daily).[38]

A backlash to Libin's appointment had already been seen in Edmonton, according to Craig, with new *Journal* and *Sun* editor Mark Iype recalled to corporate headquarters after he "raised objections that the company was not respecting the editorial independence of his newsroom."[39] Iype's reassignment to a "special projects" role came after the *Journal*'s editorial board endorsed a carbon tax brought in under Alberta's previous NDP government, which according to Craig upset management. "Postmedia corporate immediately raised the piece as an issue with Iype, arguing it strayed too far from the company's vision for its editorial content, five sources familiar with the discussions said."

Iype's abrupt ouster was symptomatic of the "poorly organized, and sometimes seemingly improvised" changes brought by Postmedia's rightward shift, noted Craig. "Two sources at Postmedia's corporate headquarters in Toronto, familiar with management's thinking, confirmed that the company was displeased with the political orientation of the paper under his watch, and did not see him as suited to managing a conservative shift." Postmedia's push to take the "progressive, civic-minded" *Journal* rightward, added Craig, was in sharp contrast to the independence the daily was allowed even under Conrad Black. "The Journal has never been a conservative newspaper," one current employee told Craig. "It's as if no one at Postmedia ever read the thing."[40]

Editors depart

Reprimanding or removing editors for being insufficiently conservative or co-operative had also been seen under Godfrey, added

Craig. After the 2015 federal election which ended almost a decade of Conservative Party rule, he noted, *Ottawa Citizen* editor Andrew Potter was called in to company headquarters in Toronto. "There, Lou Clancy — then Postmedia's senior vice president of content — told Potter that his paper was too 'anti-conservative,' according to three sources," reported Craig. "When Potter asked for specific examples of coverage that could be improved upon, Clancy could only cite a single editorial cartoon."[41] Potter left the *Citizen* in early 2016 for a position at McGill University, part of an exodus from the newspaper's editorial pages after the fall election, as two of its editorial writers had already resigned.[42]

Leaving the *Edmonton Journal* about the same time were Goodhand and her managing editor Stephanie Coombs, who were purged as part of the 35 layoffs made in combining the newsrooms of Postmedia's duopoly dailies there. Goodhand had criticized Postmedia's election endorsement edict a few months earlier as an outdated tradition. "I truly believe the media has to be as accountable and transparent as every organization they demand it from," she told the CBC upon her departure. "So there was no way that I wasn't going to speak up."[43]

According to former journalist David Climenhaga on his blog Alberta Politics, the *Journal* editors "had been seen as insufficiently enthusiastic about head office plans to merge the Edmonton newsrooms." Their dismissal, he added, may also have had something to do with a recent *Journal* editorial pointing out that the province's NDP government could hardly be blamed for the price of oil, or the state of the economy. "As is well known, that is not a message Postmedia wants its newspapers to convey to their diminishing readership."[44]

As part of his investigation, Craig learned that *Calgary Herald* columnist and editorial page editor Licia Corbella had joined the new United Conservative Party and actually voted in its recent leadership race. After he tweeted that out, the *Herald* published a "Message to readers" and removed from its website seven columns Corbella had written about the UCP while holding party membership. "It has come to light that Postmedia columnist Licia Corbella did not disclose that she became a member of the newly formed United Conservative Party in 2017 and voted in the leadership race later that year," its message read. "The Postmedia Editorial Code of Conduct is clear that journalists should not place themselves in a conflict of interest situation by writing about people or organizations with whom they are involved."[45]

According to an analysis by PressProgress, an online publication of the Broadbent Institute, the number of deleted columns would soon reach at least thirteen, including one endorsing Jason Kenney for UCP leader that was published during the party's three-day voting period. "Corbella published a number of columns sympathetic to Kenney during the 2017 UCP leadership race," it noted. "On October 27, 2017, she wrote Kenney is 'quite simply, a force of nature — compelling, sharp, humorous, principled and articulate like few others.'"[46]

A political hitman

In March 2019, Postmedia took on a columnist who would actually turn out to be a hired political hitman, but Warren Kinsella would also keep his *Toronto Sun* column even after it emerged that he was paid to attack a political candidate. *Maclean's* dubbed the long-time consultant the "Prince of Darkness" in 2009 for being a "most gleeful practitioner" of political dirty tricks.[47] His *Sun* column attacked Trudeau regularly, but he soon also began to go after Maxime Bernier, a former Conservative Party leadership candidate who had left the party in 2018 to form the populist People's Party of Canada.

Kinsella wrote in one May column that "Bernier and his cabal have devolved into the porch-light of Canadian politics, attracting all the bugs and the creepy-crawlies."[48] Another in June described Bernier as having gone "full alt-Right" and "thereby consigned himself to the margins of Canadian politics, and the dustbin of history."[49]

On the eve of that fall's federal election, the CBC and *Globe and Mail* reported that Kinsella's four-person consulting firm had been hired by the Conservatives to discredit Bernier and keep him out of the party leader debates. "The objective of the plan, dubbed 'Project Cactus,' was to make the Conservative Party look more attractive to voters by highlighting PPC candidates' and supporters' xenophobic statements on social media," noted the CBC.[50] A Canadaland investigation counted 40 Kinsella columns the *Sun* had published by then, of which "all but a handful are explicitly critical of Trudeau, the Liberals, and/or their supporters."[51]

Postmedia issued a statement saying it was "unaware of any financial arrangement that Warren Kinsella might have had with a political party while writing a column for the Toronto Sun. If we had been aware of such an arrangement, we would have disclosed that relationship, as is our standard practice."[52] Bernier sued Kinsella for libel over comments made during the campaign, mostly on social media, but his lawsuit was dismissed and he was ordered to pay the columnist $132,000 in legal costs.[53]

Postmedia hired a new head of its Sun News division, but Toronto talk show host Mark Towhey had no background in journalism other than writing a book about the late Toronto mayor Rob Ford, for whom he had been chief of staff. "It appeared that it may have been a poorly timed, early April Fool's joke," quipped Canadaland. "Postmedia, however, has confirmed it is not."[54]

After Kenney was elected as Alberta premier the following month, Postmedia hired his campaign manager, Nick Koolsbergen, in a bid to join a planned government "war room" designed to counter negative coverage of the province's tar sands project. To fulfill a campaign promise, Kenney announced shortly after the election that he would dedicate $30 million to countering "lies and myths" about the Alberta energy industry, and Postmedia wanted in on the action. A listing in the Alberta Lobbyist Registry revealed that Koolsbergen and his newly-formed company Wellington Advocacy had been hired by Postmedia to lobby the government on its behalf and to "discuss ways Postmedia could be involved in the government's energy war room."[55]

Mount Royal University journalism professor Sean Holman found it scandalous that Postmedia would offer itself for hire to a government that wanted to suppress or punish free speech it didn't like. "A news media organization that relies on free speech should not be in the business of supporting this kind of operation," Holman told the CBC. "This is a complete abrogation of the societal mandate that Postmedia should be upholding."[56]

This is another reason for people to believe that we are actually in the business of providing biased information, and that's not good in this current post-truth era, where it's more important now than ever that the news media functions as a bastion of the truth against forces of authoritarianism that are threatening us.[57]

Native advertising

Postmedia issued a statement pointing out that any lobbying done in its newspapers on behalf of Alberta's oil and gas industry would not be editorial content but instead content marketing, which was also known as branded content or native advertising. "This is not an editorial initiative but part of the commercial content part of the business," spokeswoman Phyllise Gelfand told the *Globe and Mail*.[58] Postmedia had launched its Content Works studio in late 2015 to get in on the native advertising boom, or as its website put it, "to meet the insatiable need for engaging experiences that connect … brand messages to audiences across a myriad of touch points."[59] Postmedia's branded content writers were kept separate from its journalists, but placing commercial messages next to news in a format which looked almost exactly the same troubled many journalists.

Native advertising was something new in the newspaper business, having started online with websites like Vice and Buzzfeed, but it was so lucrative that even august dailies like the *Washington Post* and *New York Times* were offering native ads. *New York Times* executive editor Jill Abramson called native advertising "the industry's new digital Frankenstein," and her opposition to it cost her the newspaper's top job in 2014.[60]

In Canada, both the *Toronto Star* and the *Globe and Mail* set up branded content studios, with the latter even demanding unsuccessfully in 2014 that its journalists write the content.[61] Postmedia jumped aboard the gravy train enthusiastically. "Simply put, we are breaking the mold of a traditional media company selling its own brands and audiences to advertisers," said Mike Pilmer, its Content Works head. "The conversation is now about telling our customers' stories to their target audiences on any platform."[62] Postmedia's website played up the company's history of providing authoritative content as several generations of Southams rotated in their graves.

> Postmedia Content Works provides a comprehensive understanding of the landscape of content engagement through the insights gleaned from producing and delivering editorial on a daily basis to measuring the efficacy of content engagement through the services provided ... We have been producing award-winning content for more than 200 years.[63]

The industry publication *Editor & Publisher* took a keen interest in Postmedia's foray into this new endeavour that blurred the lines between journalism and advertising. "Because Postmedia represents more than 200 brands in print, online and on mobile, the company has a leg up compared to other content marketing agencies," it noted in 2016 shortly after Content Works launched. "By utilizing these strategies developed by its editorial brands, Postmedia has the unique ability to create compelling and creative content for its clients." Postmedia executive Yuri Machado told *E&P* that "it's like a big petri dish on how Canadians are consuming and engaging with content."[64]

Serious ethical issues

Others feared that what was growing in the petri dish might be spreading out of control. A 2016 study published in the journal *American Behavioral Scientist* noted that executives from journalism, advertising, and public relations agreed that native advertising raised serious ethical issues. "Native advertising potentially deceives audiences who are unaware that native advertising is paid, persuasive content versus editorial, thus contributing to the diminishing credibility of journalism."[65]

> The potential for deceiving readers and proliferation of native advertising threaten journalism's credibility along with its core boundary: the separation between editorial and advertising. For the press to function in a normative manner, as a watchdog, contributing to the public's ability to self-govern, it simply cannot participate in deception.[66]

A 2018 study by the Montreal-based Union des Consommateurs, a network of thirteen consumer rights groups, outlined "serious ethical problems" with native advertising, including "the erosion of the impenetrable wall that, in the news media, must separate editorial from advertising content."[67] The study examined native advertising produced by fifteen Canadian news organizations, including Postmedia, and concluded that although some media outlets clearly marked the content as advertising, "we found the practices of most analyzed to be reprehensible."[68]

It scrutinized in detail three *National Post* articles and found that any disclosure that it had been produced by Postmedia's commercial content division on behalf of a client was often "camouflaged." Noting that Belgium and the U.S. both required clear labeling of native advertising, "ie. the term 'advertisement' itself rather than some euphemism," the study urged similar action to tighten standards in Canada, along with strict monitoring and enforcement to "take exemplary action against culprits."[69]

One of Postmedia's native advertising campaigns even caused a stir in the Senate. Charlottetown senator Percy Downe noticed in early 2017 as part of his work on overseas tax evasion that a number of "very positive articles" on the Canada Revenue Agency suddenly began appearing in Postmedia newspapers and on their websites.

Downe well knew the CRA's terrible track record of collecting taxes from Canadians who were hiding their money overseas, as not one person has been charged with overseas tax evasion in more than a decade, much less convicted, fined, or sentenced. In fact, the agency even promised not to charge evaders in one scheme if they explained how it worked and paid what they owed. Worse yet was the CRA's history of making false or misleading statements about its efforts.

That's why Downe's antennae went up when he read the glowing Postmedia coverage. "The CRA already has a proven track record," read one article in the *Ottawa Citizen*, "with over $218 million in third party penalties against promoters and tax preparers."[70] Another claimed that the CRA had won criminal convictions against 42 Canadians for evading taxes on $34 million of income between 2011 and 2016, with $12 million in court fines and 734 months of jail time resulting.[71]

Downe demanded from the floor of the Senate to know how such disinformation could be spread by the CRA and soon learned it had paid Postmedia to spread it. "It is likely the best press the ... CRA ever received," he said later in debating Bill C-11, the Online Streaming Act.

> As it turned out, the CRA didn't so much receive that press as produced and paid for it themselves. Unable to earn any positive media for their well-known incompetence in fighting overseas tax evasion, they decided to buy some positive media coverage and try to pass it off as legitimate news, which is the problem inherent in sponsored content.[72]

Downe demanded to know how much taxpayer money had gone into deceiving Canadians about the ineptitude of their bureaucrats, and when the answer came back, he issued a press release denouncing the "shameless self-promotion" and reported its price to the penny. "The Canada Revenue Agency admitted that it had paid $288,497.36 to place these 'articles' in six print and digital newspapers," it read. "So the next time you see an article in a newspaper or online talking about how good a job the Canada Revenue Agency is doing, check to see who paid for it. It might have been you."[73] Downe's revelations got no mention in the news, but he was able to slip them into an opinion article he wrote for the *Hill Times* on the CRA's "litany of exaggeration, misinformation and outright falsehood."[74]

Petroleum propaganda

Postmedia's partnerships to publish content on behalf of advertisers predated the establishment of its Content Works studio, however. Environmentalists were outraged in 2014 after a Postmedia presentation was leaked online which outlined a campaign it planned to conduct for the Canadian Association of Petroleum Producers.[75] The Vancouver-based online publication The Observer reported that the presentation proposed a dozen full-page "joint ventures" on topics of CAPP's choosing to be written by Postmedia which would run in its nine metropolitan dailies. "We will work with CAPP to amplify our energy mandate and to be a part of the solution to keep Canada competitive in the global marketplace," it promised.[76] The presentation promised to pull out all the stops to push CAPP's vision of energy extraction. "The *National Post* will undertake to leverage all means editorially, technically, and creatively to further this critical conversation," pledged publisher Douglas Kelly, who was pictured on one slide. Other slides suggested "topics to be directed by CAPP and written by Postmedia," with stories appearing in the *National Post* and other major newspapers.[77]

To environmentalists, the revelation helped to explain the growing amount of pro-oil propaganda appearing on the pages of Postmedia newspapers, whose opinion sections had become a haven for climate change deniers.[78] Retired Vancouver talk show host Rafe Mair, an ardent environmentalist, charged that Postmedia had "sold its soul to oil and gas."[79] The Broadbent Institute pointed out that CAPP was "selling the idea that the rapid development of the tar sands without federal emissions regulations constitutes a 'balanced' approach," and noted that it had "no shortage of money to spend to try and shape the debate about Canada's energy and environmental policies."[80]

Advertorials under the heading "A Joint Venture with CAPP" began appearing in Postmedia newspapers across the country in late 2013 and seemed to be the fruit of the leaked presentation. One from 2014 was headlined "Canada's Oil Sands Innovation Alliance: Collaboration for the environment" and focused on the technologies used by petroleum companies to "accelerate the pace of environmental performance improvement."[81] The article carried a disclaimer at the end when it appeared in the *National Post* and on its website, but in some other Postmedia publications such disclosure was absent. One CAPP advertorial in the *Regina Leader-Post* carried no disclaimer, according to the Victoria-based online publication The Narwhal, an environmental journalism publication founded in 2018, and the article later disappeared from the newspaper's website.[82]

Another *National Post* article from 2013 headlined "The way forward for oil and gas" carried no disclosure when viewed on the newspaper's website in 2023. It stressed the need for access to overseas markets for liquefied natural gas and crude oil, requiring pipelines across B.C. from Alberta and oil tankers off the west coast. "Canada's oil and natural gas industry is at a critical juncture," it began, "and the actions taken over the next year will influence the success of the industry and the national economic benefits that flow from it."[83]

> The continued success of this industry, the single largest private investor in Canada, is determined by two main factors: improved market access for Canadian oil and natural gas and the ongoing importance of maintaining social licence by demonstrating resources are developed safely and responsibly.[84]

Holman called the petroleum propaganda "tragic" and claimed that the lack of disclosure undermined the value of news media. "It is eroding the societal and political value of the content that media institutions are supposed to be producing," he told The Narwhal. "I'm not sure the media has thought through the ramifications of that ... We are supposed to be serving not an advertising purpose, but a political purpose, not a business purpose, but a societal purpose."[85] The Narwhal admitted that the Postmedia presentation to CAPP "was meant to cajole an advertiser to spend big bucks, not for public eyes," and that the resulting online articles could have been left unlabelled by error. "But the fact is, it doesn't look good. Readers expect news organizations to maintain their first loyalty to citizens."[86]

Friends of Science

One article sponsored by the Calgary-based group Friends of Science was removed by Postmedia in 2016 after it appeared in major newspapers across its chain. Friends of Science was a non-profit group founded in 2002 which rejected the scientific consensus that global warming was human caused.[87] The article suggested that scientists were not worried about the impacts of climate change and blamed warming temperatures on sunshine. It claimed that warnings of a climate catastrophe had been popularized by "self-serving politicians and their bureaucracies, cause-addicted celebrities and environmental groups that form an echo chamber driven by dollars from ideologues at various foreign philanthropic funds."[88] The article criticized the Alberta government's recent decision to phase out coal-fired power plants. It quoted several prominent climate change deniers who claimed that "climate change is natural" and that "the sun drives climate change, far more than human influence or human industrial emissions of carbon dioxide."[89]

Friends of Science had earlier run billboards with the same claim that were found by Advertising Standards Canada in 2015 to be in violation of the Canadian Code of Advertising Standards because they were inaccurate and distorted science. The sponsored story soon vanished from the websites of several Postmedia newspapers, according to PressProgress, including the *Montreal Gazette*, *Ottawa Citizen*, *Calgary Herald*, and *Vancouver Sun*, along with its online hub Canada.com. The Broadbent Institute publication reported that the article then re-appeared on the Calgary Herald's website, but no versions of it could be found online in 2023.

Postmedia investigative reporter Mike De Souza, who focused on energy and the environment, obtained documents in 2011 which showed that Friends of Science was founded in 2004 with $175,000 from Calgary oil company Talisman Energy.[90] In a story for which he received a citation of merit from the National Newspaper Awards, De Souza reported that the money was funneled through University of Calgary accounts with the help of political science professor Barry Cooper, who was also a columnist for the *Calgary Herald*. The university shut down the accounts in 2007 after a complaint from a blogger prompted an audit which concluded they were being used for partisan activity.[91]

De Souza reported regularly on energy issues from Postmedia's Ottawa bureau, often exposing secretive relationships between government and the oil industry by basing his articles on documents obtained via freedom of information requests.[92] He was laid off in 2014, however, after Postmedia eliminated its five-person Ottawa bureau.[93] The leaked Postmedia presentation to CAPP appeared online the same day. De Souza went on to work for Reuters, the National Observer, and Global Television before joining the

Narwhal in 2021.[94] He filed a complaint with the National NewsMedia Council in 2016 while managing editor of the Observer over a *National Post* article which disparaged the publication and noted that it received donations from American environmentalists.[95] The complaint was dismissed, however, as the National NewsMedia Council ruled that De Souza "offered no specific examples to substantiate his allegation about deceptive, defamatory or misleading information about his work as an investigative journalist."[96]

Pipeline propaganda

Another Postmedia article in 2013 prompted a complaint to Advertising Standards Canada. The profile of a pipeline company president in the *Vancouver Sun* headlined "Born to the Challenge: Janet Holder's B.C. roots make her the perfect lead on Northern Gateway," included her claim that Canada was losing $50 million a day due to limited oil export markets.

Economist Robyn Allan wrote a response disputing the figure which she hoped the *Sun* would publish, but Advertising Standards Canada rejected her complaint on the grounds that the content was not actually news but advertising. "It was clear that the page was set up to look like arms length reporting," said Allan, a former president of the Insurance Corporation of B.C., "even more so on the web than in the printed version of the paper."[97]

The environmental group DeSmog filed a complaint with Canada's advertising regulator under a clause in the Canadian Code of Advertising Standards that prohibited disguised advertising techniques, which stated: "No advertisement shall be presented in a format or style that conceals its commercial intent."[98] Advertising Standards Canada, a self-regulating industry body established in 1957, declined to pursue the complaint. The article subsequently disappeared from the *Sun*'s website, however.[99]

In his posthumous 2017 book *Politically Incorrect: How Canada Lost Its Way and The Simple Path Home*, Mair claimed that the CAPP revelations showed media reform was needed to save democracy. "How the hell can a newspaper justify becoming partners with part of the industrial community when it is their duty to report fairly, independently, fearlessly, and accurately on that industry to the public at large?"[100]

Mair also pointed to an agreement that Postmedia's *Vancouver Province* had with Woodfibre LNG to promote its controversial liquefied natural gas refinery in the nearby coastal community of Squamish. "Would that not also take away the journalistic independence so necessary to democracy? How could it possibly report on Woodfibre LNG in an honest, ethical and unbiased way?"[101]

Another example of Postmedia's coziness with Big Oil came in 2012, when the *Vancouver Province* removed from its website an animation by its cartoonist Dan Murphy which spoofed a TV commercial for Calgary pipeline company Enbridge. "After an existing Enbridge pipeline in Alberta developed a leak," noted the *New York Times*, "Mr. Murphy took an Enbridge commercial that features bucolic watercolor animations of life after the new pipeline and interrupted it with repeated splatters of animated oil."[102]

The outraged cartoonist went public, telling the CBC that *Province* editor Wayne Moriarty informed him that Enbridge had threatened to pull millions of dollars in advertising if it didn't remove the video, and that if it wasn't taken down, Moriarty would be fired.[103] Murphy left the *Province* a few months later after his position was eliminated in a cost-saving move.[104]

News for sale?

In 2020, the website Canadaland obtained a document which suggested that the University of B.C. had offered to buy $10,000 to $15,000 worth of *Vancouver Sun* advertising in exchange for space on its opinion pages and even its news pages. The memo outlined "UBC expectations," which included "five op-eds placed and three stories produced and published in Vancouver Sun/Province during the first two weeks of September."[105]

> Partnering with Postmedia will assist the university in ensuring our key audiences — parents, government, donors, and VIPS — have insight into the benefits of online education and our plans around virtual orientation. Postmedia's platform also offers an opportunity to engage Toronto/National audiences around UBC's Back to School approach.[106]

UBC promised in exchange to provide the Postmedia papers with advance access to campus stories and to senior officials for interviews. Canadaland counted four op-eds published in the *Vancouver Sun* during the first twelve days of September which matched the topics and dates specified in the memo. "An op-ed on September 1, about the measures UBC was implementing for online education this fall," it noted, "was followed a day later with the news story on the same topic by a Postmedia reporter."[107]

A UBC spokesman admitted the authenticity of the document but told Canadaland that the *Sun* retained the right to edit or refuse its submissions and to solicit responses from other authors. The editor of the *Sun* told the *Ubyssey* student newspaper the next day that the university "did not purchase editorial" from the Postmedia paper. "The university pitched the newsroom on several back-to-school op-ed ideas and we liked three of those pitches because of the focus on Covid," said Harold Munro. "Others we rejected for various reasons. We also published op-eds from other post-secondary institutions on related topics during this time."[108]

Backlash over racism

The situation on Canada's left coast would soon boil over for Postmedia, not as a result of petroleum propaganda or the sell-out of journalism integrity but instead over the hot-button issue of the day. Racism had increasingly become a sore point across Canada, especially among young people, and the backlash against it collided head-on with Postmedia's editorial offerings. The resulting explosion resounded across the country.

The touchpaper that set off the long-simmering conflagration was a 2019 *Vancouver Sun* column written by Mount Royal University geography instructor Mark Hecht headlined "Ethnic diversity harms a country's social trust, economic well-being, argues professor."[109] It described a backlash against immigrants who failed to assimilate in Denmark, then extrapolated wildly from it. "Many western nations assumed that increasing ethnic and cultural diversity through immigration would be beneficial," it noted.

> The dogma of diversity, tolerance and inclusion assumed that all members of the society wanted to be included as equal citizens. Yet, instead of diversity being a blessing, many found that they've ended up with a lot of arrogant people living in their countries with no intention of

letting go of their previous cultures, animosities, preferences, and pretensions.[110]

Hecht argued that societies with high social trust were more economically productive and happier, but that people in Canada were becoming less trusting of one another because of the country's immigration policies. "The most successful are homogeneous countries," he wrote, "not the diverse ones."[111] Social trust was defined by the Pew Research Center, which tracked it among Americans, as "a belief in the honesty, integrity and reliability of others."[112]

Hecht cited research from the Gatestone Institute, which was described on Wikipedia as "a far-right think tank known for publishing anti-Muslim articles."[113] It claimed that at least half of Muslims polled in Europe believed that Shariah law was more important than national law. "So, is excluding certain people from one's society a requirement?" asked Hecht. "The short answer is absolutely. The long and more reasonable answer is if you do let people into your country then make sure they hold similar values."[114] He warned readers to "expect enclaves to form" in any country welcoming diversity. "We say goodbye to diversity, tolerance and inclusion if we wish to be a society that can rebuild the trust we used to have in one another and start accepting a new norm for immigration policy — compatibility, cohesion and social trust."[115]

The column caused a backlash first on social media, then in alternative media, and finally even in some mainstream media. Several *Sun* reporters quickly took to Twitter to denounce it. "That opinion piece is pathetic," tweeted reporter Nick Eagland.[116] "What a complete pile of absolute garbage that op-ed is," agreed his colleague Rob Shaw.[117] Veteran crime reporter Kim Bolan distanced herself and her colleagues from the column. "None of us had anything to do with this," she tweeted. "If I knew this was being published, I would have said something. And my co-workers would have done so too."[118] B.C.'s new human rights commissioner described the column on Twitter as a "call to hatred."[119] The head of the Canadian Anti-Hate Network called it a "white supremacist screed" and "neo-Nazi talking points."[120]

Soon Munro was on Twitter apologizing. "I agree and apologize to everyone that this was published before I had a chance to read it," he wrote. "We've taken it offline."[121] The column had already been printed in the *Sun*'s Weekend Review section, however, and it remained on the *Province* website for the next twelve hours. Munro soon published an apology to readers which said the column "contained views that do not meet the journalistic standards of The Vancouver Sun and do not represent the views of our editors and journalists."[122]

> The Vancouver Sun is committed to promoting and celebrating diversity, tolerance and inclusion. Our vibrant community and nation are built on these important pillars. We apologize for the publication of the article. We are reviewing our local workflow and editorial processes to ensure greater oversight and accountability so that this does not happen again.[123]

Newsroom revolt

That wasn't good enough for *Sun* staff, among whom a revolt quickly brewed. Tyee founder David Beers, a former *Sun* editor, obtained an e-mail one staff member sent to Munro that criticized his apology as inadequate. "It was weak & tepid & five sentences long, when it should have been a full throated refutation of racism & bigotry," the unnamed journalist wrote. "You should have explicitly stated that the piece was racist & promised that something like it would never be published again."[124]

The e-mail listed a number of similar columns the *Sun* staffer unearthed during a short search. "Oversight of the op-ed pages is clearly lacking or utterly absent," they wrote. "The retracted article was merely the latest in a series of ignorant, bigoted & racist op-eds that have been published on our site that I found in 30 minutes of browsing."[125] Instead of a perfunctory apology, the writer suggested a more positive statement. "You should have announced ... that moving forward the op-ed pages would reflect the voices of B.C. that are underserved, that are ignored & that face discrimination every day."[126]

Soon the entire Vancouver press was up in arms, especially ethnic journalists who had watched for too long as the *Sun* and *Province* peddled racist drivel on their editorial pages. Vancouver journalist Jagdeesh Mann noted that the *Sun*'s racist past extended back at least as far as the 1914 Komagata Maru incident, in which a ship full of immigrants from India was turned away from Vancouver harbour. "It would seem Vancouver's largest daily paper is still bent on stoking racial discord a century later," Mann wrote on Canadaland.[127] The newspaper's unenviable record on racism was a long one and hit another pathetic pinnacle in the mid-1970s with the rantings of columnist Doug Collins.[128] According to Mann, it had not improved much, with news coverage that alienated the city's huge South Asian and Chinese populations by focusing on negative or crime-related stories. "Based on this piece — and arguably others published by Postmedia outlets — skin colour still seems to be a threat to Canada's social harmony, or at least is too often framed as such by Canada's largest media chain."[129]

Veteran Vancouver journalist Stephen Smart called the column "disgusting" and "incredibly disturbing."[130] Vice called it "blatantly xenophobic" and compared it to Nazi propaganda.[131] An online petition demanded that Munro fire editorial pages editor Gordon Clark, who had approved the column. "There is no place in Vancouver for a xenophobic, anti-immigrant, anti-Muslim paper like the one Postmedia wants it to become," it read.[132] Holman denounced his MRU colleague's op-ed and listed several recent anti-immigration and climate denial columns to show that it was "just another example of Postmedia content that undermines journalism to propagandize for radicalized right causes."[133]

Veteran *Georgia Straight* editor Charlie Smith agreed that the column was not an aberration for the Sun's weekend opinion pages and noted that concern over anti-immigration sentiment at Postmedia newspapers had long been festering. "This daily paper and many others have been sowing mistrust of federal immigration policies and multiculturalism for quite a while."[134]

One former *Province* colleague of Clark defended him, however. "Having worked there for over three decades, I can assure readers that the current leadership team at The Vancouver Sun/Province values Canada's diversity and uses its power to promote pluralism," wrote Fabian Dawson.[135] An Indo-Canadian who had immigrated from Malaysia, Dawson wrote his defence on the Ottawa-based website New Canadian Media, which was aimed at immigrants.

Dawson pointed to Munro's swift action in apologizing and

removing Hecht's column from the newspaper websites. "These are not the actions of a publication that wants to promote hate," he wrote. "I am proud of their swift and decisive response." Dawson instead blamed publication of the column on an understaffed newsroom. "Previously, there were separate opinion page editors for The Vancouver Sun and The Province. Now there is one — Gordon Clark."[136]

Clark, who had previously received criticism for columns he'd written calling the niqab "an insult," and asking "Are we allowing too many people into Canada?", took stress leave from the paper and quit in 2021, posting a 11,000-word defence on the website Medium. In it, he claimed that Munro told him that Postmedia executives had been "stung" by a recent Canadaland exposé and that the decisions to apologize, meet with staff, and make changes to the opinion pages all came from head office.

> Munro explained that his Postmedia superiors, including CEO Andrew MacLeod, were reacting to negative social media comments about the Hecht op-ed ... sending company executives into a moral panic. Munro told me that his superiors wanted to demonstrate that the company wasn't racist. To put it another way, it seems I was caught up in a panicky, poorly thought out corporate marketing exercise.[137]

Mass shooting

The *Sun* soon became a serial unpublisher when another racist column disappeared from its website after it showed just how dangerous such inflammatory rhetoric could be. Written by the late diplomat Martin Collacott in 2017 and headlined "Canada replacing its population for no good reason," it peddled so-called replacement theory, a variant of white supremacy. The column cited research which showed that almost 70 percent of Vancouver residents would be "visible minorities" within two generations and that the non-white population of Canada would rise from 20 percent to 80 per cent in less than century. "Questions must be asked about why such drastic population replacement is taking place and who is benefiting from it," Collacott's column read. "While Canada has been helped by large-scale immigration at various times in its history, the current high intake causes more problems than benefits for our current population."[138]

> Young people in large cities such as Vancouver and Toronto are being crowded out of the housing market by sky-high prices caused largely by the ceaseless flow of new arrivals. Despite this, those who profit from mass immigration continue to laud its benefits. Their claims are not supported by the facts, however. We are not facing looming labour shortages that we can't meet with our existing workforce and educational infrastructure.[139]

The column caused a stir on Twitter and other sites online, but apparently not enough to warrant its removal at the time. "I've had to re-read these first two paragraphs many times because I cannot quite believe they were printed in a major, mainstream Canadian newspaper," wrote journalist Andrew Kurjata on Medium. "That is racist, plain and simple."[140] Collacott, who was also a senior fellow of the Fraser Institute, was a regular contributor to the *Sun*'s op-ed page under Clark until his death in 2018, according to the Vancouver alt-weekly *Georgia Straight*, and his columns on immigration were "regularly derided as racist by his critics."[141]

After a 2022 mass shooting in Buffalo, New York, which killed ten African-Americans, the perpetrator's "manifesto" was found to contain wording almost identical to Collacott's 2017 column. The *Sun* "quietly scrubbed" the piece from its website after the Buffalo shootings, noted an online journalist who noticed it was gone and asked Munro why. "The opinion piece was removed because the contents are offensive and don't reflect the standards of The Vancouver Sun," Munro said. "I was not aware the opinion piece was archived on the website, or it would have been removed earlier."[142] The column remained available online, however, having been republished by other websites.[143]

National Post unionized

Racism on Postmedia's pages even prompted *National Post* journalists to finally unionize in mid-2020. A *National Post* column by 73-year-old Rex Murphy headlined "Canada Is Not a Racist Country, Despite What the Liberals Say" lit the fuse, outraging a group of women of colour in its newsroom. "Most Canadians, the vast majority in fact, are horrified by racism," wrote Murphy.[144] One of the women wrote a rebuttal to it the next day headlined "Before You Declare Canada Is Not a Racist Country, Do Your Homework." The *Post*'s cannabis reporter Vanmala Subramaniam noted that it was "both shocking and exhausting that a column like this needs to be written in 2020."[145]

The group demanded a town hall meeting to air their grievances, to which management finally agreed. It also agreed to launch a mentorship program, broaden its pool of contributors, engage community groups in editorial board meetings, and ensure that senior editors signed off on sensitive opinion pieces. The *Post* added a disclaimer to the online version of Murphy's column, claiming there had been "a failure in the normal editing oversight that columns should be subjected to."[146] The group was still dissatisfied, according to a *Ryerson Review of Journalism* investigation. "Staff wanted their leaders to say they'd no longer allow columnists to deny the reality of systemic racism."[147]

Murphy soon re-ignited the dispute by writing in a subsequent piece: "I stand by the column. I will not apologize for it; nor apologize for any part of it, word, comma or space between words. I will even stand for the semicolons."[148] That was followed a few days later by a column written by *National Post* founder Conrad Black. "'Systemic racism' means racism throughout society and its governance and is a false description of Canada and the United States," wrote Black, who had been pardoned for his crimes the previous year by Donald Trump after writing a flattering biography of the U.S. president.[149] The *National Post* malcontents were enraged, according to the *RRJ*, and contacted Unifor about organizing a union certification drive. "Several also went on a byline strike," it noted, "withholding their names from their articles to signal their objection to the Post's handling of the Murphy affair."[150]

> Over the next five months, what began as a debate between a columnist and a beat reporter at the National Post took on new life, pitting a group of frustrated journalists against their bosses. What first started as a fight about editorial standards — about the difference between a fact and a fair interpretation — soon morphed into a fight about much more: wages, editorial direction, and opportunities for racialized staff.[151]

When the votes were counted, the unionists had won an overwhelming victory. The new bargaining unit of 40 signed a two-year collective bargaining agreement that fall with an average pay raise of 8.25 percent, and it also raised the salary of its lowest-paid members to more than $54,000 per year, which was an increase of more than $14,000 for some web editors. A ground-breaking affirmative action hiring clause was also included which required that diverse candidates get priority in considering job candidates of equal merit.[152]

Competition Bureau: "No action warranted"

The news was not all bad for Postmedia as 2021 dawned, however. The Competition Bureau quietly announced it would not pursue charges against it or Torstar for their trade and closure of Ontario community newspapers more than three years earlier. The bureau released a statement on January 7 stating that "following a review of the available evidence, the Bureau concluded that no further action was warranted." It gave no reasons for its decision, and as most media were pre-occupied with the U.S. Capitol insurrection the previous day, the news made barely a ripple. "To refer a case for prosecution under the criminal conspiracy provisions of the *Competition Act*," its statement concluded, "the Bureau must find clear evidence demonstrating that competitors reached an agreement to fix prices, allocate markets, or lessen or eliminate the supply of a product or service."[153]

MacLeod issued a statement in response that seemed the height of irony given the company's recent mis-steps. "We are happy to have this matter and the associated pressure and cost behind us and look forward to continuing the important work of keeping Canadians informed with ambitious, trusted and high-quality journalism."[154] Competition lawyer Mark Warner told The Tyee that the Competition Bureau seemed to be "making a case about why they shouldn't make a case. ...In other jurisdictions — and I've practiced in Brussels, in New York and Washington — people would investigate and bring the case."[155] One legal analysis saw the case as "the Bureau's 'one last chance' to show it could effectively regulate antitrust behaviour in the newspaper industry, but this now appears to be a missed opportunity."[156]

Ormrod's petition was also swept under the bureaucratic rug. It proved a non-starter with the government, which finally released the required response to it after more than twice the required 45 calendar days. It never addressed Ormrod's plea to restrict bail-out money to Canadian-owned media, instead merely listing all of the assistance it had given to the news media and why. "The Government recognizes the Canadian news media's essential role in maintaining a healthy democracy, especially in this time where information is vital to all Canadians," wrote MP Julie Dabrusin, the Heritage ministry's parliamentary secretary. "As the news media landscape continues to evolve, the Government will continue to provide support while safeguarding the fundamental principal of press independence thus ensuring Canadians have access to reliable information from diverse, trustworthy sources."[157]

Government support for Canada's faltering news media would soon become a hot political topic again, however, as would the fundamental principal of press independence, but that wouldn't stop Postmedia and the newspaper lobby from taking their demands for support to another level.

CHAPTER 6
SHAKING DOWN BIG TECH

Tim Bousquet could scarcely believe what he was reading. The veteran Halifax journalist was going through the federal budget released online that first day of spring 2019, which included long-awaited details of the $595 million news media bailout announced the previous fall. The bailout, which took the form of a refundable tax credit covering a portion of journalists' salaries, was supposed to provide financial assistance for struggling news organizations, but it seemed the aid was meant for some and not others.

Bousquet had started the online Halifax Examiner in 2014 with his life savings of $10,000 after leaving the *Coast* alt-weekly, where he had exposed corruption and misspending for seven years as its news editor. He had won the Canadian Association of Journalist's Don McGillivray Award for investigative reporting in 2013 for his story about then-mayor Peter Kelly's questionable management of a family friend's estate.[1]

Then the *Coast* asked him to write advertorials, and Bousquet balked. He abhorred the paid features promoting a company or product, which some newspapers had been running long before the Internet invented native advertising. "Advertorial goes against everything I stand for as a reporter," Bousquet wrote on his blog. "The editorial side of the news business — that is, the news reporting — should be separate from the advertising side of the paper because readers need to trust that reporters are not influenced by commercial concerns."[2] Bousquet quit his job at the Coast and started his own ad-free online publication that would be funded by subscriptions instead.

The subscription model had been pioneered in 2001 by allNovaScotia, which by 2013 had more than 7,000 subscribers paying $39 a month and employed 15 journalists covering business and politics. It worked so well that it launched allNewfoundlandLabrador in 2016, allNewBrunswick in 2019, and allSaskatchewan in 2021.[3] Their content was hidden behind a hard paywall, however, and could only be accessed by subscribers. Bousquet decided to make his new Halifax Examiner free for all to read, with only in-depth stories and investigative articles behind a paywall. He charged $10 a month, half-price for students, and double for businesses. He hired freelancers to write articles and continued his own investigative work.

His story published in March 2019 about a man who spent sixteen years in prison after being wrongfully convicted of murdering his girlfriend took Bousquet eleven months to research and cost him about $5,000.[4] "Because I own a smaller niche publication, I can actually spend more time and money on selected projects than can the big corporate media," he told an interviewer after winning PEN Canada's Filkow Prize for it.[5]

As part of his mission to hold the powerful to account in Halifax, Bousquet kept a close eye on the local *Chronicle Herald*. It was the city's only real newspaper since the *Daily News* had been converted into a *Metro* commuter tabloid in 2008 by Transcontinental Media, which then sold it to Torstar, which rebranded it as *StarMetro* in 2018 but folded it a year later. Bousquet regularly called out the *Chronicle Herald*, which had long been one of Canada's few remaining independently-owned dailies, for its blatant boosterism and the undeclared conflicts of interest of some of its business columnists. He called it "Canadian Pravda, unquestioningly repeating official propaganda, kowtowing to the powers that be, and airbrushing inconvenient truths out of the official record."[6] (The *Chronicle Herald*, which was owned by the local Dennis-Lever family, lost its independent status in 2017 when it bought Transcontinental's 27 community newspapers in Atlantic Canada to form a chain called SaltWire Network.)

Bousquet's disappointment grew as he read through the 2019 budget online. It explained how so-called "Qualified Canadian Journalism Organizations" would be eligible for tax credits on each journalist employed to a maximum salary of $55,000, or $13,750 apiece. A new category of charity would also be created to enable news media outlets to apply for non-profit status and thus issue tax-deductible receipts in exchange for donations. Eligibility for the tax credits would be decided by the Canada Revenue Agency. Subscribers to digital publications would also be allowed a 15 percent tax credit, which was capped at $75 a year.[7]

Details were still sketchy, but according to the budget, eligible organizations had to have been in business for at least a year, be primarily engaged in the production of original written (not broadcast) content, cover general (not specialty) news, and meet additional criteria developed by an "independent" panel. Even the initial criteria, however, excluded many digital outlets like the Examiner. It had certainly been in business long enough, produced original written content, and covered general news, but under the rules posted online, a news media outlet had to meet several other conditions to qualify for the tax credits, including that it "regularly employs two or more journalists in the production of its content who deal at arm's length with the organization."[8]

That ruled out the Examiner, which had only one full-time employee besides Bousquet, and she was an administrator, not a journalist. Any stories not written by Bousquet were from freelancers. The Examiner was a shoestring operation, as were many other digital news media outlets that would also be disqualified from receiving federal aid. "'Arms-length' means that the subsidized reporter does not control the corporation," he wrote in his column, lapsing into the third person. "So, Halifax Examiner Inc. can't receive the subsidy to offset Tim Bousquet's wages."[9]

> As the Examiner is currently organized, we'd be ineligible for any of the tax credit, as we don't pay two full-time reporters who aren't named Tim Bousquet. Again, nearly every other startup media entrepreneur — Mary Campbell in Sydney, Joey Coleman in Hamilton, etc. — would be excluded. All the money goes to the big players.[10]

Bousquet did some calculations and figured that with a newsroom of about 30, the *Chronicle Herald* would receive an annual subsidy of around $412,500. He estimated that its 27-paper SaltWire chain had about 100 reporters and would thus get about $1,375,000. Allnovascotia would receive about $275,000 to subsidize its 20 or so journalists, while *StarMetro's* three Halifax reporters would net Torstar about $41,250 yearly.

The Examiner would get nothing the way the rules were written. "The budget goes to great lengths to exclude small operations," wrote Bousquet. "It already seems designed as a big tax giveaway to legacy media."[11]

Bending over backwards

The eligibility rules for the Canadian journalism labour tax credit may have excluded many Canadian journalists, but it seemed to bend over backwards to include a foreign-owned corporation. "One provision seems specifically designed to accommodate Postmedia," noted Bousquet. A qualifying media organization could be a corporation, a partnership, or a trust. If it was a public corporation, it had to be listed on a stock exchange in Canada and not be controlled by foreigners. If it was a private corporation, it had to be at least 75 percent owned by Canadians. By those criteria, Postmedia qualified for support. "Postmedia is owned primarily by an America hedge fund," Bousquet wrote, "but the weird criteria in this provision allows it to receive the tax subsidy ... even if its budget and profit demands are ultimately dictated by the hedge fund."[12]

Bousquet's were not the only criticisms of the proposed legislation. J-Source, an online publication of Canadian journalism schools, noted that the bailout "favours legacy media and may leave some of the country's scrappiest and most noteworthy start-ups in worse shape, relative to their old-guard competitors."[13] The fact that publications had to have been in business for a year to qualify for support, noted Erin Millar of the Vancouver-based website The Discourse, specifically excluded startups. "The policy seems purpose-built to help only one kind of media: newspapers. As it stands, this package provides resources to big newspaper chains to hire journalists to compete directly with startups."[14] This approach was a far cry from the government's stated objective in 2017, she noted, of not bailing out industry models that are no longer viable and instead supporting innovation, experimentation, and the ongoing transition to digital. "The newspaper lobby clearly succeeded in changing that strategy."[15]

A quiet bailout

Former *Toronto Star* and *Boston Globe* journalist David Skok, who founded the Toronto-based tech news website The Logic in 2018, noted that the bailout package landed with hardly a mention in Canada's mainstream media. "If you missed the news, it's probably because ... there's been almost no coverage of the media (don't call it a bailout) package from the country's traditional newspapers and airwaves since it was announced."[16]

Skok had serious reservations about the rules after he surveyed digital publications in Canada and found that those under two years old were far less likely to have at least two full-time employees. "The program will hinder seed-stage journalism development by favoring mature publications," he wrote. "The mandatory full-time status for eligibility also ignores the vital role that freelance journalists play in the news ecosystem."[17] Deeming some forms of coverage worthy of subsidy but not others showed a misunderstanding of journalism's societal role, he added. "This is a problematic policy because it will have a direct impact on the daily assigning and editing of a journalism product. But worse, the policy is an insult to the audience."[18]

Some journalists were opposed to the very notion of a government panel doling out money to journalists. "Taking money from the people we cover will place us in a permanent and inescapable conflict of interest," wrote Andrew Coyne in the *National Post*. "It will produce newspapers concerned less with appealing to readers than to grantsmen ... It will solve none of our problems, but only encourage us to put off dealing with them."[19] The way the bailout was designed, he added, was not for the future of news "but the past; not the scrappy startups who might save the business, but the lumbering dinosaurs who are taking it down."[20] Coyne, noted Skok, was "one of the few voices that could be found on the topic" in the mainstream media.[21]

Some digital media outlets, such as Blacklock's Reporter and Canadaland, stated that they would not apply for the money. Canadaland founder Jesse Brown predicted that with Liberal leader Justin Trudeau campaigning for re-election as prime minister that fall, the bailout would "poison the relationship between newsreaders and journalists."[22]

Any piece of favorable, or even neutral coverage of him will be seized upon by adversaries as evidence that the Liberal government has successfully bribed Canada's professional reporters, who have already been dubbed #JustinJournos since news of the media subsidy broke ... A barrage of attacks on media credibility will result in permanent defensiveness and self-censorship on the part of journalists, and a steady erosion of public confidence in establishment news organizations.[23]

Specifics about how the funds would be dispensed were also lacking, noted a pair of journalism researchers. "How that panel will be chosen is just one of several obscure or questionable aspects of the government's approach," wrote Heather Rollwagen and Ivor Shapiro on the website The Conversation, "likely to be at the centre of debate as this election year proceeds."[24] A lack of transparency also troubled many journalists who were used to demanding it from others. The Canadian Association of Journalists found the budget short on "a number of transparency steps recommended by the CAJ including that the panel defining journalism eligibility have its terms of reference, meeting agendas and minutes be published online."[25]

The government, however, promised transparency. "The whole process will be public," Heritage Minister Pablo Rodriguez said in an interview on CTV's Question Period in May.[26] Rodriguez, who had been named to replace Mélanie Joly as Heritage minister in mid-2018, repeated the pledge later that month in Parliament. "I have been very clear since day one that everything will be transparent," he said in answering questions about the bailout.[27]

In October, however, *Maclean's* journalist Nick Taylor-Vaisey tweeted that his Access to Information request for a copy of a 27-page Department of Finance ministerial briefing note on the panel's recommendations had been refused. "The Trudeau government promised 'everything will be transparent' in regards to the bailout," noted the Post Millennial website, "but much of the process has been done behind closed doors with major industry players representatives sitting at the table."[28]

An exclusive panel

Suspicions that the bailout was not for all media, but instead for old media, only grew when the panel was announced. News Media Canada and Unifor were both given a seat on the eight-member panel tasked with deciding who qualified for government support. Six other organizations were also invited to name one panel member — the Canadian Association of Journalists, the National Ethnic Press and Media Council, and four corresponding French-language organizations. *National Post* columnist Chris Selley wrote that "people claiming to act in journalists' and journalism's best interests are climbing all over each other not just to be first in line, but to decide who goes home empty-handed. It's a nightmare." The CAJ and its French-language equivalent, he added, "ought to be ashamed to go anywhere near this farce."[29]

Unifor's involvement was particularly problematic, he added, given its political campaigning. "Now the government that benefited from Unifor's partisan largesse has asked it for help deciding who's a proper journalist and what's a proper news outlet, and thus worthy of government largesse!"[30] Unifor spokesman Howard Law defended the union's right to participate in the process. "Unifor has represented journalists for decades and we have, you know, a great deal to offer."[31]

Former *Ottawa Citizen* editor Andrew Potter called on the CAJ to refuse its offered seat on the panel because of the conflict of interest its other members were in. "The panel will be staffed by pretty much the same legacy news organizations and vested interests that have spent the last three years demanding the government bail them out in the first place," he wrote for the CBC. "It boggles the mind that the Liberals have chosen this route in helping them decide who will be eligible for the money."[32]

> If there's any good news here, it is that it is now dead clear to everyone just why the Liberals' bailout package is such a toxic initiative. The news media play a number of useful roles in a healthy democracy, but one that is often cited is the job of "holding power to account." One very common way journalists do this is by pointing out conflicts of interest — in particular, the conflicts that

arise when public money is being handed out by people who stand to gain by handing it out.[33]

The CAJ agreed to participate, but not if panelists were required to sign a confidentiality agreement, so meeting notes were posted online as a compromise. It unsuccessfully urged the panel to post a full list of applicants for funding online. "It is the CAJ's position that when public funding is sought, some privacy must be sacrificed in the public interest," it said in a statement when other panelists argued that this would be a violation of privacy. "The CAJ maintains that making public those whose applications are denied would have held the government accountable for its implementation of the tax measures."[34]

The panel also declined to recommend that explanations be provided publicly for why groups had been denied funding. "The CAJ continues to urge the government to take these basic transparency steps. Without transparency this government funding remains at risk of the perception, regardless of the reality, of partisan influence in which outlets receive or do not receive funding."[35]

Writing the bailout rules

The so-called Journalism and Written Media Independent Panel of Experts issued its report recommending the bailout rules in July. Written by its chair, News Media Canada head Bob Cox, the report first called for increased funding. "Daily newspaper ad revenues are half what they were a decade ago," it noted. "The tax credits program, as positive as it is, will not suffice to counter these disastrous effects."[36] The report urged the government to raise the salary cap for the labour tax credit to $85,000 and increase the tax credit to 35 per cent, as originally proposed by News Media Canada, and to raise the digital subscription tax credit to 25 per cent. It also included other News Media Canada demands, including that the federal government buy more advertising in Canadian newspapers and on websites instead of spending it on "foreign-owned digital companies that do not fund Canadian newsrooms."[37]

To loosen the restrictions on small websites, the report urged that those publishing for more than 10 years without two arm's-length employees be allowed to count regular freelancers.[38] The report urged the government to speed up the payment process by deciding for itself who qualified based on the criteria its report set out. "In the interests of moving quickly, we have recommended that the tax credits be implemented and administered directly by the Canada Revenue Agency."[39]

The panel recommended that the CRA should refer any questions about applying the criteria to a new panel made up of journalism academics, which resulted in the formation in 2020 of the Independent Advisory Board on Eligibility for Journalism Tax Measures.[40] "We're not determining what is journalism and what isn't journalism," its head Colette Brin, a Université Laval professor and *Shattered Mirror* collaborator, told Canadaland, "but what is the kind of journalism that is really targeted with this program?"[41]

In late 2019, the CRA released information on how media outlets could apply for the new tax credits. "Media organizations must first apply to the Canada Revenue Agency (CRA) to obtain the QCJO (Qualified Canadian Journalism Organization) designation by completing the application form and returning it to the CRA."[42]

Postmedia reported to its shareholders in mid-2019 that it expected to receive $8 million to $10 million annually from the bailout. "It's an interestingly precise forecast," noted the Tyee's Paul Willcocks, "since no details about the subsidies have been released and the panel to establish eligibility was created less than two months ago."[43] The chain did not foresee a return to profitability, he added, and continued to cut costs despite the bailout.

"Therein lies the problem," concluded Millar, noting that the supposed purpose of the bailout was to strengthen Canadian news media. "That objective runs counter to Postmedia's number one goal right now: to cut its way to a place where it can reliably service its U.S. hedge fund debt. Its plan for doing that is to do less journalism. So, as it stands, a good portion of tax dollars intended to support journalism will aid Postmedia's transition to doing less journalism."[44]

> If the journalism support package does not go beyond benefiting big chains like Postmedia — which has few plans for its future beyond cutting back on journalism fast enough to stay ahead of its collapsing print-based business model — the measures will fail on their intended policy outcome: a sustainable, diverse, independent press.[45]

It was a myth that Postmedia was not profitable, however. It was only losing money if huge "paper" losses were taken into account. Those usually took the form of writedowns on asset value, which could run to the hundreds of millions.[46] On an operating basis, Postmedia was still comfortably profitable, although debt payments to its hedge fund owners took up an increasing proportion of its earnings.

The bailout provided a boost to its profits, however. In its 2019-20 fiscal year ending in August, Postmedia profits rose 37 percent from the previous year to $67.7 million, of which $30.6 million went to servicing its debt. It received $4.5 million in tax credits from Ottawa that year as part of the bailout, plus another $700,000 in bailout money from Quebec. It also reported a receivable of $10.8 million in tax credits which it had not yet collected from the government, and it had already received $7 million from the bailout in its 2018-19 fiscal year.[47]

With the onset of Covid-19 in early 2020, the company was also able to collect the Canada Emergency Wage Subsidy, which paid 75 percent of its salaries expense. From March 15, 2020 until the end of its fiscal year on August 29, Postmedia collected $40.3 million in CEWS, which when $5.2 million in bailout money was added, meant that fully two-thirds of its profits came from government subsidies.[48]

The subsidies didn't stop Postmedia from making more layoffs, and it also used the pandemic as an occasion to further cull its herd of community newspapers. In April, it announced the closure of fifteen weeklies in Manitoba and Ontario, thirteen of which were free distribution, resulting in 30 permanent layoffs. "The products that we closed today were really on the precipice and the crisis associated with the pandemic just pushed them over the edge," said MacLeod. "If we're losing money on titles then that has an impact on the overall company."[49]

Postmedia also temporarily laid off 50 staff in sales and operations and cut the salaries of its remaining employees. MacLeod reduced his own salary by 30 per cent, cut that of his executive vice-presidents by 20 percent, senior vice-presidents by 17.5 percent, and vice-presidents by 12 percent. All staff earning more than $60,000 a year, except for advertising sales staff working on commission, received at least a 5-percent pay cut. "No subsidy can offset the declines in revenues our industry is experiencing," MacLeod said.[50] Other newspaper companies also made similar cuts as the pandemic began, with SaltWire announcing it would temporarily lay off about 40 percent of its staff and reduce the hours of others.[51]

Some community newspapers, however, reported doing well despite the pandemic. Lana Meier published several community newspapers in Manitoba that competed with closed Postmedia weeklies, including the *Selkirk Record*, *Stonewall Teulon Tribune*, and *Winkler Morden Voice*. They were surviving, she told the CBC, because there was still a need for local journalism, with more people staying home and businesses advertising their service changes.

Meier, whose family had once owned some of the newspapers Postmedia just closed, said the chain "had lost touch [with] what the community newspaper was really about."[52] She started her newspapers in 2010 because she felt the "cookie-cutter" model emphasizing digital coverage, increased national advertising, and syndicated news from elsewhere was "taking the community out of community papers."[53]

One week after Postmedia's closures, Meier began publishing the *Carman-Dufferin Standard* to replace the *Carman Valley Leader* that Postmedia had closed. "As long as you have relevant news, and people who want to read it, then the equation is there for you to be successful," she told the *Winnipeg Free Press*, which launched a new weekly of its own in Altona to replace the one Postmedia had closed there. "We're certainly not going to get rich, but we're filling a void in the market. The response has been phenomenal."[54]

In May, Postmedia laid off another 40 workers after their unions did not approve the temporary salary reductions that were imposed at the chain's non-union newspapers. CWA head Martin O'Hanlon told the *Toronto Star* that the proposed pay cut would have saved the company about $100,000, but that the union had offered to buy that much advertising, only to be ignored. "The executives, the debt holders are not going to be out a penny when this is all said and done with so why the hell would the people who put out the product, why should they bear all the burden?"⁵⁵ In November, Postmedia gave notice to its unionized Vancouver workers that it would reduce salary expenses there by 15 per cent through layoffs or voluntary buyouts.⁵⁶

Bailing for dollars

The news media bailout campaign worked so well that soon a second campaign began for Ottawa to claw back some of the revenues that digital media were taking from old media. It was started by Friends of Canadian Broadcasting, which had been founded in 1985 to defend the CBC from Conservative budget cuts and within a decade had 40,000 members.⁵⁷

To kick off its "news thief" campaign in mid-2020, it plastered downtown Toronto with wanted posters picturing Facebook founder Mark Zuckerberg and listing his alleged crime as "Theft of news content."⁵⁸ The posters, noted the *Toronto Sun*, publicized a website at newsthief.ca where the full indictment could be found. "FACEBOOK'S GETTING RICH BY TAKING WHAT'S OURS," reads the site. "Facebook makes billions selling content created by Canadians, especially journalists. They don't ask permission. They just take it."⁵⁹

> While Facebook cashes out, the people who make the news are disappearing. And with them the real news we depend on. Other countries are acting. France and Australia are forcing Facebook to pay up. But Canada is doing nothing, allowing Facebook to pocket billions on the backs of our journalists. It doesn't have to be this way. FRIENDS is the only citizens' group defending Canada's media and culture from American tech giants who take our stuff without asking.⁶⁰

Friends, as it re-branded itself, had begun campaigning during the 2019 federal election under the banner "Can Canada Survive Facebook?" and had launched a newspaper and social-media campaign calling on politicians to "Unfriend Facebook" in order to combat hate speech and so-called fake news online. "We can choose to continue this policy of 'anything goes' for Silicon Valley," its director Daniel Bernhard told the *Globe and Mail*. "We can choose to continue extremely generous exemptions, tax breaks, all kinds of benefits for the companies that have negligible or arguably negative effects on society. Or we can support Canadian broadcasting."[61]

Soon newspapers became filled with opinion columns vilifying the digital platforms. "Despite their claims to 'innovation,' Facebook and Google play the old same game," wrote Bernhard in the *Toronto Star*. "They find content that attracts attention and sell a slice of that attention to advertisers. The 'innovation' is that they don't pay for content—they just take it."[62]

The flaw in his argument was that the content was posted by newspapers and other media outlets on their websites for all to read for free. They sold ads alongside it in the hope that readers would click on it because their advertising rates were based on page views. The digital platforms, which were becoming more popular, were actually doing publishers a favour by delivering more readers to their websites. Most publishers even hired Google to sell the ads on their websites because its AdSense program was so effective in matching them to computer users because of the vast amount of individualized data it had accumulated.

It did not sell ads against articles listed on Google News searches, however, where it included only the headline and first few words of a story so users could decide whether to click on it. Facebook allowed its members to share links to news stories with their online "friends," and they were similarly displayed with just a "snippet" of their content, which was well within the fair use provisions of copyright law.

Bernhard admitted that publishers posted articles on their websites hoping that people would read them and be exposed to their ads, but he argued that they only did so under duress. Readers who shared the links, he argued, somehow created an obligation on the platforms to compensate publishers.

> Some of that news is offered up willingly by publishers and broadcasters (albeit under duress), but much of it is shared by people like you and I. Except it isn't ours to share. The platforms know when this happens. They could easily pay a fair fee for each article they circulate. But they don't, because compliant governments like ours conveniently condone their thieving. No wonder Canadian journalism is disappearing.[63]

The playbook for the campaign against Google and Facebook was published in 2019 as *The Tangled Garden*, a book by Richard Stursberg which expanded on the 2016 paper that had earned him a dinner with Godfrey that kicked off the newspaper lobby. Stursberg's book urged Ottawa to update the Broadcasting Act in order to tax and regulate online streaming services such as Netflix, Amazon, and Apple, and to force them to both program and fund Canadian content. Stursberg used the ominous acronym FAANGs — standing for Facebook, Amazon, Apple, Netflix and Google — to refer to the foreign digital media. He counted billions of dollars available to be clawed back from them to help finance government subsidies to Canadian media.

The Tangled Garden exhorted the "sleepy" Liberal government to use tax revenues to pump more money into Cancon. Making the FAANGs charge HST on their sales to Canadians would bring in $100 million a year, Stursberg estimated, while eliminating the business expense tax deduction on advertisements placed on foreign digital media would repatriate about $1.3 billion worth of ads annually. Taxes on the ads that didn't return to Canadian media would bring in an estimated $590 million a year. Making Netflix and other foreign streaming services contribute 30 per cent of their Canadian revenues to fund Cancon would add an estimated $438 million.[64]

Stursberg claimed that big media companies in Canada had suffered "losses as far as the eye can see" due to declining ad sales.[65] "If the federal government does not wake from its torpor, the major Canadian media companies are likely to collapse," he wrote. "If this happens, English Canada will be effectively annexed by the United States."[66] He claimed that their failure would bring about "the utter collapse of Canadian culture," leaving Canadians with the "arid and lifeless landscape of an abandoned culture."[67] The closure of Postmedia, which he claimed had lost money every year since 2011, "would mean that there would no longer be any local papers in many of Canada's largest cities."[68]

In fact, the biggest media companies in Canada actually made profits each year which exceeded the economic output of some countries. Because Canadians paid some of the highest prices in the world for cable, Internet, and cell phone service, Bell had made $9.5 billion in its most recent fiscal year at a profit margin of 40 per cent. Its media division, which included the CTV network, made $693 million on revenues of $2.68 billion, for a profit margin of 26 per cent. Rogers made $6 billion in profit that year, up 9 per cent, on revenues of $15.1 billion, for a profit margin of almost 40 per cent. Its media division, which included the Citytv network, made a profit of $196 million.

Even Postmedia was hardly losing money, as Stursberg claimed, having made a profit of $65.4 million that year. "Even if Postmedia went bankrupt due to debt, however, its profitable dailies would continue to publish under new ownership," noted one reviewer of *The Tangled Garden*. "You don't just close down a business that makes $65 million a year."[69]

Murdoch's gambit

The world-wide push for Google and Facebook to compensate news media for their lost advertising revenue was started by Rupert Murdoch, the Australian media mogul who owned most of the major dailies there along with UK titles like the *Sun* and the *Times* and U.S. newspapers such as the *New York Post* and the *Wall Street Journal*.

Starting early in the millennium, Murdoch began pushing for Google and Facebook to pay publishers for news stories they linked to, claiming the digital platforms were stealing their content. He called Google a "content kleptomaniac" and in 2009 threatened to licence his company's articles to Microsoft's rival search engine Bing.[70] Murdoch used his *Times* and tabloid *Sun* to campaign against the platforms in the UK. The news website Buzzfeed counted eighteen front-page stories on Facebook and Google in the *Times* alone in 2017. "They aren't afraid to use their own media properties as weapons."[71]

Murdoch had a business reason to play up any negative news about the tech platforms, noted Buzzfeed, as he had invested in a rival to Google's DoubleClick ad-matching service called AppNexus and planned his own digital advertising network.[72] He was actually knee-deep in new media, having paid US$580 million ($775 million) for the social network MySpace in 2005, only to watch Facebook eclipse it in popularity.

In Australia, where Murdoch owned fourteen of the country's 21 metropolitan daily and Sunday newspapers in addition to the Sky News television network, the campaign against Google and Facebook was notably one-sided.[73] After Murdoch's media influence helped elect a new Liberal government there, he prevailed on it in 2020 to enact a News Media and Digital Platforms Mandatory Bargaining Code, which forced Google and Facebook to license content from the country's news media. Facebook balked, refusing to run links to Australian news stories for several days until changes were made to the law allowing it to opt out of carrying links to news stories at all.

Murdoch's News Corp. signed content licensing agreements with both Google and Facebook in early 2021.[74] In its first year, the law was estimated to have benefited Australian news media by about $200 million.[75] With their five-year bailout set to end in 2023 and online advertising going mostly to the digital giants, Canadian newspapers eagerly joined Murdoch's campaign against Google and Facebook.

The U.S. and UK hesitated to follow Australia's lead over fears for press freedom, but in Canada a campaign by news media to adopt similar legislation became intense. The *Toronto Star* began running a series titled "De-fanging Big Tech" which featured stories like "Why Canada's media industry is in more danger than you think — and what we can do to save it."[76] It listed more than 250 Canadian newspapers that had supposedly ceased publication since 2013. (Even though News Media Canada's annual inventory showed that by then there were only 81 fewer community newspapers.)

Star reporter Joanna Chiu pointed to her hometown Tri-Cities area of Greater Vancouver, which comprised the suburbs of Coquitlam, Port Coquitlam and Port Moody, where two community newspapers had published until 2015. The *Tri-Cities Now* had shut down that year, however, leaving only the *Tri-City News*. She neglected to mention that the monopoly was created when Glacier

Media acquired the *News* from Black Press and closed its own *Now*. Nor did her article mention that the monopoly may have been due to a failure of anti-trust enforcement by the Competition Bureau, or that news in the area was also covered by the two Vancouver dailies.[77]

The paywall alternative

The digital giants had indeed built a better mousetrap to attract advertisers, and newspapers were struggling to compete. Publishers began to re-arrange their business models to rely less on advertising and more on reader revenue, however, raising their cover prices for print editions sharply while erecting paywalls around their online content. Murdoch had made a success of paywalls around his *Times* of London and *Wall Street Journal*. After the *Times* introduced its paywall in 2010, its profits began to rise exponentially, doubling from £26 million ($43 million) in 2020 to £52 million ($86 million) in 2021.[78]

Many newspapers hesitated to erect a paywall for fear of losing web traffic, on which their online advertising rates were based. The *New York Times* pioneered a "metered" paywall in 2011, however, which allowed most traffic through by giving readers free access to a number of articles every month before asking regulars to subscribe. By 2018, it had more than 2.6 million digital subscribers who accounted for 60 per cent of its sales.[79] According to a University of Missouri study, 77 percent of U.S. newspapers had by then erected paywalls to charge readers for online access.[80] When the *Toronto Star* erected a paywall that year, it brought to 65 percent the newspaper circulation In Canada that was behind a paywall.[81] Postmedia began erecting metered paywalls around the websites of its ten metropolitan dailies in 2011 and extended the subscription scheme to its *National Post* the following year.[82]

Regulating the Internet

In 2020, the Liberal government took steps to regulate the Internet for the first time. The Department of Innovation, Science and Economic Development received a report early that year which recommended taxing and regulating foreign streaming services by bringing them under the Broadcasting Act. The Broadcasting and Telecommunications Legislative Review panel, chaired by lawyer Janet Yale, had been established in 2018 to propose updates to Canada's media regulations. Its 235-page report titled "Canada's Communications Future: Time to Act," made 97 recommendations, including making the CBC ad-free, expanding the scope of the CRTC to regulate online media, and renaming it the Canadian Communications Commission.

The report also recommended extending the media tax credits to broadcasters and imposing a levy on media aggregators to help fund news content. The proceeds would be distributed by an "independent, arm's length CRTC-approved fund for the production of news, including local news on all platforms."[83] It also recommended that the CRTC should regulate the relationship between social media that share news and the sources of that news to ensure that the latter were "treated fairly where there is an imbalance in negotiating power."[84]

> The CRTC should have the specific jurisdiction to regulate economic relationships between media content undertakings and content producers, including terms of trade. This would include media content undertakings that make alphanumeric news content available to the public.[85]

Extending the CRTC's mandate from broadcasting to online video and podcasting was one thing, but allowing it to regulate alphanumeric, or written news content troubled many. "The BTLR report proposes to wreck what makes the internet free, popular and innovative and to make it resemble the Canadian broadcasting system," protested Timothy Denton, chair of the Internet Society of Canada.[86] Extending the CRTC's reach to written news online and requiring online news outlets to register with the government, he added, would result in a "wholesale transformation of a system of free expression into a government-directed system of licensees."

Denton had little fear that such a system of state control over free expression online would ever get off the ground, however. "Once newspapers, communications companies and ordinary citizens wake up to this massive overreach, it will become a dead letter, if it is not already. In the meantime, we can only marvel that they thought they could get away with it."[87]

Trudeau tried to reassure Parliament that the government did not intend to regulate news media. "We will not impose licensing requirements on news organizations nor will we regulate news content," he said.[88] Steven Guilbeault, who had been appointed in late 2019 as the third Heritage minister in less than eighteen months, similarly walked back talk of licensing media. "Let me be clear, our government has no intention to impose licensing requirements on news organizations, nor will we try to regulate news content," he said. "We are committed to free and independent press, which is essential to your democracy."[89]

The government's September 2020 throne speech gave notice of a campaign to rein in tax avoidance by digital platforms. "Web giants are taking Canadians' money while imposing their own priorities," it stated. "Things must change, and will change... The government will act to ensure their revenue is shared more fairly with our creators and media, and will also require them to contribute to the creation, production, and distribution of our stories, on screen, in lyrics, in music, and in writing."[90]

That November, the government introduced the first of what would become a series of bills to tax and regulate the Internet. Bill C-10, the Online Streaming Act, was designed to update the Broadcasting Act and require online streaming services to contribute as much as $830 million a year toward Canadian content.[91] It passed third reading in mid-2021 and was before the Senate when an election call halted its progress.

Leveling the playing field

News Media Canada launched a campaign in the fall of 2020 to ensure that newspapers would be included in any planned revenue sharing with the digital platforms. It released its own report, "Leveling the Playing Field," which called for the introduction of legislation similar to that in Australia, which it calculated would bring publishers $620 million a year in revenues.

According to this report, Google and Facebook had together generated $7.5 billion in global advertising revenues the previous year, up from $2.8 billion in 2014, while publishers' revenues were expected to decline by 43 per cent to $1.7 billion in 2020. "We have estimated the potential decrease in Canadian publishers' revenues between 2019 and 2023 to be between $500 million and $600 million per year," the report read.[92] It claimed that enacting a law such as Australia had would create 700 journalism jobs, or almost a quarter of all print journalists nationally. The stimulus would also have further knock-on effects for the economy. "The pathway would also support 6,900 jobs overall, $715 million in annual GDP, and $236 million in annual federal tax revenues through increased activity leading to higher tax collections."[93]

News Media Canada called on all political parties in Parliament to support the adoption of Australia's approach to confronting Google and Facebook. "In Canada, as in democracies around the world, the two American web giants control the lion's share of online advertising dollars and distribute newspaper content without compensation," it said in a press release. "The model being implemented in Australia counters these monopolistic practices and levels the digital playing field — at no cost to taxpayers and without the need for user fees or other charges."[94]

The *Toronto Star*, which had been taken over by the private equity firm NordStar Capital a few months earlier, joined the campaign the next day, calling for a "new regulatory regime to safeguard trusted journalism" and to stop the "free ride" for Google and Facebook and their "monopolistic" practices. "This is more than just an arm wrestle over digital ad revenues, the bulk of which have been snapped up by Facebook and Google," wrote its new public editor Bruce Campion-Smith. "The two companies have used their market dominance to unfair advantage to control 80 per cent of digital ad revenues while not providing 'fair' compensation for news content."[95]

Pressing forward

The dominance of newspaper publishers in the media bailout frustrated many online journalists, and their campaign to extract even more money from Google and Facebook troubled some. Jeff Elgie of Village Media, which published news websites in Ontario like the one in Orillia, told the *Toronto Star* that it would be a "huge mistake" to tax advertising on foreign digital platforms because it would disadvantage Canadians in competing globally. "Does the media industry really want to have a narrative that suggests that because they want these channels penalized, that every other business in Canada has to be penalized as well?"[96]

Elgie and other digital journalists felt uncomfortable and unwelcome as part of the newspaper lobby. "It took years for us to find acceptance with News Media Canada," he noted in 2018 during the first bailout campaign. "We still find we must fight for a 'fair' chance in the news industry."[97] The government's promise to support a "platform agnostic" approach to news didn't seem to be coming true, noted Elgie on LinkedIn. "Imagine our surprise, disappointment and (continued) frustration when we discover our government is funding a platform-specific (newspaper) program, launched by an association that we pay to be a member of."[98]

> While we champion the importance of supporting news and the integral role journalism plays in keeping citizens across the country informed, we would hope that all news organizations would be supported by our government, and not just newspapers specifically ... As an industry, we must stop perpetuating the belief that only newspapers can provide news.[99]

The criteria for receiving bailout funding and the fact it was being set largely by the newspaper lobby convinced many online journalists that they needed their own association. Erin Millar of Discourse Media expressed those concerns to the *Globe and Mail*. "It's a critical question: Who is at the table? Is this representing established outlets as well as new outlets?" she asked. "We need to ensure that this [funding] is diversifying the media industry, both who is in newsrooms and the communities that are being served. If all we are doing is growing the same system that is not addressing the full spectrum of Canadians, then we are not moving forward."[100]

News Media Canada's 2017 bailout proposal excluded blogs and websites that emphasised opinion over reporting, and its long-time head, *Winnipeg Free Press* publisher Bob Cox, regularly derided digital media and one-issue websites such as those covering the environment. "We would exclude individual blogs, and we emphasize reporting over opinion," he wrote in 2017. "No one wants to fund personal rants or political agendas."[101]

After digital media were excluded from the eight-member panel that set the bailout criteria in 2019, a group of 45 online journalists, academics, and activists brainstormed at a three-day conference in Toronto organized by Journalists for Human Rights. They unveiled their new group in late 2020 as Press Forward, which would "advocate for independent journalism organizations in Canada."[102] Included in its initial membership were websites such as the Sprawl, the Discourse, the Narwhal, Village Media, the Coast, the Observer, and the Tyee. Unlike News Media Canada, noted J-Source, the new group was truly platform agnostic, as according to its website "members can be digital-only publications, printed newspapers, radio stations, podcasts or a hybrid of any or all of these or other platforms."[103]

Blanking out

The newspaper lobby ramped up its campaign for legislation to force the digital platforms to share their revenues with them in early 2021, with newspapers across the country running blank front pages except for a short message. "Imagine if the news wasn't there when we needed it," it read. "If nothing is done, the journalism industry will disappear."[104]

The campaign was spearheaded by Torstar and News Media Canada, reported the website Media in Canada, and their message appeared on the front page and digital platforms of the *Toronto Star* and all 70 of Torstar's community newspapers. "But they have also created an alliance of other publishers to participate, including Postmedia, which is running the campaign in the *National Post* and 16 of its local dailies, and Black Press' dozens of community papers."[105] Notable by its absence, however, was the *Globe and Mail*.

The campaign also had a digital component, which allowed online readers to click on a page that let them write to their local MP. In addition to running blank front pages, the newspapers ran a full-page open letter to Prime Minister Justin Trudeau from Jamie Irving, who in late 2020 was named vice-chair of News Media

Canada, which called the threat to journalism unprecedented. "And, frankly, so shocking is the inaction of your government that it demands this unprecedented step."[106]

> For months, you and the Minister of Canadian Heritage, Steven Guilbeault, have promised action to rein in the predatory monopoly practices of Google and Facebook against Canadian news media. But so far, all we've gotten is talk. And with every passing week, that talk grows hollower and hollower.[107]

News Media Canada also ran an ad in newspapers across the country quoting Guilbeault in huge letters saying "we will table a bill in the spring," then asking: "Where is it?" MPs would go on vacation in mid-June, it noted, and there was no legislation in sight. "Every day of delay puts more journalism jobs across Canada at risk and strengthens the stranglehold of these two powerful global giants."[108]

That was too much for Andrew Coyne, who took to Twitter. "What self-serving nonsense," he wrote. "Facebook & Google don't use our content: they point readers to it. They don't 'take' our ads: they offer advertisers a better product."[109] Coyne went on a rampage known as a "tweet storm," adding reply after reply to his own tweet. "And they don't typically sell advertising off 'our' content, ie the links sending readers to our pages," read the first. "Look at Google News. See many ads there? It's ironic that the publishers should be mounting this disinformation campaign in the name of stemming the tide of 'fake news.'"[110] "Where does Google sell ads off our content?" Coyne continued. "ON OUR WEBPAGES. They sell them and place them, in exchange for a cut of the revenues. That's right: not only do they send readers our way, they sell our ads for us."[111]

> Meanwhile, what's the first thing you see atop any story on a newspaper site? A button urging readers to "share this" on Facebook, Twitter etc. Indeed, we post links to all our stories on these sites ourselves. So much for Facebook "stealing" our content.[112]

"The publishers' argument is so gaga in so many ways it's hard to know where to begin," he wrote. "What their case really boils down to is this: FacebookGoogle have a lot of money. We don't. Make them give some of theirs to us."[113] Coyne had called out News Media Canada's campaign against the digital platforms the previous September. "This has nothing to do with fairness, in other words. It's a shakedown, pure and simple. But it is hostage to its own illogic. The reality is that the news business needs Facebook and Google far more than they need us."[114]

Regulating online speech

Coyne soon saw something more sinister going on between government and press, however, pointing to a troubling initiative by the Public Policy Forum and Ottawa to combat hate propaganda but which could also prohibit otherwise lawful speech online. It was introduced in Parliament that June as Bill C-36, or what would become known as "online harms" legislation, but the bill died on the order paper when the 2021 election was called and the subject proved so contentious that it had trouble being re-introduced.

In an April 2021 column, Coyne wrote that "if the government were only putting all of the country's newspapers on its payroll, or imposing Canadian content quotas on YouTube, or snooping through people's tweets, it would be worrying enough. But as it is proposing to do all three at the same time, I think a little alarm is in order."[115]

The Public Policy Forum had set up a Commission on Democratic Expression in 2020 to "study and provide informed advice on how to reduce harmful speech on the internet."[116] Chaired by retired Supreme Court chief justice Beverley McLachlin, the seven-member commission of "eminent" Canadians conducted a study that included hearing witness testimony. With $625,000 from the Heritage ministry and additional funding from the McConnell Foundation, the Public Policy Forum also worked with Toronto consulting firm MASS LBP and the Max Bell School of Public Policy at McGill to set up a so-called Citizens' Assembly of 42 randomly selected Canadians to do the same thing.

In early 2021, the Public Policy Forum announced that both groups had reached the same conclusion. "The Canadian government must undertake urgent action to ensure that social media platforms are subject to regulation in order to adequately protect

Canadians from online harms."[117] The Commission rejected the policy of "aggressive takedown of content" seen in countries like Germany, the Public Policy Forum announced, in favour of a "citizen-centric approach that places responsibility for hateful and harmful content firmly on the shoulders of platforms and its creators." Such a program, it added, would "not only protect but enable democratic participation." The commission called for a new legislated duty on platforms to act responsibly, a regulator to oversee and enforce this Duty to Act Responsibly, a Social Media Council to serve as a forum for reducing harms, and a "world-leading transparency regime."[118]

The *Globe and Mail* reported that the panel's call for creating a federal "e-tribunal" to hear complaints about social media posts would be modelled on the B.C. Civil Resolution Tribunal, an online body that resolved disputes over small claims and motor vehicle accidents. To be effective, the *Globe* noted, the proposed regulator would have the power to penalize digital platforms with "massive fines and possible jail time for executives."[119] The *Toronto Star* reported that the fines would be based on "severity, frequency and repetition, as well as the size and reach of the regulated party in question." It noted that Guilbeault had told the House of Commons that "there will be a new regulator, and their task will be to implement the new rules and also to monitor work carried out by platforms," and that "the regulator will be able to impose financial penalties for non-compliance."[120]

Breaking ranks

Facebook signed a licensing deal in the spring of 2021 with fourteen Canadian publishers to pay them for republishing news stories. The agreement covered several online news outlets, such as the Observer, the Narwhal, the Tyee, and the Sprawl in Alberta, along with Village Media in Ontario and Discourse Media. It also included French-language newspapers such as *Le Devoir*, *Le Soleil*, and *Le Droit*, along with FP Newspapers, which published the *Winnipeg Free Press* and the *Brandon Sun*, along with Saltwire Network and the *Coast* in Atlantic Canada. It notably did not include large dailies such as Postmedia's, Torstar's, or the *Globe and Mail*. Facebook called the program a "news innovation test," which would "help promote a healthy news ecosystem, elevate authoritative journalism, and deliver a valuable experience for people on Facebook who are interested in news."[121]

Google reached licensing agreements the following month with six Canadian publishers, including the *Globe and Mail*, Black Press, SaltWire, the *Winnipeg Free Press*, and Glacier Media. The agreements also included digital training for 5,000 journalists and workshops for small and medium-sized outlets.[122] The deals were part of parent company Alphabet's $1.3-billion Google News Showcase launched in 2020. Conspicuously absent from the list were Postmedia and Torstar. Google had signed three-year non-negotiable contracts for a newsfeed with hundreds of publishers in 15 countries during the program's first year, reported the UK website Press Gazette, but a minority were "holding out for more."[123]

In July, the *Globe and Mail* reported that a rift had developed between news companies over how to get Google and Facebook to pay them, with Postmedia wanting to bargain collectively with the platforms rather than individually. "Andrew MacLeod at Postmedia Network Canada Corp., wants to see the Canadian government emulate Australian regulators and create a framework that forces tech platforms to pay all news organizations for access to their work," noted the *Globe*.[124] MacLeod responded by saying the deals signed with Google and Facebook would hurt the bargaining position of smaller publishers and added that the industry needed to stand together. "I think it's disappointing when you have an iconic company and a uniquely Canadian company like the Globe and Mail deciding to do a deal with the giants."[125]

> I respect the right of all companies to be doing what's in their self interest and I understand the financial pressure that some players feel and the urgency they feel relative to creating more certainty in their financial environment, but I think that speaks to the need for the government to enact the promised legislation.[126]

Coyne laid responsibility for the problem on MacLeod and the newspaper lobby, who "seemed as exercised by those publishers who, deserting their industry brethren (i.e. Postmedia), had signed side deals with FacebookGoogle as he was with the alleged content thieves themselves."[127] His column noted that Unifor president Jerry Dias was even blunter about the need for Ottawa to introduce legislation to force the digital giants to pay publishers. "'They better get it done,' he mused, noting there was an election coming. He accused the breakaway publishers of 'panicking,' and thus undermining the kind of 'solidarity' that 'forces governments to react quickly.'"[128] The accusation that Facebook and Google were stealing newspaper content by linking to it was never what the dispute had been about, Coyne concluded. "Rather, it is about tilting the negotiating table in our favour. It's about forcing them to pay more than they would willingly negotiate. A shakedown, in other words."[129]

Another election

The snap election called for the last day of summer would surely settle things. Conservative leader Erin O'Toole promised to cancel the ongoing bailout if he was elected prime minister. "While we support Canadian media outlets, they should not be directly receiving tax dollars," the Conservative Party's platform stated. "Government funding of 'approved' media undermines press freedom, a vital part of a free society."[130] The Liberals for their part promised to introduce legislation based on the Australia model within 100 days of forming a new government to make digital platforms such as Facebook and Google collectively negotiate and pay a share of their revenues to Canadian news publishers.[131]

But bailing out Canada's media, either by government or the digital platforms, never became an election issue. Just like during the 2019 election campaign, reporters seemingly didn't want to question support for their own industry. Wikipedia's list of "issues on the campaign trail" included foreign policy, climate change, Covid-19, and gun control.[132] Perhaps the biggest issue was why the election was called at all less than two years after the previous one, and during a pandemic at that. It didn't change anything, as the Liberals were again returned with a minority.

Trudeau got the support of NDP leader Jagmeet Singh to form a coalition government, however, and together they might be able to push through legislation, including several bills aimed at regulating the Internet and forcing the digital giants to pay up.

As for Tim Bousquet, the pandemic and his coverage of the 2020 mass shootings in Nova Scotia doubled the number of subscribers to his Halifax Examiner, allowing him to hire two full-time reporters and become a Qualified Canadian Journalism Organization.[133] The Examiner received a tax credit of $26,179 for 2021, according to its tax return posted online.[134]

CHAPTER 7
A PERFECT MARRIAGE

The only newspaper monopoly in Canada worse than Postmedia's in the West was in New Brunswick, where the Irving family's Brunswick News owned all of the dailies and almost all of the weeklies. Four generations of Irving industrialists monopolized that province's news media and used it to benefit their business empire, which grew to employ one in every twelve working New Brunswickers and extended across Atlantic Canada into New England.

The Irving name was everywhere in the Maritimes, adorning 700 gas stations and a fleet of tanker trucks. What started with one gas station in 1924 turned into a web of more than 300 privately-held companies engaged in oil and gas, forestry, real estate, retailing, construction, shipping, trucking, shipbuilding, and other businesses. The Irvings owned sawmills, pulp and paper mills, hardware stores, marine terminals, shipyards, and oil tankers. They owned Canada's largest oil refinery, which accounted for more than 40 percent of the country's petroleum exports. By 2008, the secretive family was the second richest in Canada, behind only the even more secretive Thomsons, who were perhaps not coincidentally also a newspaper family.[1] By 2022, the Irvings owned all three of the province's daily newspapers, eighteen of its 25 community newspapers, and four of its radio stations.

The family's stranglehold on media in New Brunswick has been the target of government inquiries dating back to the 1970 Senate report on mass media, which described the province as a "journalistic disaster area."[2] The 1981 report of the Royal Commission on Newspapers recommended breaking up the chain, along with other regional newspaper monopolies. A 2006 Senate report on News Media described the Irving empire as "an industrial-media complex that dominates the province."

And because the Irving interests are privately owned, they do not even have to provide the level of public reporting that publicly traded corporations are required to provide. This situation is, as far as the Committee could determine, unique in developed countries.[3]

Investigative reporter Bruce Livesey noted that "the Irvings' media monopoly has been a source of frustration for decades in New Brunswick, largely over concerns about what their newspapers omit — specifically any critical coverage of the Irvings and their companies."[4] Mount Allison University professor Erin Steuter, a long-time Irving critic, noted that the family's newspapers "routinely publish their own press releases as news stories."[5] A study in the *Canadian Journal of Communication* found that the family used its "considerable editorial and advertising clout to lobby the government, and to advocate for particular policies and regulations that support both its short and long-term business interests [which] include changes to regulations impacting energy markets as well as rules impacting the forestry industry."[6]

> The degree of control and influence exerted by the Irving papers makes it difficult to get to the bottom of many important and highly consequential stories, such as those surrounding industrial pollution, or the substantial public subsidies periodically awarded to Irving companies.[7]

One "hardy perennial of the editorial pages of the Brunswick News papers," noted the study, was "the importance of maintaining low power rates for large industrial users. Indeed, few issues have received more frequent mention in recent years. More troublingly, none of these editorials carried any disclaimer about the fact that the owner of the papers was... the single largest electricity user in the province."[8]

The fact that oil baron K.C. Irving had been gobbling up the province's most influential news media was actually kept a closely-guarded secret for a quarter century. After Irving bought the *Saint John Telegraph-Journal*, its *Evening Times-Globe* sister paper, and local radio station CHSJ in 1944, he retained their management and made no announcement of his purchase. Irving, a life-long Liberal, repeated the manoeuvre a few years later when he bought both Moncton dailies, the morning *Times* and the evening *Transcript*.[9]

A biography noted that Irving's newspapers "shied away from any meaningful investigation of industrial pollution in New Brunswick" while maintaining a "long-standing conspiracy of silence about Irving's business dealings," including "secrecy about its own ownership."[10] Irving's picture was never to appear in the newspapers, noted journalist Jacques Poitras, and if an oil spill or similar mishap involved Irving Oil, it was to be referred to as simply "a local oil company."[11]

In 1957 Irving quietly bought a minority interest in the province's only other daily, the *Fredericton Gleaner*, and took it over in 1968, again secretly. This time, however, the purchase was dramatically revealed by New Brunswick Senator Charles McElman in a speech from the floor.

In 1969, Liberal Senator Keith Davey was named to head a Special Senate Committee on Mass Media to investigate it and the ever-tightening ownership of the rest of Canada's media which held hearings across Canada for five months and called 125 witnesses. It found that Irving controlled 92.7 percent of New Brunswick's English-language daily newspaper circulation, which it called "about as flagrant an example of abusing the public interest as you're likely to find in Canada."[12] The Combines Investigation Branch raided the offices of Irving's newspapers the following year, along with his home and those of several of his executives, seizing almost 4,000 documents.

Irving was charged with monopoly in 1972 by the Restrictive Trade Practices Commission, but he moved to Bermuda for tax purposes before his trial started, so the judge, prosecutor, and a stenographer had to fly there to take his testimony.[13] Irving was convicted at trial, fined $150,000, and ordered to sell both Moncton dailies within a year, but the conviction was overturned on appeal in a case that went all the way to the Supreme Court of Canada in 1976.

Prior to his departure, Irving restructured his companies and transferred their control to his three sons.[14] The Irvings merged their two Moncton dailies in 1983 as the *Times-Transcript*, and after their father died in 1992, his sons closed the Saint John *Evening Times-Globe* in 2001.

The family's holdings were restructured in 2005 to give control of their four radio stations to son Jack, and by 2020 his Acadia Broadcasting had added another five in Nova Scotia and six more in Northern Ontario. The newspapers went to son J.K., who also headed the family's forestry and transportation companies. Brunswick News had embarked on an expansion at the millennium, acquiring a dozen New Brunswick weeklies, half of which were published in French. Son Arthur headed Irving Oil.

Crushing the competition

One thing the Irvings apparently could not stand was competition.

After journalist Mark Leger quit the *Telegraph-Journal* to found the Saint John alt-weekly *here* in 2001, and expanded to Moncton in 2004, Brunswick News launched a similar newspaper called *Metro Marquee* that offered discounted or even free advertising.

This predatory pricing forced Leger to sell out to Brunswick News, which closed *Metro Marquee,* and its too-good-to-be-true advertising rates, expanding *here* into Fredericton. It also watered down the alt-weekly's critical content and demolished the wall it had kept between advertising and editorial.[15] "The new owners exercised their editorial control immediately by cancelling the sex column," noted Steuter, "and not long after the new editor was fired for running a cover story on breast feeding."[16]

That was nothing compared with what happened to Ken Langdon after he quit as publisher of the Irving-owned twice-weekly *Woodstock Bugle-Observer* in 2007 to start his own newspaper, the *Carleton Free Press*. Brunswick News secretly went to court and got a rare civil search warrant which allowed private investigators and forensic accountants to raid Langdon's home in search of any company documents Langdon may have taken with him. According to the *New York Times*, they even went through his wife's lingerie.[17] A court order that blocked Langdon from contacting *Bugle-Observer* advertisers, writers, readers, and distributors was lifted after a judge ruled that "Brunswick News Inc. cannot claim a monopoly over advertisers or its customers."[18]

The first issue of the *Carleton Free Press* carried more than fifteen pages of advertising, which soon grew to 20. The Canadian Association of Journalists awarded Langdon its 2008 President's Award for contributions to journalism.[19] Six months after it started, the *Carleton Free Press* had almost as many readers as the *Bugle-Observer*, which began to discount its advertising rates and slash its subscription prices "to try to drive the Carleton Free Press out of business," noted the *Toronto Sun*.[20] Langdon filed a complaint with the Competition Bureau alleging anti-competitive business practices and "abuse of dominance" by Brunswick News. "It's hard for an advertiser to give you $500 for an ad when they can buy it for $200 from your competition," he told the Canadian Press.[21]

The Competition Bureau dismissed Langdon's complaint, however, saying it could not conclude that Brunswick News had "been engaged in the practice of anti-competitive acts or that there has been a substantial lessening or prevention of competition."[22]

Predatory pricing could only be demonstrated, it added, if the dominant firm was pricing below its "average avoidable costs," and it did not have such evidence. "Given that BNI is able to share resources such as printing, between several publications, their avoidable costs would be minimal."[23]

> We have concluded that we cannot show that BNI's behaviour constitutes predatory pricing or that such behaviour results in harm under the Act. This, taken together with the Bureau's need to focus our investigative efforts where they can be most effective in contributing to the prosperity of Canadians requires us to discontinue our investigation on this matter.[24]

The *Carleton Free Press* ceased publication in October 2008 after not quite a year in print. A copy of its unpublished final front-page story, which chronicled its own demise, was obtained by the CBC. "Concentration of ownership and big money," it said, "finally wore us down."[25]

The Irving media monopoly in New Brunswick and their often-questionable business practices made rather ironic a March 2021 *National Post* column by Jamie Irving that accused Google and Facebook of "medieval practices." His column compared the millions of dollars the online platforms were paying Canadian news media to the indulgences paid by sinners to the Catholic church during the Middle Ages to secure their place in heaven. "In Europe and Australia, governments and legislatures are pushing back on the monopolies and standing up for local news," Irving's column read. "They take content created through the hard work of journalists across the country and distribute it without compensation."[26]

Facebook's recently-announced $8-million fund for Canadian journalists, Irving complained, did not even constitute a rounding error when compared to its reported 2020 revenues of more than $105 billion. "Google and Facebook were once scrappy upstarts, disrupting established wealth and power structures," he concluded, touting the Australian solution to rein in the digital giants. "Now they are the wealth and power. And they are badly in need of some disruption of their own."[27]

Irving's column appeared not only in the *National Post* but also in about two dozen other Postmedia publications across the country, many of which now carried an inserted section from the company's national newspaper. Irving wrote it in his capacity not only as vice-president of Brunswick News, but also as the new vice chair of News Media Canada, for which he was an increasingly strident spokesman.

Riding the fast track

As the first Irving to ever show any interest in the family's newspaper business, fourth-generation Jamie had been fast-tracked to power, serving first as a summer reporter for the *Telegraph-Journal* while attending the University of Ottawa. According to Poitras in his 2014 book *Irving vs. Irving*, Jamie had "caught the journalism bug" from being around the *Telegraph-Journal* as a youngster. "The whole newsroom action was kind of exciting," he told interviewer Kim Kierans for a CBC radio documentary. "I got to watch all this stuff unfolding: yelling, and excitement, and deadlines. It was fun."[28]

Fellow reporter Carolyn Ryan found him a natural writer. "Jamie's writing was clean and clear from the beginning," she said.[29] Shy and awkward, he apprenticed as a reporter under the late *Telegraph-Journal* editor Neil Reynolds, a legendary figure in Canadian journalism who had earlier turned the *Kingston Whig-Standard* into a dynamo and would go on to edit the *Ottawa Citizen* and *Vancouver Sun*.

Some family members, including his father, disapproved of Jamie's foray into a side of the business they often treated like an unwanted stepchild, but crucially his grandfather J.K. was supportive. "Remarkably in a family that placed a premium on marching in lockstep with their forbears," noted Poitras, "Jamie Irving seemed determined to go his own way."[30]

Morale at the Irving newspapers was abysmal, and any talk of forming a union was enough to get you fired. Reporters narrowly avoided having to wear uniforms like those of the family's gas station attendants, according to Poitras. Due to Jamie's keen interest in journalism, some of its staff began to see the 23-year-old as a "potential saviour" of the newspaper.

> As the *Telegraph-Journal* reporters saw their paper's one-time greatness diluted into the corporate fold, they became convinced the only person who could save its reputation, its *independence*, was Jamie Irving ... Two visions of the Irving press — two incompatible visions — were on a collision course.[31]

A young publisher

After completing a Master's degree in Journalism in 2001 at Columbia University in New York, Jamie was appointed publisher of the newly-acquired weekly *Kings County Record*, then general manager of the community newspaper division of Brunswick News. Still only 27, he was named publisher of the company's flagship *Telegraph-Journal* in 2004, but his personal style was off-putting to staff, according to Poitras. One reporter described him as "one of the most awkward people I've come across... He can't say good morning, he can't chit-chat, he can't look you in the eye."[32]

His aspirations for the *Telegraph-Journal* were lofty, however, as he told staff he wanted it to be the *Globe and Mail* or *Wall Street Journal* of New Brunswick. As if to demonstrate his independence, Jamie soon took a stand against one of the family's grandest projects, a new LNG superport planned for Saint John, for which a global consortium that Irving Oil headed had secretly negotiated a 90-percent tax concession from the city.

A *Telegraph-Journal* editorial criticized city council's vote in favour of the deal, which was expected to cost the city an estimated $112 million in lost tax revenue over the next 25 years. "The paper rapped Irving Oil again," noted Poitras, "when a company press release condemned a group of citizens who disrupted a subsequent city council meeting to demand the decision be reversed."[33]

> The tax concession "opened old and deep wounds in the city," it said, criticizing Irving Oil's "aggressive and defensive" public relations strategy and its "facetious" [and] "unprofessional" press release that amounted to bully tactics. The newspaper went on to urge council to rescind its decision.[34]

Jamie's independence, which according to Poitras caused a rift in the family, wouldn't last. "When the stories moved closer to home — with the focus on Jamie's father, Jim, lobbying the province to cut power rates for his pulp mills — the *Telegraph* was baldly supportive."[35]

Neither would Jamie last as publisher of the *Telegraph-Journal*, after a series of embarrassing mis-steps in mid-2009 saw him replaced by his father atop the newspaper's masthead and Reynolds brought out of retirement as an "editor at large." When he returned six weeks later, Jamie held the lesser post of vice-president of Brunswick News.[36] "In a bizarre reporting arrangement," noted a 2010 study, "the announcement noted that 'Jamie Irving will continue to be responsible for the day-to-day operations of the newspapers. Mr. Irving will report to Mr. Reynolds on matters related to editorial policies, standards, and journalistic practices.'"[37]

A string of blunders

The series of unfortunate events that led to Jamie's demotion began when an intern was fired in May over a few minor errors in his front-page scoop that 100 University of New Brunswick faculty and staff had signed a letter protesting the school's decision to award an honorary degree to then-premier Shawn Graham. They included misspelling a name, getting an administrator's title wrong, and reporting that the premier had an degree in education instead of physical education. "Far more experienced journalists have repeatedly made worse mistakes and kept their jobs," noted the *Columbia Journalism Review*.[38]

UNB faculty boycotted the newspaper as a result, refusing to provide it with any political commentary until the student graduated the following spring. After a former editor of the *Telegraph-Journal* suggested on local radio that Irving was trying to appease the governing Liberals, the newspaper responded with a story headlined "CBC runs baseless story with no regard for facts or truth."[39]

Then in June, Saint John mayor Ivan Court charged in a city council meeting that Irving had told him that the *Telegraph-Journal*'s tough coverage of his administration would change if it lowered taxes and replaced the city manager.[40] "Why is Jamie Irving hell-bent on the destruction of City Hall, its mayor, and its management staff?" Court asked.[41]

Finally in July, a scandal erupted that became known as "Wafergate." The *Telegraph-Journal* was forced to issue a rare front-page apology for a story that falsely accused then-prime minister Stephen Harper of pocketing a communion wafer rather than consuming it during mass following the funeral of former Governor General Roméo LeBlanc.[42]

The incident was not included in the reporter's account, but was added by senior editors on the basis of a rumour and an inconclusive video. The scandal prompted Jamie's suspension and editor Shawna Richer's firing. "The paper was offside, and Jamie had to be responsible for that," his father later told Poitras. "It was bad judgment, all around."[43]

The *Telegraph-Journal* had lost its hoped-for saviour and quickly went back to its old ways. In a cost-cutting move, a central editing desk soon "pounded out pages for the weeklies and the dailies, cookie-cutter style," noted Poitras.[44] Reporters were required to file 1,500 words a day, he added, "and managers were counting. Quality didn't matter as long as they hit the quota; if they didn't, they were called in for a chat."[45]

By 2015, the *Telegraph-Journal* was editorializing against reconsideration of the city's tax concessions to Irving Oil. "Could council in 2005 have negotiated a better deal? Perhaps," one editorial argued without acknowledging any conflict of interest. "Is Saint John better off from having the capital investment, jobs and extra tax revenue from Canaport? Absolutely. Poor economic performance has created Saint John's fiscal difficulty, not a decade-old tax deal."[46]

Columnizing for cash

If Jamie Irving couldn't be the saviour of the *Telegraph-Journal*, perhaps he could help save Postmedia and the rest of the newspaper industry in Canada. Elected as Chair of News Media Canada in May 2021, he wrote numerous columns advocating for legislation to force Google and Facebook to pay publishers for carrying links to their news stories. In mid-2021, he co-authored a *National Post* column with NMC president and CEO Paul Deegan headlined "Why Canada must fight Big Tech's unregulated monopoly power: The future of journalism depends on it."[47] It pointed out that Denmark had recently allowed media outlets there to bargain collectively with Google and Facebook and that the competition regulator in France had fined Google 500 million euro ($750 million) for not bargaining in good faith with publishers. The problems that the Online Streaming Act was then having getting passed in the Senate, they argued, made a fund "politically challenging."[48]

> It raises serious issues around journalistic independence. Who decides where the money goes: Google? Facebook? Government? A fund would also be administratively expensive. For example, the Canada Media Fund is forecast to have expenses of more than $20 million in 2021-22. That's not newspaper box change.[49]

The column ran not only in the *National Post*, according to a search on the database Canadian Newsstream, but also in more than two dozen other Postmedia newspapers across the country. It ran in major metropolitan dailies like the *Edmonton Journal*, the *Calgary Herald*, the *Montreal Gazette*, and the *Vancouver Sun*. It ran in small city newspapers like the *Windsor Star*, the *London Free Press*, and the *Kingston Whig-Standard*. It ran in small-town newspapers like the *Brantford Expositor*, the *Sarnia Observer*, the

Chatham Daily News, the *Brockville Recorder and Times*, the *St. Thomas Times-Journal*, and the *North Bay Nugget*.

It promoted the Australian approach to making the digital giants pay up. "Experience elsewhere has shown, it is only through this collective approach that the digital playing field can be levelled between platforms and publishers who hire the journalists and produce content."[50]

The two NMC executives stepped up their campaign during the 2021 federal election with a column that again appeared in dozens of Postmedia publications across the country, headlined "Time to put a filling in truth decay: Australia leads way with a strong news publishing business." It cited the RAND Corporation think tank's 2018 book *Truth Decay*, which noted that newspapers and broadcasters were accountable for the news they published, unlike social media and Internet platforms, because they could be sued and regulated.

Their column began by noting the apparent lack of interest in the subject on the campaign trail, which they took as acquiescence. "It's increasingly rare that Canada's major political parties agree on anything, especially during a federal election campaign," they wrote. "Yet all agree that we should look toward Australia to ensure the long-term commercial viability of Canada's news publishing business."[51]

In October 2021, NMC began an advertising campaign which held out newspapers as "champions" of the truth. "Ads are running this week in 350 participating local, regional and national newspapers," noted the website Media in Canada, which also carried a branded content article sponsored by NMC. "It also includes a key media buy in *Chatelaine*, both English and French, comprised of print ad units, homepage takeovers and newsletter ad placements."[52]

Selling out to Postmedia

Many in New Brunswick rejoiced in early 2022 when the shock announcement was made that Postmedia was buying Brunswick News for $16.1 million. The Irving family was finally quitting the media business, Jim Irving announced in a news release, saying that the sale "represents an exit from the media business by J.D.

Irving, Ltd."[53]

Then it was pointed out that, under ownership by Postmedia, New Brunswick newspapers were likely going from bad to worse. St. Thomas University professor Michael Camp, a former Irving journalist, doubted that Postmedia would maintain all of its newly-acquired publications. "I regret very much that we're losing this local news presence," he told the CBC. "I also feel badly for the people who will be displaced from their jobs. And I wonder about the future of journalism in New Brunswick."[54]

Less than half of the purchase price was paid in cash, however, with the rest coming in the form of Postmedia shares, and the more than 4 million shares the Irvings received put them among the company's largest Canadian shareholders. It wasn't so much a purchase as a merger, which was amply demonstrated when a second shock announcement was made a few months later that Jamie Irving would be named executive chairman of Postmedia's board of directors when Paul Godfrey stepped down at the end of the year.[55]

The 83-year-old Godfrey actually wasn't going anywhere, however. A major shareholder himself from all of the stock options he had received while CEO, Godfrey would be staying on as a paid special adviser to the board and CEO Andrew MacLeod, which could include advocacy work with government. "I'm going to be there doing a lot of the same things that I've done in the past," Godfrey told the *Globe and Mail*. "I realize a lot of people are going to think this is a retirement. I'm not retiring."[56]

So Postmedia got New Brunswick, Canadians from coast to coast got an Irving to head their largest newspaper chain, and Godfrey got to stick around and steer home the third leg of his Postmedia rescue plan. There was certainly more work to be done.

Despite the new Liberal minority government's promise to introduce Australian-style legislation within 100 days to force Google and Facebook to bail out the country's newspapers, the government was having trouble getting its planned Internet controls passed. It had forced the Online Streaming Act through Parliament in 2021 by invoking closure to cut off debate, but members of the Senate, where the bill died with an election call, were more skeptical and in no hurry to pass it.

The Shattered Mirror Revisited

Two weeks after Postmedia's merger with Brunswick News, the Public Policy Forum issued a report that was part five-year retrospective and part victory lap, all sponsored by Unifor and the Atkinson and McConnell foundations.

In *The Shattered Mirror Revisited*, Greenspon first took credit for the bailout tax credits despite his original report having eschewed them, instead recommending a fund to which publishers would have had to apply. "Following the release of *The Shattered Mirror* in January 2017, PPF workshopped it with a variety of interested parties," Greenspon wrote in a Foreword. "Out of that process was born the Journalistic Labour Tax Credit, which would be brought forth in the 2019 federal budget and is arguably the most important and least intrusive form of support for news organizations."[57] More self-serving revisionist history followed.

> And then, of course, there was the report's foundational recommendation, which boiled down to the creation of a special tax or levy upon sellers of digital advertising within Canada who did not re-invest in journalism. The thinking behind the recommendation is addressed by the so-called Australian model promised by the Canadian government.[58]

Of the *Shattered Mirror*'s dozen recommendations, Greenspon counted fully half that had seen or were about to see the light of day in one form or another. "*The Shattered Mirror* also sounded an early alarm bell about the rising dangers to democratic societies from online disinformation and hate, and how this content was purposely amplified by digital platforms indifferent to truth and devoid of civic ethos."[59]

Greenspon co-authored *The Shattered Mirror Revisited* with several others, including Christopher Dornan, a former head of Carleton University's journalism school who had worked with him on the original, and David Moscrop, author of the 2019 book *Too Dumb for Democracy?*

It contained a detailed policy prescription for adapting the Australian code to Canada. "Transparency should be part of any scheme backstopped by government," it argued. "It is imperative funding from platforms, just as from government, is accompanied by guardrails of transparency and by mechanisms to ensure the payers do not have the means to play favourites, punish those out of favour, or skew coverage."[60]

To ensure that Google and Facebook were not able to exercise media influence by deciding who got the money, the report urged that the recipients should instead be determined using the QCJO process. "Fortunately, Canada enjoys the advantage over Australia of already having a mechanism in place."[61]

Negotiations with the platforms should be conducted collectively, it added, and not one-on-one. "Therefore, all QCJOs would qualify and benefit equally; there would be no leeway for either platforms or news associations to determine who is in or out."[62] Whether the money that Google and Facebook had already committed to Canadian news media should count under this system would be for government to decide. "Policymakers will have to determine whether to grandfather these deals or whether the rules of a Canadian Mandatory Bargaining Code should supersede them."[63]

The report recommended that the funding should be distributed through the Local Journalism Initiative program, which was set to expire soon. "The moment will be ripe for a LJI relaunch, not because it's a bad program but because it's a good one. The time is ripe to consider how it can be made more impactful." A renewed and strengthened LJI would lock in long-term government funding to "diversify the sources of funds into the program."

LJI funding decisions would be redirected to "a mission-driven entity allowing for multiple streams of funding both collected into the pot and paid out of the pot." The new granting agency, "likely a non-profit corporation, charity or charitable trust," would have a "fully arm's length governance structure" to separate news decisions from both government and industry associations. "Think of it as LJI+."[64]

Throwing good money

The Local Journalism Initiative, which had been funded with $50 million over five years in 2018, was then extended for another two years in 2022. The Heritage ministry also announced that a Special Measures for Journalism component of its Canada Periodical Fund for community newspapers and magazines would dispense another $40 million over three years.[65]

It was getting hard to keep up with all of the government money flowing to Canada's news media. The $50-million trickle which began with the LJI had turned into a $595 million torrent with the 2019 bailout and then a veritable flood with CEWS, which of course all Canadian businesses could access to help weather the pandemic. Federal money seemed to be pouring in to all corners of the print news media.

On the eve of the 2021 election call, Blacklock's Reporter revealed that Ottawa had quietly showered another $60.8 million of "emergency support" on news media through its Aid to Publishers program. It asked for details but hit a bureaucratic stone wall. "Staff would not answer repeated requests for names of publishers and the amounts they received under the ad hoc program called Emergency Support For Cultural Industries."[66]

Canadaland got the list and published it, however, as the money turned out to have been dispensed under the government's long-standing Canadian Periodical Fund, and as such the payments were publicly posted on the Heritage website. The recipients of emergency funding included Postmedia, which got $355,871 for 21 news outlets.[67]

The money just kept on coming, Canadaland reported, publishing a list of news media that benefitted from a $10-million "Special Measures for Journalism" top-up for 2021-22. "Certain Postmedia outlets applied for multiple pools of funding," it noted. "The largest individual recipient of the top-up fund from Postmedia was *Ontario Farmer*, taking $116,496. *Ontario Farmer* received $213,814 from the emergency relief fund."[68]

As for the Canadian journalism tax credit, however, that was seemingly a state secret. Not only could journalists not find out who was getting how much, neither could elected MPs. Alberta MP Chris Warkentin tried, asking in the House of Commons: "How much funding has each outlet ... received to date?"[69] Minister of National Revenue Diane Lebouthillier replied that the Canada

Revenue Agency refused to say. "The confidentiality provisions under section 241 of the Income Tax Act prevent the CRA from releasing taxpayer information unless an exemption exists."[70]

> No exemption exists to permit the disclosure of information related to QCJO designations or taxpayer information related to the Canadian journalism labour tax credit. As such, the CRA is able to provide neither a list of organizations that have been designated as QCJOs nor information on organizations that have claimed the Canadian journalism labour tax credit on their income tax returns.[71]

The CRA had made public the list of digital news subscriptions that qualified for a consumer tax credit, added Lebouthillier, along with the names of Qualified Canadian Journalism Organizations the legislation established, but it would not reveal who got how much. CWA president Martin O'Hanlon criticized the program and its lack of transparency. "This is skewed heavily in favour of entrenched newspapers and their managers," he told Blacklock's. "If this was supposed to be open and transparent, I don't think that happened here. They chose the people they wanted to get the answers they wanted."[72]

The only payments under the refundable tax credit that were made public were those to publicly-traded news media companies because they had to report their income, but these were getting fewer and fewer. Blacklock's reported in 2019 that the *Toronto Star* had estimated that its payroll rebates from the tax credits would be $115,385 a week.[73] Its parent company Torstar was taken over by private equity firm NordStar Capital the following year and de-listed from the Toronto Stock Exchange, however, so it no longer had to disclose any financial information.

Publicly-traded FP Newspapers, which published the *Winnipeg Free Press* and the *Brandon Sun*, received $822,000 in bailout funding in 2020 and $5.4 million in CEWS, which Blacklock's noted accounted for 54 percent of the company's $11.4 million in profit that year.[74]

An Ottawa-based subscription news service, Blacklock's refused to apply for the tax credit and was one of the few news media in

Canada that regularly scrutinized the program. Several other media outlets licensed Blacklock's content, including Postmedia, but readers wouldn't find any of its bailout coverage in Canada's largest newspaper chain.

Blacklock's also cast a sharp eye on News Media Canada, reporting in 2018 that it had received a federal grant of almost $385,000, or more than half of its annual budget, to encourage people to buy newspapers.

Documents it obtained under to Access to Information laws showed the funding went to cover costs such as hiring publicists at $160 an hour to encourage celebrities to pose for Instagram photos reading a newspaper. News Media Canada's grant application proposed to seek endorsements from unidentified "high-profile Canadians, from traditional media 'influencers' to authors to politicians to business leaders, to showcase their passion for newspapers on their social media channels by asking them to share a photo of themselves on Instagram reading their favourite newspaper."[75]

News Media Canada's campaign, Blacklock's reported, was "designed to drive consumers to take action, showing their support for the Canadian newspaper industry by signing an online petition. The success of this campaign will subsequently be leveraged with advertisers to encourage them to advertise in newspapers." The lobby group also suggested that local papers sponsor screenings of the Academy Award-winning 2015 film *Spotlight*, which chronicled investigative reporting by the *Boston Globe*, in order to promote the essential role of newspapers in society.

The campaign also proposed to spend $75,000 on Facebook ads, noted Blacklock's, even though NMC's grant submission complained that American social media like Facebook got too much advertising. "We simply don't have the resources to plan and execute campaigns of this scope and scale on our own," wrote NMC head Bob Cox in a letter to the Department of Canadian Heritage. "Even well-informed people often do not realize what is at stake... This is the most serious crisis we have faced in our history."[76]

Founded in 2012 by a half dozen Ottawa Press Gallery reporters and named after long-time Parliament Hill correspondent Tom

Blacklock, the scrappy news service delighted in shining a light on the bailout's hypocrisies and conflicts of interest, and especially its lack of promised transparency.

As chair of the Local Journalism Initiative's "independent" judging panel of experts from the news media industry, Blacklock's reported in 2020 that Cox personally signed off on LJI funding for his own newspaper to hire two reporters. "We will tell stories that need to be on the public record from around the province," the *Free Press* promised in its application. "We do it on the farm. We do it in the oil patch. We do it where the permafrost is melting."[77]

In late 2022, Blacklock's cited government records obtained under Access to Information in reporting that 35 publishers had attended a confidential 2020 teleconference with CRA and Department of Finance officials to discuss terms of the $595-million bailout. "Publishers submitted questions in advance," it noted. "None reported it."[78] All of the names were censored in the 622 pages of highly-redacted documents it said it had sought from Finance Canada for more than two years.

A few days later, Blacklock's was evicted from the Parliamentary Press Gallery in Ottawa by its governing executive. The eviction letter "stated *Blacklock's* managing editor Tom Korski was 'impolite,' 'disturbs the journalists around him' and 'streams parliamentary committee hearings on his computer.'"[79]

Blacklock's claimed the eviction, the first of its kind in the history of the National Press Building, was in "clear reprisal over its continued protests against media subsidies." It filed suit in Ontario Superior Court seeking reinstatement and monetary damages.[80]

There ought to be a Law

One social media outlet that regularly promoted the bailouts was the MediaPolicy.ca blog set up in 2017 by Howard Law, Unifor's Media Director who retired in 2021. One entry in late 2021 countered Canadaland's exposé of the $10-million "Special Measures for Journalism" top-up for 2021-22 by pointing out several errors. "The story neglects to mention that media companies owning multiple publications can only claim from *one fund for any single publication*," Law pointed out in the blog post, which carried the logo of Canadian Heritage. "And there are four federal funds dedicated to four different types of publications."[81]

Law also found misleading Canadaland's contention that Postmedia had recorded a $52.8 million quarterly profit that January. "The very big and very right-wing Postmedia is a favourite piñata for mainstream media haters," Law wrote. "I suppose the implication is that Postmedia is lining its profitable pockets with federal cash." The $52.8-million figure was cherry-picked from one quarterly report, he added, and resulted from a one-time $63-million non-cash accounting gain from the merger of its pension plans. "I have posted below a spreadsheet of key debt, dividend, cost-cutting, revenue, profit and loss figures from Postmedia's annual reports over the last four fiscal years ending August 31," Law added. "You can draw your own conclusions."[82]

He was right that the $52.8-million figure overstated Postmedia's earnings for the three months. When stripped of all extraordinary items, including a $13.4 million writedown of asset value and a $2.9 million restructuring charge, it recorded a $17.1 million profit, compared to $21.3 million in the same quarter a year earlier.

Law took issue with Andrew Coyne's reaction to the bailout details revealed in the 2019 budget, calling it an "acquiescence to ignorance and the destruction of liberty."[83] When the panel which would decide who qualified for the tax credit was announced, Law dismissed as "Puritan objection to media subsidies" widespread criticism of the $595 million package. "I get, and accept, that a media rescue package is controversial," he wrote. "The idea that government is buying media support with its modest subsidy designed to mitigate further newspaper closures is fear mongering."[84]

Law sought to allay fears about the bailout impinging on press freedom by making a promise he obviously soon forgot. "The Minister has promised transparency for the entire process," he wrote. "As much as anyone, we will hold him to it."[85]

Law also had a MediaPolicy.ca account on Twitter which he used to promote his blog and anything else favourable to media bailouts. Numerous other Twitter accounts of media consultants and Cancon devotees similarly promoted government media assistance.

As the 100-day deadline for the promised legislation came and went, the chorus of voices calling for it reached a crescendo. The long-running campaign that began in 2016 with Godfrey inviting Stursberg to dine with Postmedia's board of directors, and then added Greenspon and Unifor, had already paid off big in 2018 with the $595 million bailout. Now with Friends and others on board, it looked like it would pay off even bigger in the spring of 2022.

One of its original members, however, would not be there to celebrate at the finish line. Unifor president Jerry Dias, the author of such 2020 *National Post* columns as "Zuckerberg's self-serving push for regulation" and "How to save Canadian journalism," had certainly done his part.[86] When the weekly Goderich, ON *Signal Star* finally picked up the latter column six days later, it brought to three dozen the number of Postmedia newspapers it had appeared in.

Dias may have set the record, however, for his May 2020 column "Take on Big Tech to save journalism," which hit 40 after appearing in even non-Postmedia papers like the *Winnipeg Free Press* and the *Saint John Telegraph-Journal*.[87] Dias retired from Unifor's presidency in March 2022, however, after a union investigation alleged he had taken a $50,000 bribe for promoting a supplier of COVID-19 test kits to employers.[88]

Bill C-18 — The Online News Act

Bill C-18, which like the Australian code would force digital platforms to pay publishers for posting links to their news stories, was shocking to some when it was introduced in April 2022. Rather than creating a new entity to supervise the transfer of Google and Facebook revenues to Canadian news media, like the non-profit corporation, charity, or charitable trust which *The Shattered Mirror Revisited* had suggested was needed to create separation from government, it gave the job instead to federal bureaucrats.

The Online News Act proposed that the Canadian Radio-television and Telecommunication Commission supervise collective bargaining between news outlets and tech companies and step in only if the parties could not agree on the appropriate magnitude of wealth redistribution. It suggested that $8.5-million come out of the federal budget over two years for the CRTC to establish a new legislative and regulatory regime to oversee the bill. While any disputes would go to independent arbitrators who would choose the fairest of each side's final offer, the CRTC would oversee the new regime and could levy fines of up to $15 million a day from platforms that didn't comply.

Even former CRTC members were aghast. Konrad von Finckenstein, who was its chair from 2007 to 2012, said that while CRTC had great expertise in broadcasting and telecommunications, "you are really asking them to make a decision on the basis of competing businesses and whether ... the pie being sliced between them is fair or not."[89]

Peter Menzies, a former CRTC vice-chair and *Calgary Herald* publisher, noted that putting the CRTC in charge of making deals between news outlets and tech companies was "like putting a baseball umpire in charge of a soccer game." With public trust in both government and news media cratering, he added, making journalists beholden to bureaucrats was ill-advised. "Government nosing around, however benignly they say they are doing it, is just not a good look."[90]

There was certainly good reason for a lack of public trust in the CRTC. Under its regulation, ownership of Canada's broadcasting industry was among the most highly-concentrated in the world, and telecommunications services such as cable TV, Internet access, and cellular telephony were among the most expensive. Many scholars were convinced that the CRTC had long since fallen victim to the seemingly inevitable phenomenon of "regulatory capture," in which the private interests of regulated parties prevailed over those of the public.[91]

There was a well-known revolving door between the CRTC and industry, with regulators becoming lobbyists and vice-versa. Perceptions of a conflict of interest were fuelled in 2021 when a photo that went viral on social media showed CRTC chair Ian Scott, a former lobbyist, having a beer with Bell CEO Mirko Bibic in an Ottawa pub after a ruling that lowered wholesale internet rates was reversed in favour of large telecoms.[92]

There were more than a few problems with the Online News Act, the first of which was fairness. "This elaborate sham is intended to apply a veneer of due process to what is in fact nothing more than a crude revenue grab," wrote Andrew Coyne in a 1,600-word *Globe and Mail* column which ran on its front page. "The actual rationale for forcing Facebook and Google to underwrite the Canadian newspaper industry is very simple. It is . . . because that's where the money is."[93]

> FaceGoogle didn't take anything from the newspaper industry. They simply offered advertisers a better product. Rather than adapt and improve, however, the industry cried to government, first for direct subsidy . . . now for indirect subsidy, to be extracted from their competitors.[94]

Howard Law responded on his MediaPolicy.ca blog that the columnist was "romanticizing" the Internet while ridiculing the Liberal government's impulse to regulate it. "No one is asking Mr. Coyne or his many libertarian confederates to curb their appetites for a wide open Internet," he wrote. "Just leave room for achieving policy goals like a strong cultural footprint for Canadian news, information, sports and entertainment." Bill C-18, he added, "deserves the support of all Canadians concerned by the economic strangulation of news journalism."[95]

Google protested that requiring payment for linking to online content contradicted how the internet worked and set a bad precedent. Bill C-18, it added, gave too much power to the CRTC to regulate news, decide which publishers would be paid, and define who is a journalist.[96] It warned that language in Bill C-18 prohibiting platforms from giving "undue or unreasonable preference" to specific news items would "break" its search engine. "The ability to link freely between websites is fundamental to how the internet works," it said in a statement. "Canadians expect that when they search for information, they will have access to ALL the content the internet has to offer. Requiring payment for links risks limiting Canadians' access to the information they depend on. The Online News Act would break this critical principle of the internet for everyone."[97]

Bell Canada's chief regulatory officer called Google's criticisms "misplaced, disingenuous and highly exaggerated" in a guest column in the *Globe and Mail*. "In Canada, our highly dynamic and intensely competitive communications market is subject to extensive regulation," wrote Robert Malcolmson. "It has become clear that additional regulatory oversight is the best way to ensure Canadian news publishers... are able to continue reflecting the interests, concerns and perspectives of Canadians."[98]

The *National Post* ran guest columns supporting the Online News Act with headlines like "Great news for Canadian journalism," which appeared in ten Postmedia papers, "Bill C-18 will redress market imbalance," which was published in 30, and "Online News Act will be good for journalism," which ran in 27.[99]

Noting that a recent poll had found that most Canadians knew nothing about the proposed legislation, Warren Kinsella made Bill C-18 simple enough to understand for even *Toronto Sun* readers who might not exactly be policy wonks. "C-18 isn't a handout," he wrote. "It simply requires Google and its cabal to finally pay something for the hard work of others. Because, right now, they pay nothing."[100]

> They swipe stories that are the product of hard work by reporters and editors, suggest it is their own, and then get paid billions in advertising dollars. That's not fair. Hell, it's essentially theft. And it's killing our news media — and, in the process, actually putting democracy in peril.[101]

One of the best critiques of Bill C-18 barely saw the light of day, however. "There is no evidence that shows news outlets are worse off because of Google, Facebook and other aggregators," wrote Queen's University business economist Gil Ricard on the website The Conversation. "If anything, evidence (and lots of it) shows that, overall, news outlets would be in worse shape without these digital platforms."[102]

The Conversation allowed academics to present their research on topical issues, and Ricard had researched the 2014 shutdown of Google News in Spain after it enacted a link tax. From his research, he concluded that Bill C-18 was based on the false premise that news outlets were not already being compensated for links to their articles. "We found that after the shutdown, Spanish news outlets experienced a reduction in the number of daily visits of between eight and 14 per cent," he wrote. "To add insult to injury, advertisers stopped placing ads on their sites, causing a collapse in ad revenues. Particularly hard hit were smaller news publishers — lower-ranked sites with a larger share of casual readers."[103]

> During the same period, Germany instituted a link fee as well. In this case, Google News required German publishers to waive the linking fee. A study from the University of Munich found that publishers deciding to opt out from Google indexing faced disastrous consequences: daily visits to their sites significantly dropped and traffic was diverted to competing sites that opted into indexing.[104]

If Bill C-18 passed, Ricard predicted that "we can expect big publishers to receive most of the funds — that's what happened in Europe and Australia. Smaller media outlets with low brand awareness will suffer unless they band together and bargain collectively with the digital giants."[105] Articles published on The Conversation were distributed over the Canadian Press news service, and could be reprinted by any member news outlet.[106] A search of the Canadian Newsstream database, however, showed that not one picked up Ricard's cogent analysis. This was only one example of a disturbing trend that became apparent during the debate over Bill C-18: Almost all of the coverage in newspapers was favourable to the bill, while the online coverage was more balanced.

Bill C-18 "an embarrassment"

University of Ottawa professor Michael Geist, an authority on intellectual property and Internet law, followed the Bill C-18 hearings closely and was appalled by what he saw. "This represents nothing less than a government-backed shakedown that runs the risk of undermining press independence, increasing reliance on big tech, and hurting competition and investment in Canadian media," he wrote on his eponymous blog. "The government's plans effectively require compensation without something deserving of compensation. That is best described as a shakedown."[107]

Geist lamented both "the lobbying campaign for the bill, which included over 100 registered lobbyist meetings by News Media Canada over the past three years," and the "skewed coverage of the issue in which the overwhelming majority of news stories backed government intervention."[108] Geist deemed Bill C-18 "shamefully over-broad, an embarrassment to the news media lobby that demanded it, and unworthy of a government that sees itself as a model for the rest of the world on media freedoms."[109]

The worst part of the lobbying campaign, however, was the corporate censorship Geist said he experienced first-hand. He revealed on his blog that he had submitted an opinion article in 2021 to a newspaper he did not name, and it was accepted by its opinions editor. "I was told it was ready for publication and then I waited. And waited. And was then told the piece was spiked by upper management given the subject matter and the campaign for legislative support from Canadian Heritage."[110]

When the House of Commons voted to approve Bill C-18, Geist noted that while "media lobbyists will no doubt celebrate the milestone, it should not go unremarked that the legislative process for this bill has been an utter embarrassment."[111]

> Bill C-18 is the product of an intense lobbying campaign from some of Canada's largest media companies... Years of one-sided editorials — even devoting full front pages to the issue — had its effect. Indeed, Canadian newspapers would be exhibit #1 for how government intervention in the media space has a direct impact on an independent press.[112]

Geist wasn't the only one to suffer from corporate censorship. The same thing happened more than once to Dwayne Winseck of Carleton University, who said he was asked by a *Toronto Star* editor in 2021 to write a column on Australia's code, only to have it spiked on orders from above, although he managed to place that one in the National Observer.[113] He had a second piece spiked in 2022 after it was accepted by the *National Post*, which he subsequently posted on his blog.[114]

Winseck was generally supportive of Bill C-18, seeing Google and Facebook as too powerful and unscrupulous, but he was apparently not enthusiastic enough about it for the newspaper lobby. Never one to mince words, Winseck tweeted that the rot in Canadian media "spreads out from the news publishers to the media industries as a whole who have lined up, hands out, to get what they want."[115]

Others were in favour of Bill C-18 and even censorship to help make it happen. David Skok of The Logic, who opposed the legislation at first, became an enthusiastic proponent of Bill C-18 and saw nothing wrong with newspapers spiking contrary or even balanced opinion to get their way. "The rejection of an op-ed is entirely within a publisher's traditional remit," he wrote, "and it's a leap to suggest it's a suppression of free speech."[116] Skok took pains to disclose that The Logic was not affiliated with any industry lobby group, but he failed to mention its 2019 partnership with Postmedia.[117]

Transparency lacking

Another problem with the Online News Act was that it seemed to provide no more transparency than the $595-million bailout or the Google News Showcase agreements. Under the proposed legislation, the CRTC would be required to have an independent auditor prepare an annual report on the bill's impact, including the total value of agreements, but not which newsrooms got how much.

That was a vital omission, according to Erin Millar, because a lack of clarity disadvantaged smaller outlets. "There's absolutely no transparency around ... how much these payments are," said the Discourse founder who had since started Indiegraf, a platform that helped launch local news startups. "I've raised this many times with Google," Millar told the *Toronto Star*. "We don't even know how to participate in the conversation, because we don't have the basic facts."[118]

Digital journalists banded together to form an ad hoc group to lobby on Bill C-18. The group of 106 warned in a *Globe and Mail* online column that by lacking transparency, the bill risked shutting out small, medium-sized, and independent publishers. "There have been a series of secret, backroom deals between Big Tech and the largest newspapers in Canada, along with a handful of small to medium-size publishers," they noted. "An unintended but likely consequence of Bill C-18 as currently structured may be to cement these inequities and this secrecy, which threatens the public's already-frayed trust in journalism."[119]

The same rules that shut out many small community newspapers from the Local Journalism Initiative and the $595-million bailout would also prevent them from qualifying for payments under Bill C-18. "I run five newspapers, but each newspaper has anywhere from a part time to one full-time reporter," Chris Ashfield, president of the Saskatchewan Weekly Newspapers Association, told the Heritage committee debating the bill. "Under the current situation, we would actually not qualify," he said. "We don't qualify for things like the Local Journalism Initiative, because we don't have two full-time reporters."[120] The executive director of the Alberta Weekly Newspapers Association testified that about half of all media outlets in that province may not be big enough to participate in the scheme. "It does put us in a bit of an awkward spot," said Dennis Merrell.[121]

Conservative MP Kevin Waugh, a member of the Commons Heritage committee and a former journalist, warned that the threshold of two staff journalists would exclude most community papers in Saskatchewan. "When this bill came out it was for newspapers, but 70 per cent of papers in Saskatchewan would not qualify." As a result, NDP MPs on the committee joined with Conservatives to propose amendments to Bill C-18 that would include newspapers or other news media outlets employing only one full-time journalist or relying on freelancers.[122]

A subsequent amendment that further expanded eligibility, according to Geist, opened the door to some media outlets that might not even produce news, such as campus radio stations, but included at least 15 percent "spoken word" programming. "As a result, the bill faces another potential trade challenge as it evolves into a straight subsidy model," noted Geist.[123]

Another problem Geist saw with Bill C-18 was that it undermined Canadian copyright law and international treaty obligations. "Platforms may link to the news, feature a headline with the link or sometimes offer a one-or-two sentence summary or quote from the article," he noted in a blog post. "The reality is that these uses are generally permitted under Canada's fair dealing copyright law rules and does not require a licence or compensation."[124]

For the government to set aside the right to limited reproduction would not only violate Canadian copyright law, added Geist, it would also breach the international treaty that governs copyright law. "Article 10(1) of the Berne Convention creates a positive obligation to include a right of quotation within national copyright law, specifically citing the right to quote news articles: 'It shall be permissible to make quotations from a work which has already been lawfully made available to the public.'"[125]

Another problem with Bill C-18 that had international implications was that Google and Facebook were U.S. companies, and Canada was attempting to regulate them. NAFTA, which had been renegotiated in 2018 as the Canada-U.S.-Mexico Trade Agreement at the insistence of then-president Donald Trump, included a "cultural exemption," noted Geist, but invoking it would allow the U.S. to retaliate with levies of "equivalent commercial effect."[126]

In late 2022, as both Bill C-11 and Bill C-18 made their way through Senate, the U.S. trade representative to Canada expressed concern about the proposed new laws, saying they "could impact digital streaming services and online news sharing and discriminate against U.S. businesses."[127] In early 2023, U.S. senators called on the Biden administration to get tough on Canada for planning to unfairly punish U.S. tech companies.[128] Members of the U.S. Senate finance committee also complained about Canada's "troubling policies," which they said targeted U.S. companies. According to the *Globe and Mail*, the CRTC's lack of experience in regulating print media and digital platforms was also an issue with the Americans.[129]

As Bill C-18 was making its way through Parliament in mid-2022, Postmedia announced it had signed a content deal for an undisclosed amount with Google News Showcase, the company's US$1-billion global content licensing program. "It means that we are now being compensated by Google for the content that we create that is disseminated on their platforms," said Postmedia CEO Andrew MacLeod.

Facebook balks

Facebook was another matter, however. When the Heritage committee debating Bill C-18 closed the list of witnesses in late 2022 without hearing from Facebook, Geist called out its "disturbing anti-democratic tactics" as "particularly problematic given the importance of the bill."[130]

Facebook then issued a statement saying it was considering blocking Canadian news stories from its platform if the legislation passed. It said the bill was "based on false assumptions that defy the logic of how Facebook works" and would saddle it with "globally unprecedented forms of financial liability for news links."[131]

A Facebook official claimed its platform sent Canadian news media more than 1.9 billion clicks a year which, at 12 cents apiece, were worth $230 million in "free marketing." Only 3 percent of Facebook posts included links to news articles, he added, and Canadians had indicated they wanted less news and politics.[132]

Facebook's online statement expanded on its concerns. "We believe the Online News Act misrepresents the relationship between platforms and news publishers," it said. "The framework of the current legislation presumes that Meta [Facebook's parent company] unfairly benefits from its relationship with publishers, when in fact the reverse is true."[133]

> We are being asked to acquiesce to a system that lets publishers charge us for as much content as they want to supply at a price with no clear limits. No business can operate this way. If this draft legislation becomes law, creating globally unprecedented forms of financial liability for news links or content, we may be forced to consider whether we continue to allow the sharing of news content on Facebook in Canada.[134]

The Heritage committee then invited Facebook officials to testify in what was a tense extra day of hearings, with Liberal MPs accusing the witnesses of threatening Canadians with "modern-day robber baron tactics."[135] Kevin Chan of Meta, protested that Bill C-18 was unfair because the platform could not control what links people posted on their pages. "We would be forced to pay publishers for giving them free marketing on Facebook," he said.

"This would be a most peculiar and unorthodox arrangement."[136]

Chan emphasized the importance of hyperlinks to the free flow of information online. "Simply put, links are really the lifeblood of the Internet," he said. "We have never seen anywhere else in the world an attempt to regulate the free flow of information by putting into scope effectively a toll for links."[137] The agreements that Facebook had signed with news media in Australia and Canada, Chan added, were not for content but instead to help them develop new innovation models. "We're not paying for links. We've never paid for links."[138]

Bill C-18 also ran counter to a 2011 Supreme Court of Canada decision, Chan noted, a short portion of which he read out. " 'The Internet cannot, in short, provide access to information without hyperlinks. Limiting their usefulness would have the effect of seriously restricting the flow of information and as a result freedom of expression.' " The ruling in the case of *Crookes v. Newton* involved posting links to defamatory material, but the court ruled that simply linking to information did not amount to publishing it. "A hyperlink, by itself, should never be seen as 'publication' of the content to which it refers."[139] Such a precedent from the highest court in the land could easily be used by the digital platforms for a legal challenge to any requirement that they pay for posting links in Canada.

Facebook's threat to quit Canada was hardly hollow, as it had blocked links to news stories in Australia in 2021 until amendments were made to its legislation which allowed it to opt out of carrying links at all. Google had quit Spain for eight years until returning in 2022. Heritage Minister Pablo Rodriguez admitted that Facebook and Google would have every right to refuse to run links to Canadian news stories if they were required to pay for doing so. When he testified before the Heritage committee debating Bill C-18, Rodriguez said that would be "a business decision to be taken by the platform."[140]

Riches to rags

A series of announcements by the Parliamentary Budget Office that fall must have caused whiplash in newspaper company boardrooms. It first estimated that Bill-C18 would generate $329 million a year for Canadian news media and cover almost a third of the costs of its production.[141] Two weeks later, a supplementary report was released by the PBO, which does financial analyses to support the work of MPs. It showed that more than three quarters of the expected payments from Bill C-18, or almost a quarter of a billion dollars, would go to broadcasters, including the publicly funded CBC.[142] Newspapers could get less than $81 million a year, which would be well short of the $150 million they had hoped for.[143]

Finally, in late 2022, *Globe and Mail* publisher Phillip Crawley further broke with the newspaper lobby and asked the government to amend the Online News Act to ensure that the CRTC's role would be strictly administrative. "Bill C-18 is the problem, in its present form," he wrote. "It contains language that could allow the newspaper industry to be subject to arbitrary regulation by a quasi-government body. Politicians of all parties should be wary of going there."[144]

Crawley noted that newspapers had never been regulated by the CRTC, and the broadcasters that were "employ squads of lawyers and lobbyists to manage that relationship, to their benefit."[145] He noted that the *Globe*'s success in evolving into a subscription-driven business, in which two-thirds of its revenue came from more than 300,000 paying readers, gave it an advantage with digital platforms like Apple and Google that paid for its content. "But many others would like to join the club, with C-18 providing powers to force the digital giants to the negotiating table."[146]

Crawley was understating the *Globe*'s success in growing its reader revenue, as earlier in the year he had told a group of publishers that the *Globe and Mail* was forecasting a $30 million increase in its revenues for 2023. "While others cut back on print, we decided it was a good time to invest," he told the World Association of News Publishers. "It does make a difference. Readers notice. As do advertisers."[147]

When he became *Globe and Mail* publisher in 1999, Crawley added, 70 percent of its revenue came from advertising, but for 2023 it was projecting that 62 percent would come from subscribers, 69 percent of whom were digital-only. Print still contributed "significant profitability to our business," Crawley said, "and while several media players have gone completely digital, we like giving our readers a choice." While the *Globe*'s digital subscription revenue jumped 20 percent in 2021, he said, its print advertising revenue rose by 8 percent and its print subscription revenue by 1 percent, helping its print product to an 18-percent profit margin. "We're confident people will pay for access to good quality, trustworthy content."[148]

Similar success seemed to be eluding Postmedia, however, as despite all of the government subsidies and now funding from Google, its outlook for 2023 was dire. Its merger with the Irving group was intended to give it more runway to achieve digital liftoff, but with a sudden downturn in revenues, it appeared it might soon crash. As Bill C-18 passed third reading in Parliament just before Christmas and went to the Senate for review, its outlook was uncertain. "The Senate is not in the business of rubber-stamping bills," said Senator Paula Simons, a former *Edmonton Journal* columnist who told the *Globe and Mail* that she had "grave misgivings" about the "dubious" bill.[149]

CHAPTER 8
THE TIPPING POINT

Andrew MacLeod could hardly have been more different from Paul Godfrey. MacLeod had no background in journalism before he joined Canada's largest newspaper chain in 2014, instead coming from the tech sector, where he had been BlackBerry's managing director for North America. When BlackBerry was forced to rapidly downsize in 2013 and 2014, laying off more than 2,000 workers in Ontario alone, one former colleague said MacLeod was deeply affected and tried to meet with as many laid-off workers as he could.[1] If he was going to do that with every Postmedia employee he would soon have to jettison, it was going to mean an awful lot of meetings.

Canadaland's Sean Craig did a deep dive on Postmedia's new boss as part of his 2019 investigation into MacLeod's hard right-turn political strategy. "Several employees at Postmedia headquarters told me that, in just seven months, MacLeod has articulated a more sensible and coherent vision for the company than they have heard in years," noted Craig. "At 48, he is a more dynamic and hands-on leader than the company is used to."[2] Several sources, he added, characterized MacLeod's personal convictions as middle-of-the-road. "One said he wouldn't stand out in a Canadian focus group, in that he has a combination of progressive social values and business-friendly fiscal views that could align with several political parties."[3] Rather than pushing a political agenda, they said, it was just as likely that MacLeod was pushing a business model. "Something many employees at Postmedia gather ... is that MacLeod has ambitions. But just what those ambitions are can only be speculated upon."[4]

> Some see his directive to unify the political voice of Postmedia's publications as a totally pragmatic audience strategy: capture the mainstream conservative audience

segment while competitors fight for other pieces of the pie, and figure out how to monetize it. Others have read the strategy as a sign of different ambitions . . . The most extreme version of this assessment, which a handful of employees shared, is the Fox News model.[5]

MacLeod, however, cast his political re-positioning of Postmedia as more of a marketing strategy. "We looked at the media landscape in Canada and we found there was a shortage of viewpoints that come from a pro-innovation, pro-free-market, smaller-tax, smaller-government perspective," he told an interviewer in 2019. "We saw an opportunity to fill that from a strategic point of view."[6] He took exception to suggestions that this was damaging the journalistic integrity of his newspapers. "This has absolutely nothing to do with the centralization of editorial strategy. And it in no way, shape or form touches on journalistic integrity or credibility. We want to fill that market opportunity and we want to make sure that we offer a wide range of voices that aren't always represented in the media landscape."[7]

Critics like Canadaland came from a point of view, MacLeod argued, which was often about providing a counterbalance to corporate-owned media or promoting a progressive agenda. "The critics have an agenda," he said. "I do take umbrage at the fact that they want to correlate a business endeavour with the integrity of our newsrooms."[8] Perhaps as a result of his background in tech, MacLeod saw Postmedia as providing a product to be consumed rather than a service that readers expected and most journalists aspired to provide. "I look at the *Toronto Star* and the Atkinson Principles and they espouse views around social justice and the necessary role of government," he argued. "No one is suggesting the Atkinson Principles in any way taint the integrity or journalism of the journalists at the *Toronto Star*. It's simply a framework within which that team operates."[9] The *Toronto Star* was one newspaper, however, and MacLeod's team stretched across the country. Many of his newspapers, and more importantly their readers, were not used to being dictated to by head office about how to slant the news they provided.

The bigger concern for MacLeod, however, was existential. If any newspaper company was going to survive in the 21st century, it was going to have to reinvent itself as a viable online enterprise. Part of the attraction MacLeod provided as Postmedia's new leader was his familiarity with the digital world and the disruption it brought. "He's grown digital advertising double digits for the last eight quarters," Godfrey noted in passing him the torch. "There's nobody in Canada and very few in the U.S. that have performed like that."[10] MacLeod's experience at BlackBerry, where he had worked for thirteen years before joining Postmedia, could come in handy in several ways as Postmedia navigated its way in the brave new online world.

The firm that began life in Waterloo, Ontario, as Research in Motion made pagers before finding a very profitable niche making personal digital assistants, which became popular at the millennium. In addition to scheduling your appointments, recording voice memos, and even taking pictures like other PDAs, RiM's BlackBerry came with a built-in keyboard and could even receive e-mail, which was the first "killer app" of the Internet. The company's handheld devices became so popular that they earned the nickname "CrackBerry." Aides had to practically pry Barack Obama's BlackBerry out of his hands for security reasons when he took office as U.S. president in 2009 because he had become so addicted to its "always on" technology.

The rapid demise of BlackBerry, however, showed how disruptive new digital products could be. The better mousetrap that arrived with Apple's iPhone in 2007 attracted users with its touchscreen technology and doomed the Canadian company. The same kind of digital disruption began visiting the newspaper industry almost as soon as MacLeod joined Postmedia, as Google and Facebook began gobbling up more and more online advertising with their better mousetrap of individualized marketing enabled by vast amounts of consumer data. "It's really about trying to find ways to reinvent yourself in an environment that's very much dominated by these large apex predators, the Silicon Valley players," MacLeod told the *Globe and Mail* in 2017. "How do you learn to co-exist with the dominance of Google and Facebook?"[11]

The strategy was simple, as devised by Godfrey and the rest of the newspaper lobby. They would use their political power to persuade the government to force the digital giants to subsidize their dying industry. If they made it to the other side as a digital survivor, so much the better. Otherwise, they would live off the success of Google and Facebook as platform content providers. They might still be able to acquire more runway to achieve digital liftoff, like Postmedia did by buying up Sun Media in 2014 and then Brunswick News in 2022. There was still the SaltWire chain in Nova Scotia. "There can be no doubt that Postmedia is looking at the SaltWire network of papers," wrote Stephen Kimber after Postmedia bought Brunswick News.[12]

Then there was Torstar. Rumours abounded when it was taken over by NordStar Capital in 2020 that it could wind up merging with Postmedia. After all, the money to buy Torstar came from none other than Canso Investment Counsel, which had financed Postmedia's purchase of Sun Media in 2014. Then when NordStar's private equity partners cited irreconcilable differences in splitting the company up in 2022, it was revealed that there had indeed been merger talks. "Some time after the sale, Torstar engaged in discussions with Postmedia about a potential combination with the company, according to two people familiar with the matter," reported the *Globe and Mail*. "A deal between the two newspaper publishers has long been rumoured in the industry, as it could potentially lead to significant cost savings."[13] A merger of the country's largest and most liberal daily and its largest and most conservative chain would surely bring pressure on Ottawa to block the combination.

Taking on water

The biggest problem was that Postmedia suddenly started sinking in 2022. Taking more newspapers aboard might simply result in them all going down. The chain had managed for more than a decade to keep its head above water through cost cutting and layoffs, not to mention government bailouts. It even continued to generate enough annual earnings to keep paying its loans, but that all changed in 2022. In its fiscal year ended August 31, Postmedia reached a point at which its annual earnings no longer covered its loans. Its profits plunged from $67 million in 2020 to $37 million in

2021, to only $13 million in 2022, of which $9.9 million came from federal aid. Its debt payments were more than $30 million a year.

TABLE 2: Postmedia Network (millions)

	REVENUES	EARNINGS	MARGIN%	DEBT	PAYMENTS
2022*	458.2	13.0	2.8	274.0	31.0
2021	442.3	37.0	8.3	256.4	30.4
2020	508.4	67.7	13.3	274.4	30.6
2019	619.6	49.3	7.9	255.2	28.5
2018	676.3	65.4	9.6	275.5	27.5
2017	754.2	54.6	7.2	343.0	32.7
2016	877.1	82.3	9.3	655.1	72.6
2015	750.2	111.4	14.8	682.2	69.1
2014**	674.2	109.5	16.1	497.5	61.9
2013	751.6	130.4	17.3	497.8	61.9
2012	831.9	144.3	17.3	527.8	65.4
2011	1,019	201.1	19.7	627.9	80.3

Earnings before interest, taxes, depreciation, and amortization (EBITDA), fiscal year ending 31 August.
* bought Irving newspapers
** bought Sun Media

The first quarter of its 2022-23 fiscal year was not much better, bringing $4.8 million in profit compared to $11.9 million in the same quarter the year before. With an interest expense of $7.7 million, it was still under water. The only bright spot was $9.1 million in revenue added by is parcel delivery service, which Postmedia had started in 2021. Its new Postmedia Parcel Services division, MacLeod had announced, was intended to leverage its built-in distribution network to expand services across trucking, sorting, and the distribution of small parcels. "Extending our offerings and trusted relationships in the communities we already serve, through this new partnership, aligns to our corporate strategy," he said.[14] The company further diversified in late 2022 by getting in on the sports betting boom with Betting Essentials, which would run across its websites as a betting hub.[15]

To make its outlook worse, a recession was expected to begin in 2023 as a result of interest rate hikes intended to cool the inflation that had been fuelled by all of the federal injections into the money supply during the pandemic. Recessions were always a time of retrenchment for newspapers as advertising inevitably dried up, but this time Postmedia's dire financial position made drastic action urgent. It could declare bankruptcy, but that would immediately end the payments flowing to Chatham and its other hedge fund owners. It might even be able to rearrange its debt again, as it had in 2016, with the hedge funds taking more shares in exchange for cancelling their second-lien notes, but they already owned 98 percent of the company. Instead it appeared time for the final phase of the harvesting strategy, in which as many people and now properties as necessary would be thrown overboard to keep the ship afloat and generating interest payments.

It began in early 2023 with another dozen Alberta community newspapers moving to online-only publication and the sale of its *Calgary Herald* building for $17.25 million to U-Haul, which planned to convert it into storage lockers. It had been mostly vacant since the pandemic began, except for a few movie shoots, with staff working remotely from home. Postmedia also announced it would outsource printing of its Saskatchewan dailies, put its *Saskatoon StarPhoenix* building up for sale, and sublet its rented *Regina Leader-Post* premises, leaving its employees there to work remotely.[16] It further announced that the editor of its *Calgary Herald*, *Calgary Sun*, *Edmonton Journal*, and *Edmonton Sun* would also assume leadership of its Saskatchewan dailies.[17]

Cutting to the bone

Its next announcement, however, shook Postmedia to its foundations. In order to continue making ends meet, it told employees in a company-wide video conference that it would have to cut 11 percent of its staff. Particularly hard-hit would be the *Montreal Gazette*, which expected ten layoffs, or a quarter of its staff. The company first asked for volunteers, and in a sure sign of the future, the grisly details emerged first online. "They have a number of cuts they need to reach and they don't care how much damage they inflict on their newspapers in order to reach it," one long-time *Gazette* journalist told Christopher Curtis for his Substack blog

The Rover. "With these voluntary layoffs, they're pitting us against each other. There's some tension between younger reporters who feel their senior colleagues should step aside and save the future. And I get that. But older workers have a right to work too."[18]

Curtis said he interviewed ten sources inside Postmedia. "A half dozen sources at the *Gazette* describe a paper on its last legs," he reported. One former Postmedia executive put his finger on the biggest problem. "Here's the crazy part in all this," he said. "The Montreal Gazette still turns a profit. Why would Postmedia let it go?" What made a sale awkward is that if a local buyer could persuade Postmedia to sell the *Gazette*, it would then have to staff the paper. "Because so much of the production cycle happens in Toronto and Hamilton, the *Gazette* isn't really its own paper anymore," the source told Curtis. "They don't have their own layout team, line editors and they need Postmedia's arts, life and sports stories just to fill the paper. And it's not exactly a thick paper."[19]

An ad-hoc group calling itself Friends of the *Gazette* enlisted local, provincial, and federal politicians to help and launched an online petition that quickly gained more than 2,000 signatures. Montreal MP Anthony Housefather, a member of the Heritage committee that had just approved Bill C-18, said he had spoken with both MacLeod and Jamie Irving in hopes of mitigating the damage. "We've had multiple conversations and they've been productive," said Housefather. "I can't get into specifics because I don't want to harm any of these talks but we want to see if we can save some jobs and get the community more involved with the newspaper."[20] Montreal businessman Mitch Garber offered to buy "all or part" of the *Gazette*, only to be rebuffed by MacLeod. "Garber even offered to let Postmedia keep whatever government grants the *Gazette* might receive from Ottawa once Bill C-18 is adopted," noted Curtis.[21]

Meanwhile, the Online News Act which disappeared into the Senate before Christmas didn't appear ready to emerge until spring. Postmedia announced in February that it would be outsourcing the printing of its *Windsor Star* to a press in Toronto, from where the papers would first be shipped to a plant in London for the inserting of flyers, and then finally to Windsor for distribution.[22]

Whether its landing was hard or soft, Postmedia was going down. The only question seemed to be how much could be salvaged from the wreckage. In the end, it was probably best to let Postmedia fail rather than keeping it alive through serial bailouts so it could keep paying off the debt held by its New Jersey hostage takers. From the ashes might emerge a new type of journalism, one that wouldn't be for sale to any advertiser who wanted to buy positive coverage. What Postmedia produced mostly wasn't journalism anyway, but instead a perversion of journalism. Its would be no big loss, hopefully to be followed by something better.

ENDNOTES

PREFACE

1. Jesse Brown, "Nobody's a Critic: Who Holds Journalists to Account in Canada?" *The Walrus*, June 2014. URL: http://thewalrus.ca/nobodys-a-critic/
2. Lawrence Martin, "It's not the economy, stupid. It's the media," *Globe and Mail*, September 8, 2022, p. A13. URL: https://www.theglobeandmail.com/opinion/article-its-not-the-economy-stupid-its-the-media/
3. Ibid.

CHAPTER 1 — A QUESTION OF CONTROL

1. Teresa Tedesco, "How Postmedia met Quebecor," *National Post*, October 7, 2014, p. A1. URL: https://financialpost.com/news/fp-street/how-the-postmedia-quebecor-deal-unfolded-starting-with-a-secret-visit-in-2012; Carys Mills, "Postmedia Meets With Mayors About Sun Media Acquisitions," J-source.ca, December 4, 2014. URL: https://j-source.ca/postmedia-meets-with-mayors-about-sun-media-acquisitions/
2. Margo Goodhand, "Above the Fold," *The Walrus*, February 4, 2016. URL: https://thewalrus.ca/above-the-fold/
3. Canada, House of Commons. Standing Committee on Canadian Heritage. Evidence, May 12, 2016, p. 3. URL: https://www.ourcommons.ca/Content/Committee/421/CHPC/Evidence/EV8266619/CHPCEV15-E.PDF
4. Ibid.
5. Sunny Dhillon, "Councillor, OLG chair bicker over placement of possible Toronto casino," *Globe and Mail*, January 8, 2013. URL: http://www.theglobeandmail.com/news/toronto/councillor-olg-chair-bicker-over-placement-of-possible-toronto-casino/article7067274/
6. Enzo Dimatteo, "Paul Godfrey overplays his hand," *Toronto NOW*, May 21, 2013. URL: https://nowtoronto.com/paul-godfrey-overplays-his-hand
7. Evidence, May 12, 2016, p. 3.
8. Ibid.
9. Jacquie McNish and Jacqueline Nelson, "The US hedge funds financing 'Project Canada,'" *Globe and Mail*, October 7, 2014, p. A1. URL: https://www.theglobeandmail.com/report-on-business/us-junk-bond-specialists-behind-postmedias-project-canada/article20957729/
10. Evidence, May 12, 2016, p. 3.
11. Ibid.

12. Ibid.

13. Evidence, May 12, 2016, p. 7.

14. Ibid.

15. James Bradshaw, "S&P cuts Postmedia's credit rating, warns capital structure 'unsustainable,'" *Globe and Mail*, December 1, 2015. URL: https://www.theglobeandmail.com/report-on-business/postmedia-credit-rating-cut-on-looming-debt-maturities/article27541893/

16. Michael Lewis, "Paul Godfrey wants more foreign ownership: source," *Toronto Star*, January 30, 2016, p. B1. URL: https://www.thestar.com/business/2016/01/30/postmedia-pushing-for-looser-foreign-ownership-rules.html

17. Ari Altstedter, "Postmedia Bond Plunge Signals End of Godfrey's U.S. Debt 'Noose,'" *Globe and Mail*, April 6, 2016. URL: https://www.theglobeandmail.com/report-on-business/postmedia-bond-plunge-signals-end-of-godfreys-us-debt-noose/article29541466/

18. James Bradshaw and Tim Kiladze, "Top Postmedia shareholder seeks to sell," *Globe and Mail*, March 15, 2016, p. A1. URL: https://www.theglobeandmail.com/report-on-business/goldentree-in-talks-to-sell-stake-in-postmedia-report/article29219247/

19. James Bradshaw, Tim Kiladze, and Christina Pellegrini, "Tough sell: GoldenTree's Postmedia pitch," *Globe and Mail*, March 16, 2016, p. B1. URL: https://www.theglobeandmail.com/report-on-business/streetwise/goldentree-faces-major-obstacles-in-bid-to-sell-postmedia-stake/article29254097/

20. See Marc Edge, *Asper Nation: Canada's Most Dangerous Media Company*. Vancouver: New Star Books, 2007. URL: http://www.marcedge.com/Asper_Nation_3W.pdf

21. Christine Dobby and James Bradshaw, "Competition Bureau clears way for Postmedia to buy Sun Media papers," *Globe and Mail*, March 26, 2015. URL: https://www.theglobeandmail.com/report-on-business/competition-bureau-clears-postmedia-deal-for-sun-media-papers/article23610481/

22. Christine Dobby, "Paul Godfrey: Evolution of a Canadian media mogul," *Globe and Mail*, October 24, 2014. URL: https://www.theglobeandmail.com/report-on-business/paul-godfrey-evolution-of-a-media-mogul/article21304029/

23. See Marc Edge, *Pacific Press: The Unauthorized Story of Vancouver's Newspaper Monopoly*. Vancouver: New Star Books, 2001. URL: http://www.marcedge.com/pacpress.pdf

24. Jamie Bradburn, "Nominated for: turning the country's largest newspaper chain into a laughingstock during the federal election," *Torontoist*, January 2015. URL: https://torontoist.com/2016/01/2015-villain-paul-godfrey/

25. Phil Lind, *Right Hand Man: How Phil Lind Guided the Genius of Ted Rogers, Canada's Foremost Entrepreneur*. Toronto: Barlow Books, 2018, p. 418.

26. Dobby, "Paul Godfrey: Evolution of a Canadian media mogul."

27. Malcolm Johnston, "Q&A: Paul Godfrey, chair of the OLG, is on a mission to bring a Las Vegas–style casino to Toronto," *Toronto Life*, June 4, 201. URL: https://torontolife.com/city/qa-with-paul-godfrey/

28. See Marc Edge, "Enabling Postmedia: Economists as the 'rock stars'

of Canadian competition law." *Canadian Journal of Communication* 45(2) 2020, 287-303. URL: https://www.researchgate.net/publication/342728243_Enabling_Postmedia_Economists_as_the_Rock_Stars_of_Canadian_Competition_Law

29. Jennifer Ditchburn, "Panel of MPs to examine issue of local news crisis, media concentration," CBC News, February 17, 2016. URL: https://www.cbc.ca/news/politics/federal-committee-newsroom-closures-1.3451513

30. David Olive, "As long as it continues to live, Postmedia is blight to readers," *Toronto Star*, January 30, 2016, p. B1. URL: https://www.thestar.com/business/2016/01/30/the-problem-with-postmedia-olive.html

31. Ibid.

32. Ibid.

33. David Olive, "Postmedia and the high price of survival," *Toronto Star*, January 24, 2015, p. B1. URL: https://www.thestar.com/business/2015/01/23/postmedia-and-the-heavy-price-it-pays-to-survive-olive.html

34. Ibid.

35. Olive, "As long as it continues to live."

36. James Bradshaw, "Andrew Coyne exits editor role at National Post over endorsement," *Globe and Mail*, October 20, 2015. URL: https://www.theglobeandmail.com/report-on-business/andrew-coyne-exits-editor-role-at-national-post-will-remain-columnist/article26868832/

37. Bradburn, "Nominated for."

38. John Barber, "Postmedia's support for Conservatives leaves it out of step with the public," *The Guardian*, November 1, 2015. URL: http://www.theguardian.com/media/2015/nov/01/election-blow-canada-postmedia-stephen-harper

39. Benjamin Mullin, "Canadian newspapers run huge political ads on front pages," Poynter, October 19, 2015. URL: http://www.poynter.org/2015/canadian-newspapers-run-huge-political-ads-on-front-pages/379543/

40. Jenny Uechi and Matthew Millar, "Presentation suggests intimate relationship between Postmedia and oil industry," Vancouver Observer, February 5, 2014. URL: https://www.vancouverobserver.com/news/postmedia-prezi-reveals-intimate-relationship-oil-industry-lays-de-souza.html

41. Sean Holman, "At the Gate of Disaster: A Case Study on the Promotion of Climate Science Rejectionism by Mainstream News Outlets and E-Commerce Companies," *Facts and Frictions* 1(2), 2022. URL: https://factsandfrictions.j-schoolscanada.ca/wp-content/uploads/2022/03/Holman.pdf

42. James Bradshaw, "Postmedia brass pocketed bonuses for Sun acquisition," *Globe and Mail*, November 27, 2015, p. B5. URL: https://www.theglobeandmail.com/report-on-business/postmedia-brass-pocketed-bonuses-for-sun-acquisition/article27497598/

43. Anonymous, "After Closing Newspapers and Laying Off Journalists, Postmedia Executive Pay Hits New High in 2017," PressProgress, December 18, 2017. URL: https://pressprogress.ca/after-closing-newspapers-and-laying-off-journalists-postmedia-executive-pay-hits-new-high-in-2017/

44. Quoted in Ibid.

45. Malcolm Johnston, "Q&A: Paul Godfrey, the CEO who's presiding

over the Postmedia newspaper chain's rapid decline," *Toronto Life*, February 7, 2017. URL: https://torontolife.com/city/qa-paul-godfrey-ceo-whos-presiding-postmedia-newspaper-chains-rapid-decline/

46. Edmund Lee, "Fund's Chain Has Shrunk. It's Acquiring Another One," *New York Times*, July 18, 2020, p. B1. URL: https://www.nytimes.com/2020/07/16/business/media/hedge-fund-chatham-mcclatchy-postmedia-newspapers.html

47. James Bradshaw, "Senior U.S. hedge fund manager stepping down from Postmedia board,'" *Globe and Mail*, December 1, 2015. URL: https://www.theglobeandmail.com/report-on-business/streetwise/senior-hedge-fund-manager-stepping-down-from-postmedia-board/article27545163/

48. James Bradshaw, "Postmedia appoints board to review business as GoldenTree seeks an exit," *Globe and Mail*, April 7, 2016. URL: https://www.theglobeandmail.com/report-on-business/postmedia-appoints-special-board-to-review-struggling-business/article29552772/

49. Andrew Willis, Susan Krashinsky, and Grant Robertson, "New life for CanWest papers, but debt remains," *Globe and Mail*, May 11, 2010. URL: https://www.theglobeandmail.com/report-on-business/new-life-for-canwest-papers-but-debt-remains/article1367874/

50. Altstedter, "Postmedia Bond Plunge Signals End of Godfrey's U.S. Debt 'Noose.'"

51. Lewis, "Paul Godfrey wants more foreign ownership."

52. Jacqueline Nelson and Boyd Erman, "Low-profile Canso takes Postmedia deal's lead," *Globe and Mail*, October 8, 2014, p. B4. URL: https://www.theglobeandmail.com/globe-investor/low-profile-canso-takes-postmedia-deals-lead/article20973953/

53. Andrew Willis, "A Postmedia dust-up is likely – and Canadians will win," *Globe and Mail*, June 7, 2016, p. B1. URL: https://www.theglobeandmail.com/report-on-business/streetwise/postmedia-debt-dust-up-likely-to-see-canso-victorious/article30312635/

54. Lee, "Fund's Chain Has Shrunk."

55. Ibid.

56. Paul Willcocks, "Who Still Believes Postmedia Is Canadian-Controlled?," They Tyee, July 8, 2016. URL: https://thetyee.ca/Mediacheck/2016/07/08/Who-Believes-Postmedia-Canadian/

57. Ian Gill, *No News is Bad News: Canada's Media Collapse – and What Comes Next*. Vancouver: Greystone Books, 2016, p. 37.

58. Ibid., p. 49.

59. Aleksandra Sagan, "Union demands Postmedia executives return $2.3M in bonuses," *Toronto Star*, November 24, 2016. URL: https://www.thestar.com/business/2016/11/24/union-demands-postmedia-executives-return-23m-in-bonuses.html

60. CWA Canada, "Postmedia execs must return bonuses: media union [press release]," CWA Canada, November 11, 2016. URL: https://www.cwa-scacanada.ca/EN/releases/161124_pr_bonus.shtml

61. Ibid.

62. Josh O'Kane, "National Post's Ontario newsroom workers look to unionize," *Globe and Mail*, September 13, 2017. URL: https://www.theglobeandmail.com/report-on-business/national-post-newsroom-workers-

look-to-unionize/article36242466/

63. H.G. Watson, "Final vote on National Post union will be determined by Labour Board hearing," J-source, October 3, 2017. URL: https://j-source.ca/final-vote-national-post-union-will-determined-labour-board-hearing/

64. Tannara Yelland, "How Postmedia defeated a union drive at the National Post," Canadaland, June 6, 2018. URL: https://www.canadaland.com/how-postmedia-defeated-a-national-post-union/

65. "Secret Office Memos: Rats on the rope at the National Post," *Frank*. URL: https://frankmag.ca/2017/09/25145/

66. Ian Vandaelle, "Postmedia and Bombardier not in the same boat on exec pay: Godfrey," BNN Bloomberg, April 10, 2017. URL: https://www.BNN Bloomberg.ca/postmedia-isn-t-in-the-same-boat-as-bombardier-on-executive-compensation-godfrey-1.720368

67. Johnston, "Q&A: Paul Godfrey, the CEO who's presiding over the Postmedia newspaper chain's rapid decline."

68. Vandaelle, "Postmedia and Bombardier not in the same boat on exec pay."

69. Ibid.

70. James Bradshaw, "Postmedia reports major drop in revenues, Conrad Black scolds leaders," *Globe and Mail*, July 9, 2015. URL: https://www.theglobeandmail.com/report-on-business/postmedia-reports-wider-loss-as-advertising-circulation-revenues-weaken/article25386520/

71. Johnston, "Q&A: Paul Godfrey, the CEO who's presiding over the Postmedia newspaper chain's rapid decline."

72. Ibid.

73. Kate Taylor, "New system for funding Canadian content would rely on tax credits," *Globe and Mail*, November 4, 2016. URL: https://www.theglobeandmail.com/arts/television/new-system-for-funding-canadian-content-would-rely-on-tax-credits/article32679807/

74. Richard Stursberg, *The Tangled Garden: A Canadian Cultural Manifesto for the Digital Age*. Toronto: James Lorimer & Co., 2019, p. 169.

75. Ibid., p. 168.
76. Ibid., p. 169.
77. Ibid.
78. Ibid., pp. 170-171.
79. Ibid., p. 171.
80. Ibid., p. 172.
81. Ibid., p. 173.
82. Ibid., pp. 173-174.

83 Canada, Standing Committee on Canadian Heritage, *Disruption: Change and Churning in Canada's Media Landscape*, June 2017, p. 58. URL: https://www.ourcommons.ca/Content/Committee/421/CHPC/Reports/RP9045583/chpcrp06/chpcrp06-e.pdf

84 Ibid., p. 7.

85 Daniel Leblanc, "Liberal MPs to call for broadband Internet tax to fund Canadian media," *Globe and Mail*, June 14, 2017. URL: https://www.theglobeandmail.com/news/politics/liberal-mps-call-for-5-per-cent-tax-on-streaming-services/article35313367/

86 Ibid.

87   Andy Blatchford, "Trudeau rejects call for 5% tax on broadband Internet services," *Toronto Star*, June 15, 2017. URL: https://www.thestar.com/news/canada/2017/06/15/trudeau-rejects-call-for-5-tax-on-broadband-internet-services.html

88   Laura Ryckewaert, "'Obviously he hasn't read it,' Grit MP Hedy Fry says of PM Justin Trudeau dismissing part of a committee report that suggested new taxes on internet service providers," *Hill Times*, June 26, 2017. URL: https://www.hilltimes.com/2017/06/26/liberal-heritage-committee-chair-fry-stresses-importance-recent-recommendations-laments-misinformation/111592

89   "Joly Says no to Internet Tax [transcript]," Power Play with Don Martin, CTV Television, June 15, 2017.

90   Andrew Coyne, "Why the media should say no to a government bailout," *National Post*, June 16, 2017. URL: https://nationalpost.com/opinion/andrew-coyne-why-the-media-should-say-no-to-a-government-bailout

91   Mélanie Joly, "Launch of Creative Canada," September 28, 2017. URL: https://www.canada.ca/en/canadian-heritage/news/2017/09/creative_canada_-avisionforcanadascreativeindustries.html

92   Postmedia Network, "Postmedia Announces Community Newspapers Transaction with Torstar [press release]," Postmedia.com. URL: https://www.postmedia.com/2017/11/27/postmedia-announces-community-newspapers-transaction-with-torstar/#:~:text=(%E2%80%9CPostmedia%E2%80%9D%20or%20the%20%E2%80%9C,to%20sell%2015%20of%20Postmedia's

93   Susan Krashinsky Robertson, "Torstar, Postmedia talked job cuts before deal, Competition Bureau says," *Globe and Mail*, March 22, 2018, p. A1. URL: https://www.theglobeandmail.com/report-on-business/documents-reveal-competition-watchdogs-concerns-over-torstar-postmedia-deal/article38316813/

94   Susan Krashinsky Robertson, "Postmedia, Torstar to swap and shutter dozens of local newspapers," *Globe and Mail*, November 28, 2017, p. A1. URL: https://www.theglobeandmail.com/report-on-business/torstar-postmedia-swap-community-papers-many-to-close/article37092456/

95   Elizabeth Renzetti, "From the grave of local news, fresh hope rises," *Globe and Mail*, December 2, 2017, p. O2. URL: https://www.theglobeandmail.com/opinion/hold-the-obits-page-local-news-isnt-dead-yet/article37165918/

96   Dan Healing, "Newspaper numbers will keep shrinking: Postmedia CEO," *National Post*, December 6, 2017 p. B5. URL: https://financialpost.com/pmn/business-pmn/postmedia-ceo-paul-godfrey-says-newspapers-will-survive-but-with-reduced-numbers

97   Emily Jackson, "36 Newspapers to close under Postmedia, Torstar deal," *National Post*, November 28, 2017, p. B8. URL: https://www.pressreader.com/canada/ottawa-citizen/20171128/282046212414069

98   Adam Ward, "Barrie Examiner, Orillia Packet & Times to close after newspaper swap," CTV Barrie, November 27, 2017. URL: https://barrie.ctvnews.ca/barrie-examiner-orillia-packet-times-to-close-after-newspaper-swap-1.3695851

99   Marcus Gee, "The last edition," *Globe and Mail*, December 10,

2017. URL: https://www.theglobeandmail.com/news/national/orillia-packet-and-times-local-journalism-torstar-postmedia/article37282001/

100   "Community Media Alive and Thriving, despite Postmedia and Torstar Closures," Quebec Community Newspapers Association, November 30, 2017. URL: https://www.newswire.ca/news-releases/community-media-alive-and-thriving-despite-postmedia-and-torstar-closures-660989963.html

101   Martin Cash, "Metro Winnipeg axed in Torstar, Postmedia deal," *Winnipeg Free Press*, November 27, 2017. URL: https://www.winnipegfreepress.com/business/2017/11/27/metro-winnipeg-free-daily-paper-dies-in-torstar-postmedia-deal

102   Ibid.

103   Jill Slattery, "24 hrs Vancouver newsroom shut down by Postmedia," Global News, September 29, 2016. URL: https://globalnews.ca/news/2973971/24-hrs-vancouver-newsroom-shut-down-by-postmedia/

104   Andy Blatchford and Joanna Smith, "Red Ink: Feds urged to help ailing newspaper industry amid closure announcements," *Prince George Citizen*, November 28, 2017, p. A17.

105   Dwayne Winseck, "Media and Internet Concentration in Canada, 1984-2019," Canadian Media Concentration Research Project, 2020, " p. 84. URL: http://www.cmcrp.org/wp-content/uploads/2020/12/Media-and-Internet-Concentration-in-Canada-1984%E2%80%932019-16122020.pdf

106   Ibid.

107   Healing, "Newspaper numbers will keep shrinking."

108   "Postmedia CEO says he didn't know Torstar was going to cut papers as well," BNN Bloomberg, November 27, 2017. URL: https://www.BNN Bloomberg.ca/executive/video/postmedia-ceo-says-he-didn-t-know-torstar-was-going-to-cut-papers-as-well~1271779

109   Ibid.

110   Ibid.

111   Ibid.

112   Jackson, "36 Newspapers to close."

113   "Postmedia CEO Paul Godfrey on Torstar swap," CBC News On the Money with Peter Armstrong, December 4, 2017. URL: https://youtu.be/UwIWpGWKzUQ

114   Ibid.

115   Ibid.

116   David Milstead, "Torstar, Postmedia and the arrogance of the deal," *Globe and Mail*, March 23, 2018, p. B4. URL: https://www.theglobeandmail.com/report-on-business/rob-commentary/torstar-postmedia-and-the-arrogance-of-the-deal/article38336159/

CHAPTER 2 — THE ROAD TO FINANCIALIZATION

1. John Morton, "Why Are Newspaper Profits So High?" *American Journalism Review*, October 1994, p. 72.

2. Ibid.

3. Ibid.

4. Will Slauter, "The Rise of the Newspaper," in Richard R. John and

Jonathan Silberstein-Loeb, eds., *Making News: The Political Economy of Journalism in Britain and America from the Glorious Revolution to the Internet*. Oxford: Oxford University Press, 2015, p. 30.

5. M. C. Barrès-Baker, *An Introduction to the Early History of Newspaper Advertising*. Brent Museum and Archive occasional publications No. 2, 2006. URL: https://authorzilla.com/KNd5X/history-of-british-newspapers.html

6. Kevin Williams, *Read All About It: A history of the British newspaper*. Abingdon: Routledge, 2010.

7. Barrès-Baker, *An Introduction to the Early History of Newspaper Advertising*, p. 21

8. Jurgen Habermas, *The Structural Transformation of the Public Sphere: An Inquiry into a category of Bourgeois Society*. Cambridge: MIT Press, 1991.

9. Gerald J. Baldasty, *The Commercialization of News in the Nineteenth Century*. Madison: University of Wisconsin Press, 1992.

10. Minko Sotiron, *From Politics to Profit: The Commercialization of Canadian Daily Newspapers, 1890-1920*. Montreal: McGill-Queen's University Press, 1992.

11. Ralph Negrine, *Politics and the mass media in Britain* 2nd ed. London: Routledge, 1994, p. 166.

12. Andrew Crisell, *An introductory history of British broadcasting* 2nd ed. London: Routledge, 2003, p. 108.

13. See Richard Siklos, *Shades of Black: Conrad Black and the world's fastest growing press empire*. Toronto: McClelland & Stewart, 1996.

14. Conrad Black, *A Life in Progress*, Toronto: Key Porter, 1993, p. 405.

15. Ibid., p. 378.

16. Peter C. Newman, "The inexorable spread of the Black Empire," *Maclean's*, February 3, 1992, p. 68.

17. Dallas W. Smythe, *Dependency Road*. Norwood, NJ: Ablex, 1981.

18. Ibid., p. 4.

19. Canada, *The Uncertain Mirror: Report of the Special Senate Committee on Mass Media*, Vol. I. Ottawa: Information Canada, 1970, p. 63.

20. Ibid., p. 47.

21. Ibid., p. 71.

22. Keith Davey, *The Rainmaker: A Passion for Politics*. Toronto: Stoddart, 1986, p. 153.

23. Canada, Royal Commission on Newspapers, *Report*. Ottawa: Minister of Supply and Services, 1981, pp. 215, 218.

24. Peter J. S. Dunnett, *The World Newspaper Industry*. London: Croom Helm, 1988, p. 199.

25. Marc Edge, "The never-ending story: Postmedia, press concentration, and the Competition Bureau." *Canadian Journal of Media Studies* 14(1), pp. 53-81. URL: https://uottawa.scholarsportal.info/ottawa/index.php/CJMS-RCEM/article/view/6474/5222

26. C. Ann Hollifield, "Effects of foreign ownership on media content: Thomson papers' coverage of Quebec independence vote," *Newspaper Research Journal*, 20(1), 1999, p. 65. URL: https://journals.sagepub.com/doi/abs/10.1177/073953299902000106?journalCode=nrja

27. Charles Bruce, *News and the Southams*. Toronto: Macmillan, 1968.
28. Alan Freeman, "Chain skirts media control policy," *Globe and Mail*, June 18, 1990, p. B6.
29. Ibid.
30. See Marc Edge, "How the camel got in the tent: The 1990s Canadian assault on Australia's foreign media ownership limits," *Media International Australia 132*, August 2009, pp. 42-53. URL: https://journals.sagepub.com/doi/abs/10.1177/1329878X0913200106
31. Black, *A Life in Progress*, p. 46.
32. Canada, Standing Senate Committee on Transportations and Communications, *Final report on the Canadian news media*, Vol. 1, p. 24. URL: http://www.parl.gc.ca/content/sen/committee/391/tran/rep/repfinjun06vol1-e.pdf
33. Thomas I. Palley, "Financialization: What It Is and Why It Matters." Working Paper No. 525, The Levy Economics Institute, Bard College, Annandale-on-Hudson, NY, December 2007, p. 2. URL: http://www.levyinstitute.org/pubs/wp_525.pdf
34. Ibid.
35. Rana Foroohar, *Makers and Takers: The Rise of Finance and the Fall of American Business*. New York: Crown Business, 2016, p. 5.
36. Ibid., p. 7.
37. Ibid., p. 8.
38. Nuria Almiron, *Journalism in crisis: Corporate media and financialization*. Cresskill, NJ: Hampton Press, 2010, p. 159.
39. Ibid., p. 154.
40. Ibid., p. 174.
41. Ibid., pp. 175-176.
42. Carol J. Loomis, "The Jones Nobody Keeps Up With," *Fortune*, April 1966, p. 237–242.
43. David Skeel, "Behind the Hedge," *Legal Affairs*, November/December 2005. URL: https://www.legalaffairs.org/issues/November-December-2005/feature_skeel_novdec05.msp
44. Ibid.
45. Penelope Muse Abernathy, *The rise of a new media baron and the emerging threat of news deserts*. Chapel Hill: University of North Carolina Press, 2016. URL: https://www.usnewsdeserts.com/wp-content/uploads/2016/09/07.UNC_RiseOfNewMediaBaron_SinglePage_01Sep2016-REDUCED.pdf
46. Ibid., p. 8.
47. Robert Kuttner and Hildy Zenger, "Saving the free press from private equity," *American Prospect* 29(1), pp. 22-29.
48. Anna Nicolaou, James Fontanella-Khan, and Lindsay Fortado, "US 'ghost newspapers' struggle for life," *Financial Times*, February 26, 2019, p. 7. URL: https://www.ft.com/content/e234b40a-292f-11e9-a5ab-ff8ef-2b976c7
49. Ken Doctor, "Alden Global Capital is making so much money wrecking local journalism it might not want to stop anytime soon," Nieman Lab, May 1, 2018. URL: https://www.niemanlab.org/2018/05/newsonomics-alden-global-capital-is-making-so-much-money-wrecking-local-journalism-it-

might-not-want-to-stop-anytime-soon/

50. Penelope Muse Abernathy, *The expanding news desert*. Chapel Hill: University of North Carolina Press, 2018. URL: https://www.cislm.org/wp-content/uploads/2018/10/The-Expanding-News-Desert-10_14-Web.pdf

51. See Marc Edge, *Greatly Exaggerated: The Myth of the Death of Newspapers*. Vancouver: New Star Books, 2014.

52. "Steven Shapiro," The Org, undated. URL: https://theorg.com/org/goldentree-asset-management-lp/org-chart/steven-shapiro

53. Harry Glasbeek, *Class Privilege: How Law Shelters Shareholders and Coddles Capitalism*. Toronto: Between the Lines, 2017, p. 161.

54. Ibid., pp. 161-162.

55. Katherine Burton, Sridhar Natarajan, and Shahien Nasiripour, "National Enquirer Owner Chatham Asset Management Plays Starring Role in Tabloid-Worthy Stories," *Fortune*, March 18, 2019. URL: https://fortune.com/2019/03/18/chatham-asset-management-michael-cohen-ipayment-holdings-lawsuit/

56. Ibid.

57. Adam Hayes, "What Is a Credit Default Swap (CDS)?," Investopedia, August 25, 2022. URL: https://www.investopedia.com/terms/c/creditdefaultswap.asp

58. "U.S. Manager Preps Short Credit Fund," *Derivatives Week*, June 28, 2004, p. 1. URL: https://www.globalcapital.com/article/28mwt9p82de8r-fr8pqadc/derivatives/u-s-manager-preps-short-credit-fund

59. Burton, Natarajan, and Nasiripour, "National Enquirer Owner Chatham Asset Management."

60. Ibid.

61. Carleton English, "Ex-CEO wins $11M after sex-drenched suit over his ouster," *New York Post*, August 31, 2017. URL: https://nypost.com/2017/08/31/ex-ceo-awarded-11m-after-suing-over-theft-allegations/

62. Ibid.

63. Ibid.

64. Ibid.

65. Ibid.

66. Ken Doctor, "The McClatchy auction ends not with a bang, but only more whimpers," NiemanLab, July 13, 2020. URL: https://www.niemanlab.org/2020/07/newsonomics-the-mcclatchy-auction-ends-not-with-a-bang-but-only-more-whimpers/

67. Joshua Benton, "McClatchy files for bankruptcy, likely ending 163 years of family control and setting up more consolidation in local news," NiemanLab, February 13, 2020. URL: https://www.niemanlab.org/2020/02/mcclatchy-files-for-bankruptcy-likely-ending-163-years-of-family-control-and-setting-up-more-consolidation-in-local-news/

68. Sridhar Natarajan, "Hedge Fund Gambit Stirs Fresh Controversy in Besieged CDS Market," BNN Bloomberg, April 30, 2018. URL: https://www.BNN Bloomberg.ca/hedge-fund-gambit-stirs-fresh-controversy-in-besieged-cds-market-1.1068987

69. Ibid.

70. Ibid.

71. Mark Rendell, "Toronto Star abandons Star Touch tablet app, lays

off 30 staff members," *Globe and Mail*, June 26, 2017. URL: https://www.theglobeandmail.com/report-on-business/toronto-star-abandons-star-touch-tablet-app/article35473859/

72. James McLeod, "Torstar shuts commuter papers less than two years after 'major' expansion," *National Post*, November 20, 2019. URL: https://business.financialpost.com/telecom/media/torstar-shuts-commuter-papers-less-than-two-years-after-major-expansion

73. Josh Rubin, "Torstar Being Sold in Deal That Begins 'New Chapter,'" *Toronto Star*, May 27, 2020, p. A1. URL: https://www.thestar.com/business/2020/05/26/torstar-to-be-sold-taken-private-in-52-million-deal.html

74. Andrew Willis and Jeffrey Jones, "Toronto private lender Canso funds Torstar takeover bid, after backstopping two of its print media rivals," *Globe and Mail*, May 28, 2020. URL: https://www.theglobeandmail.com/business/article-toronto-private-lender-canso-funds-torstar-takeover-bid-after/

75. "Torstar's new owners are selling off parts of the company — for more than they paid for the whole thing," CBC News, June 21, 2021. URL: https://www.cbc.ca/news/business/torstar-verticalscope-company-sale-1.6073484

76. Joe Castaldo, "Torstar owner seeks to wind up company because of rift with partner," Globe and Mail, 30 September 2022, p. A1. URL: https://www.theglobeandmail.com/business/article-torstar-owners-deadlocked-in-feud-over-direction-of-company-including/

77. Jason McBride, "Star Wars: Inside the vicious battle for control of the country's largest newspaper," *Toronto Life*, February 8, 2023. URL: https://torontolife.com/city/star-wars-inside-the-vicious-battle-for-control-of-the-countrys-largest-newspaper/

78. Philip Meyer, *The Vanishing Newspaper: Saving journalism in the information age*. Columbia: University of Missouri Press, 2004.

79. Marc Edge, *Greatly Exaggerated: The Myth of the Death of Newspapers*. Vancouver: New Star Books, 2014.

80. Keith L. Herndon, "Profitability in newspapers: Industry benchmarking data shows newspaper industry makes money and is less risky following layoffs and restructuring." Paper presented to the Association for Education in Journalism & Mass Communication Annual Convention, August 6-9, 2015, San Francisco, pp. 26-27.

81. Miriam van der Burg and Hilde Van den Bulck, "Why are traditional newspaper publishers still surviving in the digital era? The impact of long-term trends on the Flemish newspaper industry's financing, 1990-2014," *Journal of Media Business Studies*, 14(2), pp. 82-115. URL: https://www.tandfonline.com/doi/abs/10.1080/16522354.2017.1290024

82. Patrick-Yves Badillo and Dominique Bourgeois, "The Swiss press model: Democracy, concentration and digital diversification," *Recherches en communication 44*, 2017, pp. 9-30. URL: https://www.researchgate.net/publication/321974301_The_Swiss_press_model_Democracy_concentration_and_digital_diversification

83. Marc Edge, *Re-examining the UK Newspaper Industry*. London: Routledge, 2023.

84. Werner J. Severin and James W. Tankard Jr., *Communication The-*

ories: *Origins, Methods and Uses in the Mass Media* 4th Ed. New York: Pearson, 1997.

85. James W. Carey, "Harold Adams Innis and Marshall McLuhan," *The Antioch Review* 27(1), 1967, pp. 5-39. URL: https://www.jstor.org/stable/4610816

86. Gary Wolf, "The Wisdom of Saint Marshall, the Holy Fool," *Wired*, January 1, 1996. URL: https://www.wired.com/1996/01/saint-marshal/

87. Stefano DellaVigna and Ethan Kaplan, "The Fox News Effect: Media Bias and Voting," *Quarterly Journal of Economics* 122 (3), 2007, pp. 1187-1234. URL: https://academic.oup.com/qje/article-abstract/122/3/1187/1879517

88. Robert Kuttner and Hildy Zenger, "Saving the Free Press From Private Equity," *American Prospect*, December 27, 2017. URL: http://prospect.org/article/saving-free-press-private-equity

89. Michael E. Porter, *Competitive Strategy: Creating and Sustaining Superior Performance*. New York: Free Press, 1998, p. 311.

90. See Abernathy, *The rise of a new media baron and the emerging threat of news deserts*; and Abernathy, *The expanding news desert*.

91. Margaret Sullivan, *Ghosting the News: Local Journalism and the crisis of American democracy*. New York: Columbia Global Reports, 2020, p. 95.

92. John Lester, "Business Subsidies in Canada: Comprehensive Estimates for the Government of Canada and the Four Largest Provinces," University of Calgary School of Public Policy Publications Research Paper 11(1), 2018, p. 11, 25. URL: https://www.policyschool.ca/wp-content/uploads/2018/01/Business-Subsidies-in-Canada-Lester.pdf

93. "Government subsidies for business are greater than Canada's entire defence budget," CBC Radio, May 24, 2019. URL: https://www.cbc.ca/radio/sunday/the-sunday-edition-for-may-26-2019-1.5146999/government-subsidies-for-business-are-greater-than-canada-s-entire-defence-budget-1.5148266

94. Roberta Lexier and Avi Lewis, "Corporate welfare bums: It's payback time," The Conversation, December 5, 2018. URL: https://theconversation.com/corporate-welfare-bums-its-payback-time-107306

95. David Lewis, *Louder Voices: The Corporate Welfare Bums*. Toronto: Lorimer, 1972, p. 11.

CHAPTER 3 — THE BAILOUT CAMPAIGN

1. Kady O'Malley, "Globe yanks Greenspon from Parliamentary bureau," *Hill Times*, April 19, 1999, p. 10.

2. Sheldon Kirshner, "A 'general' in Canada's newspaper war," *Canadian Jewish News*, May 25, 2000, p. 11.

3. Chris Cobb, *Ego and Ink: The Inside Story of Canada's National Newspaper War*. Toronto: McClelland & Stewart, 2004, p. 167.

4. Ibid.

5. Ibid., p. 168.

6. Ibid., p. 167.

7. Ibid., p. 36.

8. Melinda Mattos, "The Scoop on Ed," *Ryerson Review of Journalism*, Summer 2003. URL: https://rrj.ca/the-scoop-on-ed/
9. Ibid.
10. Alec Scott, "Searching for Certainty: Inside the New Canadian Mindset [book review]," *Quill and Quire*. URL: https://quillandquire.com/review/searching-for-certainty-inside-the-new-canadian-mindset/
11. Paul Wells, "Tweeting the firing of Ed Greenspon," *Maclean's*, May 26, 2009. URL: https://www.macleans.ca/politics/ottawa/tweeting-the-firing-of-ed-greenspon/
12. Canadian International Council, "Open Canada: A Global Positioning Strategy for a Networked Age [press release]," May 2011. URL: https://thecic.org/research-publications/reports/open-canada-a-global-positioning-strategy-for-a-networked-age/
13. Shannon Rupp, "Should Your Taxes Subsidize Big Media?" The Tyee, August 15, 2016. URL: https://thetyee.ca/Mediacheck/2016/08/15/Taxes-Big-Media/
14. Public Policy Forum, "Former Globe and Mail and Bloomberg journalist Edward Greenspon to lead Public Policy Forum [press release]," Canada NewsWire, March 3, 2016. URL: https://ceo.ca/@newswire/former-globe-and-mail-and-bloomberg-journalist-edward-greenspon-to-lead-public-policy-forum
15. Bruce Cheadle, "Public Policy Forum will assess the state of Canada's struggling news industry," Macleans.ca, June 21, 2016. URL: http://www.macleans.ca/politics/ottawa/liberals-seek-outside-advice-as-they-mull-policy-help-for-news-media/
16. The Canadian Press, "Five things to know with Canada's news media industry under public policy review," *Brandon Sun*, June 21, 2016. URL: http://www.brandonsun.com/national/breaking-news/five-things-to-know-with-canadas-news-media-industry-under-public-policy-review-383860061.html
17. Ibid.
18. Dean Beeby, "Ottawa cuts newspaper ad spending amid worries about sector," CBC News, September 1, 2016. URL: http://www.cbc.ca/news/politics/newspapers-canadian-heritage-public-policy-forum-digital-news-gathering-internet-1.3743580
19. Public Policy Forum, *The Shattered Mirror: News, Democracy and Trust in the Digital Age*. Ottawa: Public Policy Forum, 2017, p. 104. URL: https://shatteredmirror.ca/download-report
20. Andrew Potter, "What should be done about the state of the news media? [blog entry]," In Due Course, June 28, 2016. URL: http://induecourse.ca/what-should-be-done-about-the-state-of-the-news-media/
21. Ibid.
22. Ibid.
23. Bruce Johnstone, "No consensus at debate on whether gov't has role in supporting media," *Regina Leader Post*, September 7, 2016, p. B7.
24. Dean Beeby, "Squeeze cash from Facebook, Google, say Canadian news media leaders," CBC News, January 11, 2017. URL: http://www.cbc.ca/news/politics/newspapers-news-media-digital-public-policy-forum-google-facebook-tax-1.3929356

25. Ibid.
26. Ibid.
27. Ibid.
28. Public Policy Forum, *The Shattered Mirror*.
29. Ibid., p. 96.
30. Ibid.
31. Ibid., p. 96-97.
32. Ibid., p. 9.
33. Daniel Leblanc, "Canada's media industry needs major federal cash injection: report," *Globe and Mail*, January 26, 2017. URL: https://www.theglobeandmail.com/news/politics/canadian-media-need-major-federal-investment-report/article33771170/
34. Beatrice Britneff, "Public Policy Forum report on media crisis 'flawed': Professor," iPolitics, February 12, 2017. URL: https://ipolitics.ca/2017/02/12/public-policy-forum-report-on-media-crisis-flawed-professor/
35. "CAJ supports Public Policy Forum proposals for sustainable journalism [press release]," Canadian Association of Journalists, January 30, 2017. URL: https://www.newswire.ca/news-releases/caj-supports-public-policy-forum-proposals-for-sustainable-journalism-612164973.html
36. "Feds must take 'urgent' action on news industry report," CWA Canada [press release], January 26, 2017. URL: https://cwacanada.ca/2017/01/26/feds-must-take-urgent-action-on-news-industry-report/
37. Rafe Mair, *Politically Incorrect: How Canada Lost Its Way and The Simple Path Home*. Comox, BC: Watershed Sentinel Books, 2017, p. 155.
38. Ibid.
39. Andrew Coyne, "Here's the news, whatever that is," *National Post*, January 28, 2017, p. A7. URL: https://nationalpost.com/opinion/andrew-coyne-report-on-struggling-news-business-is-responsible-high-minded-and-profoundly-wrong
40. Simon Houpt, "Will fake news provide an excuse for the feds to help Canadian media solve their real financial woes?" *Globe and Mail*, January 26, 2017. URL: https://www.theglobeandmail.com/arts/television/will-fake-news-provide-an-excuse-for-the-feds-to-help-canadian-media-solve-their-real-financial-woes/article33788496/
41. Ibid.
42. Marc Edge, "'Shattered' mirror more like a funhouse mirror [blog entry]," Greatly Exaggerated, February 6, 2017. URL: http://greatlyexaggerated.blogspot.com/2017/02/shattered-mirror-more-like-funhouse.html
43. Ibid.
44. Ibid.
45. Public Policy Forum, *The Shattered Mirror*, p. 103.
46. Ken Goldstein, "Canada's Digital Divides," Communic@tions Management Inc., August 20, 2015, p. 6. URL: http://media-cmi.com/downloads/CMI_Discussion_Paper_Digital_Divides_082015.pdf
47. Ibid.
48. "Guelph Mercury halts print production," *Toronto Star*, January 26, 2016, p. S9. URL: https://www.thestar.com/business/2016/01/25/metroland-media-to-close-print-edition-of-guelph-mercury.html
49. "Nanaimo Daily News to cease operations Jan. 29," *Nanaimo Daily*

News, January 23, 2016. URL: http://www.nanaimodailynews.com/our-town/366304751.html

50. Marc Edge, "Conspiracy to commit murder? Canadian newspaper trades and closures, 2010-17," *Canadian Journal of Media Studies* 16(1), 2018, pp. 28-45. URL: https://uottawa.scholarsportal.info/ottawa/index.php/CJMS-RCEM/article/view/6454/5211

51. Garcia-Molina, Hector, Joglekar, Manas, Marcus, Adam, Parameswaran, Aditya, & Vasilis, Verroios, "Challenges in data crowdsourcing," *IEEE Transactions on Knowledge and Data Engineering* 28(4), 2016, pp. 901–911.; Zhengy, Yudian, Li, Guoliang, Li, Yuanbing, Shany, Caihua, & Chengy, Reynold, "Truth inference in crowdsourcing: Is the problem solved?" *Proceedings of the VLDB Endowment* 10(5), 2017, pp. 541–552.

52. Lindgren, April, Corbett, Jon, and Hodson, Jaigris, "Mapping change in Canada's local news landscape: An investigation of research impact on public policy," *Digital Journalism* 8(6), 2020, p. 758.

53. Public Policy Forum, *The Shattered Mirror*, p. 79.

54. Dwayne Winseck, "Shattered mirror, stunted vision and squandered opportunities [Blog entry]," February 9, 2017. Mediamorphis. URL: https://dwmw.wordpress.com/2017/02/09/shattered-mirror-stunted-vision-and-a-squandered-opportunities/

55. Ibid.
56. Ibid.
57. Ibid.
58. Ibid.
59. Ibid.

60. News Media Canada, "Canada's Newspaper Industry Unites to Advocate for Canadian Journalism Fund [press release]," Business Wire, June 16, 2017. URL: https://www.businesswire.com/news/home/20170616005625/en/Canada%E2%80%99s-Newspaper-Industry-Unites-to-Advocate-for-Canadian-Journalism-Fund

61. Harvey Schachter, "Revolution from within," *Canadian Business*, November 1994, p. 30.

62. Terence Corcoran, "A night in the swamp," *National Post*, April 26, 2017, p. FP9. URL: https://financialpost.com/opinion/terence-corocoran-i-barely-survived-a-night-inside-the-liberal-partys-undrained-policy-swamp

63. Ibid.
64. Ibid.
65. Ibid.
66. Ibid.

67. Duff McDonald, *The Firm: The Story of McKinsey and Its Secret Influence on American Business*. New York, Simon & Shuster, 2013, p. 8.

68. Walt Bogdanich and Michael Forsythe, *When McKinsey Comes to Town: The Hidden Influence of the World's Most Powerful Consulting Firm*. New York: Doubleday, 2022.

69. Tristin Hopper, "What is McKinsey, and is it a shadow government that secretly runs Canada?" *National Post*, January 12, 2023, p. A6. URL: https://nationalpost.com/opinion/first-reading-canada-the-latest-country-accused-of-handing-outsized-power-to-mckinsey

70. Romain Schué and Thomas Gerbet, "L'influence de McKinsey explose sous Trudeau, surtout à l'immigration," Radio-Canada, January 4, 2023. URL: https://ici.radio-canada.ca/nouvelle/1945915/mckinsey-influence-canada-trudeau-immigration-conseils

71. Corcoran, "A night in the swamp."

72. Ibid.

73. James G. McGann, "2017 Global Go To Think Tank Index Report," University of Pennsylvania, January 31, 2018. URL: https://repository.upenn.edu/think_tanks/13

74. "What can a little birdie (Twitter) tell us about think tank ideology?" *Policy Options*, November 19, 2014. URL: https://policyoptions.irpp.org/2014/11/19/what-can-a-little-birdie-twitter-tell-us-about-think-tank-ideology/

75. Ibid.

76. Daniel Yergin and Joseph Stanislaw, *Commanding Heights: The Battle for the World Economy*. New York: Simon & Schuster, 2002.

77. Diane Stone, *Capturing the Public Imagination: Think Tanks and the Policy Process*. (Portland, OR: Frank Cass), 1996.

78. James G. McGann, *The Fifth Estate: Think Tanks, Public Policy, and Governance*. Washington, DC: Brookings Institution Press, 2016.

79. Ibid., p. 30.

80. Ibid., p. 19.

81. Ibid., p. 30.

82. Trudy Lieberman, *Slanting the Story: The Forces that Shape the News*. New York: New Press, 2000, p. 3.

83. Ibid., p. 20.

84. Donald E. Abelson, *Do Think Tanks Matter? Assessing the Impact of Public Policy Institutes*. Montreal: McGill-Queen's University Press, 2002.

85. Donald Gutstein, "Who funds the Fraser Institute?" *Straight Goods*, October 28, 2004, p. 31.

86. Wendy McLellan, "Study paints journalists as left-wing, biased messengers," *Media*, Winter 2003.

87. Campbell Clark, "Think-tanks changing their minds," *Globe and Mail*, August 20, 2005, p. F2.

88. Abelson, *Do Think Tanks Matter?*, p. 185.

89. Gutstein, "Who funds the Fraser Institute?"

90. Donald Gutstein, *Not a Conspiracy Theory: How Business Propaganda Hijacks Democracy*. Toronto: Key Porter, 2009, p. 12.

91. Ibid.

92. Ibid., p. 32.

93. Ibid.

94. Ibid., pp. 32-33.

95. Carey, *Taking the Risk Out of Democracy: Corporate Propaganda versus Freedom and Liberty*. Sydney, University of New South Wales Press, 1995, p. 18.

96. Gutstein, *Not a Conspiracy Theory*, p. 19.

97. Carey, *Taking the Risk Out of Democracy*.

98. Walter Lippmann, *Public Opinion*. New York: MacMillan, 1922.

99. Jacques Ellul, *Propaganda: The formation of men's attitudes*. New

York: Vintage Books, 1965, p. 57.
100. Ibid., p. 60
101. Adolf Hitler, *Mein Kampf*. Munich: Franz Eher, 1925, p. 196.
102. Garth Jowett and Victoria O'Donnell, *Propaganda and Persuasion* 4th ed., Thousand Oaks, CA: Sage, 2006.
103. Stanley Cunningham, *The Idea of Propaganda*, New York: Praeger, 2002, p. 13.
104. Paul Adams, "Postmedia's death will be a catastrophe — and nobody knows what to do about it," iPolitics, June 15, 2017. URL: http://ipolitics.ca/2017/06/15/postmedias-death-will-be-a-catastrophe-and-nobody-knows-what-to-do-about-it/
105. Bob Cox, Jerry Dias, and Edward Greenspon, "Journalism matters more than ever. We need help to save it," *Globe and Mail*, September 14, 2017, p. A15. URL: https://www.theglobeandmail.com/opinion/journalism-matters-more-than-ever-we-need-help-to-save-it/article36248690/
106. Ibid.
107. Ibid.
108. Peter Mazereeuw, "'We're going to be every bit as active in this federal election,'" *Hill Times*, January 21, 2019. URL: https://www.hilltimes.com/2019/01/21/unions-undeterred-new-pre-election-ad-spending-limits-will-every-bit-active-last-election-says-dias/184132
109. Cox, Dias, and Greenspon, "Journalism matters more than ever."
110. Edward Greenspon, "Unfinished business for Canadian journalism," *Policy Options*, October 2, 2017. URL: http://policyoptions.irpp.org/magazines/october-2017/unfinished-business-for-canadian-journalism/
111. Ibid.
112. Ibid.
113. Ibid.
114. Marc Edge, "Year of reckoning looms for Canada's newspapers," The Conversation, January 1, 2018. URL: https://theconversation.com/year-of-reckoning-looms-for-canadas-newspapers-89066

CHAPTER 4 — PROJECT ICE

1. "Hammill named regional advertising director," *Orillia Packet and Times*, November 17, 2016. URL: https://www.simcoe.com/news-story/8480510-hammill-named-regional-advertising-director/
2. "John Hammill knows the secret to running a successful media outlet," Lakehead University Alumni Spotlight, October 14, 2021. URL: https://www.lakeheadu.ca/alumni/news/spotlight/archive/node/67159
3. Bryan Carney, "Whistleblower's suspicious termination notice similar to three more turned up by Tyee," The Tyee, December 4, 2018. URL: https://thetyee.ca/News/2018/12/04/Investigation-Torstar-Postmedia-Newspaper-Swap/
4. Marcus Gee, "The last edition," *Globe and Mail*, December 10, 2017. URL: https://www.theglobeandmail.com/news/national/orillia-packet-and-times-local-journalism-torstar-postmedia/article37282001/
5. Ibid.
6. Mitchell Sleeman, "Recognition of the Historical Significance of

the Archives of the Orillia Packet & Times [petition]," Change.org. URL: https://www.change.org/p/torstar-corporation-recognition-of-the-historical-significance-of-the-archives-of-the-orillia-packet-times

7. Carney, "Whistleblower's suspicious termination notice."
8. Ibid.
9. Susan Krashinsky Robertson, "Torstar, Postmedia talked job cuts before deal, Competition Bureau says," *Globe and Mail*, March 22, 2018, p. A1. URL: https://www.theglobeandmail.com/report-on-business/documents-reveal-competition-watchdogs-concerns-over-torstar-postmedia-deal/article38316813/
10. "Village Media expands to Orillia," *Northern Ontario Business*, January 3, 2018. URL: https://www.northernontariobusiness.com/regional-news/sault-ste-marie/village-media-expands-to-orillia-803991
11. Carney, "Whistleblower's suspicious termination notice."
12. "John Hammill knows the secret to running a successful media outlet."
13. Marc Edge, "Conspiracy to commit murder? Canadian newspaper trades and closures, 2010-17," *Canadian Journal of Media Studies* 16(1), 2018, pp. 28-45. URL: https://uottawa.scholarsportal.info/ottawa/index.php/CJMS-RCEM/article/view/6454/5211
14. Jacob Parry, "Who is killing the community newspaper?" *B.C. Business*, July 22, 2015. URL: https://www.bcbusiness.ca/who-is-killing-the-community-newspaper
15. Edge, "Conspiracy to commit murder?"
16. David Parkinson, "Postmedia deal will force regulator to rethink mandate," *Globe and Mail*, October 6, 2014. URL: https://www.theglobeandmail.com/report-on-business/rob-commentary/executive-insight/postmedia-deal-forces-regulator-to-rethink-mandate/article20942578/
17. "U.S. hedge funds strengthen ownership of Canadian papers," *Toronto Star*, October 7, 2014. URL: httpus://www.thestar.com/opinion/editorials/2014/10/07/us_hedge_funds_strengthen_ownership_of_canadian_papers_editorial.html
18. John Ivison, "Postmedia-Sun merger no longer unthinkable as newspaper industry struggles," *National Post*, October 7, 2014. URL: https://nationalpost.com/opinion/john-ivison-postmedia-sun-merger-no-longer-unthinkable-as-newspaper-industry-struggles
19. Ibid.
20. Competition Bureau, "Proposed acquisition of the English-language newspapers of Quebecor Media Inc. by Postmedia Network Inc.: Position Statement," Canada.ca, March 25, 2015. URL: https://ised-isde.canada.ca/site/competition-bureau-canada/en/how-we-foster-competition/education-and-outreach/position-statements/proposed-acquisition-english-language-newspapers-quebecor-media-inc-postmedia-network-inc
21. Ibid.
22. Ibid.
23. "Postmedia buys Sun Media for $316M," *Toronto Sun*, October 6, 2014. URL: https://torontosun.com/2014/10/06/postmedia-buys-sun-media-for-316m
24. Christine Dobby and James Bradshaw, "Competition Bureau clears

way for Postmedia to buy Sun Media papers," *Globe and Mail*, March 26, 2015. URL: https://www.theglobeandmail.com/report-on-business/competition-bureau-clears-postmedia-deal-for-sun-media-papers/article23610481/

25. John Shmuel, "Postmedia Network Canada Corp to integrate Sun Media properties this year: Godfrey," *National Post*, April 14, 2015. URL: https://financialpost.com/news/postmedia-to-integrate-sun-properties-this-year-godfrey

26. Competition Bureau, "The Competition Bureau's Work in Media Industries: Background for the Senate Committee on Transport and Communications," Competition Bureau, 2003. URL: http://www.competitionbureau.gc.ca/eic/site/cb-bc.nsf/eng/01985.html

27. Standing Senate Committee on Transportations and Communications, *Final report on the Canadian news media*, Vol. 1, 2006, p. 24. URL: https://sencanada.ca/Content/SEN/Committee/391/tran/rep/repfinjun-06vol1-e.pdf

28. Ibid., p. 63.

29. Ibid., p. 17.

30. Ibid., p. 24.

31. Competition Bureau, "The Competition Bureau's Work in Media Industries."

32. Marc Edge, "Public benefits or private? The case of the Canadian Media Research Consortium," *Canadian Journal of Communication 38*(1), pp. 5-34. URL: https://www.researchgate.net/publication/314392411_Public_Benefits_or_Private_The_Case_of_the_Canadian_Media_Research_Consortium

33. Tervita Corp. v. Canada. (Commissioner of Competition) (2015). SCC 3, [2015] 1 S.C.R. 161, January 22, p. 58. URL: https://scc-csc.lexum.com/scc-csc/scc-csc/en/item/14603/index.do

34. W. Michael G. Osborne, "Efficiencies Save Landfill Merger, Supreme Court Rules," The Litigator, February 18, 2015. URL: http://www.thelitigator.ca/2015/02/efficiencies-save-landfill-merger-supreme-court-rules/

35. Peter A. Bryan, "A Rare Supreme Court Decision on Merger Review and The Potential Impacts for the Oil and Gas Industry," Canlii Connects, March 18, 2015. URL: https://canliiconnects.org/fr/commentaires/36416

36. Michelle Lally, Peter Franklyn, Peter Glossop, Christopher Naudie, and Shuli Rodal, "Supreme Court of Canada's Tervita decision provides important guidance on Canada's merger laws," Osler Update, January 30, 2015. URL: https://www.osler.com/en/resources/regulations/2015/supreme-court-of-canada-s-tervita-decision-provide

37. Roger Ware and Ralph A. Winter, "Merger efficiencies in Canada: Lessons for the integration of economics into antitrust Law," *The Antitrust Bulletin 61*(3), 2006, p. 367. URL: https://journals.sagepub.com/doi/abs/10.1177/0003603X16657216?journalCode=abxa

38. John Pecman, "Remarks by John Pecman, Commissioner of Competition: Speech to Bennett Jones LLP, Toronto, Ontario," Competition Bureau, February 17, 2015. URL: http://www.competitionbureau.gc.ca/eic/site/cb-bc.nsf/eng/03873.html

39. Thomas Ross, "The Evolution of Competition Law in Canada," *Review of Industrial Organization 13*, 1998, p. 1. URL: https://www.jstor.

org/stable/41798790

40. Paul S. Crampton, "The Treatment of Efficiency Gains in Canadian Merger Analysis." In Organization for Economic Co-operating and Development, *Competition Policy and Efficiency Claims in Horizontal Agreements*. Paris: OECD, 1995, p. 59. URL: https://www.oecd.org/competition/mergers/2379526.pdf

41. Ibid., p. 64.

42. Ibid., p. 60.

43. Canada, *The Uncertain Mirror: Report of the Special Senate Committee on Mass Media*, Vol. I, 1970. Ottawa: Information Canada, p. 80.

44. Toby D. Couture, "Without Favour: The Concentration of Ownership in New Brunswick's Print Media Industry," *Canadian Journal of Communication* 38(1), 2013, pp. 57-81. URL: https://cjc.utpjournals.press/doi/full/10.22230/cjc.2013v38n1a2578

45. M. T. MacCrimmon, "Controlling Anticompetitive Behavior in Canada: A Contrast to the United States," *Osgoode Hall Law Journal* 21(4), 1983, p. 590. URL: https://digitalcommons.osgoode.yorku.ca/ohlj/vol21/iss4/1/

46. Ian Austen, "The case against the media giants," *Maclean's*, October 3, 1983, p. 40. URL: https://archive.macleans.ca/article/1983/10/3/the-case-against-the-media-giants

47. Ian Austen, "An acquittal for the press lords," *Maclean's*, December 19, 1983, p. 34. URL: https://archive.macleans.ca/article/1983/12/19/an-acquittal-for-the-press-lords

48. See Marc Edge, *Pacific Press: The Unauthorized Story of Vancouver's Newspaper Monopoly*. Vancouver: New Star Books, 2001. URL: http://www.marcedge.com/pacpress.pdf

49. Competition Bureau, "The Competition Bureau's Work in Media Industries."

50. Christine Dobby, "Sun Media sells 74 community newspapers to Transcontinental for $75-million," *National Post*, December 5, 2013. URL: https://financialpost.com/technology/sun-media-transcontinental-quebec

51. Linda Nguyen, "Transcontinental will try to sell 34 newspapers for approval in Sun Media deal," *Canadian Business*, May 28, 2014. URL: https://archive.canadianbusiness.com/business-news/coming-soon-cbs-new-website-is-launching-this-week/

52. Bertrand Marotte, "Transcontinental ending publication of 20 Quebec weekly newspapers," *Globe and Mail*, September 3, 2014. URL: https://www.theglobeandmail.com/report-on-business/transcontinental-to-end-publication-of-20-weekly-newspapers-in-quebec/article20319966/

53. Budget Plan, "Equality + Growth," Canada.ca, p. 184. URL: https://www.budget.canada.ca/2018/docs/plan/budget-2018-en.pdf

54. Stuart Thomson, "'Band-Aid solution': Ottawa sets aside $50 million to support local journalism," *National Post*, February 27, 2018. URL: https://nationalpost.com/news/politics/band-aid-solution-ottawa-sets-aside-50-million-to-support-local-journalism

55. Bob Cox, "Local news receives minnow's share of funding in federal budget," *Winnipeg Free Press*, March 3, 2018, p. A13. URL: https://www.winnipegfreepress.com/opinion/analysis/2018/03/03/local-news-receives-

minnows-share-of-funding-in-federal-budget

56. Thomson, "'Band-Aid solution.'"
57. Susan Krashinsky Robertson, "Budget media provisions disappointing, industry says," *Globe and Mail*, March 1, 2018, p. B3. URL: https://www.theglobeandmail.com/report-on-business/budget-media-provisions-disappointing-industry-says/article38157515/
58. Ibid.
59. Ibid.
60. "PM's plan to boost local journalism," CBC On the Money, February 28, 2018. URL: https://twitter.com/i/status/968974263758696448
61. Ibid.
62. Bruce Campion-Smith, "Budget falls short, media advocates say," *Toronto Star*, February 28, 2018, p. A12. URL: https://www.thestar.com/news/canada/2018/02/27/federal-budget-fails-to-provide-real-help-to-canadian-media-industry-officials-warn.html
63. Karen K. Ho and Mathew Ingram, "Canada pledges $50 million to local journalism. Will it help?" *Columbia Journalism Review*, February 28, 2018. URL: https://www.cjr.org/business_of_news/canada-journalism-fund-torstar-postmedia.php
64. Andrew Coyne, "We don't get the money, but some do," *National Post*, March 3, 2018, p. A10. URL: https://nationalpost.com/opinion/andrew-coyne-the-good-news-is-we-dont-get-the-50m-the-bad-news-is-someone-else-does
65. Sarah Scire, "In Canada, a government program to support local news tries to determine who's most deserving," NiemanLab, May 8, 2020. URL: https://www.niemanlab.org/2020/05/in-canada-a-government-program-to-support-local-news-tries-to-determine-whos-most-deserving/
66. Krashinsky Robertson, "Torstar, Postmedia talked job cuts before deal."
67. Ibid.
68. Canada, Competition Act, 1985, p. 54. URL: https://laws.justice.gc.ca/PDF/C-34.pdf
69. Krashinsky Robertson, "Torstar, Postmedia talked job cuts before deal."
70. Ibid.
71. Ibid.
72. Ibid.
73. Ibid.
74. Susan Krashinsky Robertson, "Watchdog forges ahead with Torstar, Postmedia probe as pursuit of merger provisions questioned," *Globe and Mail*, March 16, 2018, p. B1. URL: https://www.theglobeandmail.com/report-on-business/as-watchdog-forges-ahead-with-torstar-postmedia-probe-pursuit-of-merger-provisions-questioned/article38294249/
75. "CWA Canada hails Competition Bureau raid of Postmedia-Torstar, says feds should block newspaper swap deals," CWA Canada, March 14, 2018. URL: https://cwacanada.ca/2018/03/14/cwa-canada-hails-competition-bureau-raid-of-postmedia-torstar-says-feds-should-block-newspaper-swap-deals/
76. David Milstead, "Torstar, Postmedia and the arrogance of the deal," *Globe and Mail*, March 23, 2018, p. B4. URL: https://www.theglobeand-

mail.com/report-on-business/rob-commentary/torstar-postmedia-and-the-arrogance-of-the-deal/article38336159/

77. Ibid.

78. Vanessa Lu, "Executive from National Enquirer parent joins Postmedia board," *Toronto Star*, October 19, 2016. URL: https://www.thestar.com/business/2016/10/19/executive-from-national-enquirer-parent-joins-postmedia-board.html

79. Milstead, "Torstar, Postmedia and the arrogance of the deal."

80. Nicole Hong, "David Pecker, CEO of National Enquirer Publisher, Granted Immunity in Michael Cohen Case," *Wall Street Journal*, August 24, 2018. URL: https://www.wsj.com/articles/pecker-granted-immunity-in-cohen-case-1535041976?mod=e2tw

81. Gerry Smith, "David Pecker Exits Postmedia Board Following Cohen Controversy," BNN Bloomberg, August 28, 2018. URL: https://www.BNN Bloomberg.ca/david-pecker-exits-postmedia-board-following-cohen-controversy-1.1129976

82. John Honderich, "Where is Ottawa's help for Canada's newspapers?" *Toronto Star*, October 9, 2018. URL: https://www.thestar.com/news/canada/2018/10/09/where-is-ottawas-help-for-canadas-newspapers.html

83. John Honderich, "Media and Canadian democracy deserve better than studied indifference," *Hamilton Spectator*, January 27, 2018. URL: https://www.thespec.com/opinion/contributors/2018/01/27/media-and-canadian-democracy-deserve-better-than-studied-indifference.html

84. Ibid.

85. Ibid.

86. Bruce Campion-Smith, "Upcoming federal budget could contain measures to help Canada's ailing media organizations but how much help and how it might be delivered remain a question mark," *Toronto Star*, February 13, 2018. URL: https://www.thestar.com/news/canada/2018/02/09/ottawa-weighs-financial-help-for-canadian-media.html

87. Ibid.

88. Andrew Coyne, "Newspaper owners shamelessly pleading for cash only make bailouts look worse," *National Post* February 15, 2018. URL: https://nationalpost.com/opinion/andrew-coyne-newspaper-owners-shamelessly-pleading-for-cash-only-makes-bailouts-look-worse

89. Ibid.

90. Emily Jackson, "Postmedia to close six community newspapers," *Ottawa Citizen*, June 27, 2018, p. B8. URL: https://nationalpost.com/news/national/postmedia-to-close-six-community-newspapers-offers-buyouts-to-editorial-staff

91. "Press Hired Liberal Lobbyist," Blacklock's Reporter, August 28, 2019. URL: https://www.blacklocks.ca/press-hired-liberal-lobbyist/

92. Jason Kirby, "Behind closed doors: The 12 most powerful lobbyists in Ottawa," *Maclean's*, November 23, 2014. URL: https://www.macleans.ca/news/canada/behind-closed-doors-the-12-most-powerful-lobbyists-in-ottawa/

93. Susan Krashinsky Robertson, "Paul Godfrey steps down as Postmedia CEO, will remain executive chair," *Globe and Mail*, January 10, 2019. URL: https://www.theglobeandmail.com/business/article-paul-godfrey-steps-

down-as-postmedia-ceo-will-remain-executive-chair/
94. Derek Abma, "Newspapers seek federal help, major lobbying push made in recent months," *Hill Times*, October 10, 2016. URL: https://www.hilltimes.com/2016/10/10/newspapers-seek-federal-help-major-lobbying-push-made-recent-months/83145
95. "Press Hired Liberal Lobbyist."
96. "Local News & Democracy," Public Policy Forum, undated. URL: https://ppforum.ca/project/local-news-democracy/
97. Christine Schmidt, "Democracy is cracking and platforms are no help. What can we do about it? Some policy suggestions," NiemanLab, August 15, 2018. URL: https://www.niemanlab.org/2018/08/democracy-is-cracking-platforms-are-no-help-what-can-we-do-about-it-some-policy-suggestions/
98. Terry Pedwell, "Local news cut in half, not-for-profit funding models emerging, reports say," *Globe and Mail*, September 25, 2018. URL: https://www.theglobeandmail.com/canada/article-local-news-cut-in-half-not-for-profit-funding-models-emerging-2/
99. Ibid.
100. Daniel Leblanc, "Media sector gets $595-million package in Ottawa's fiscal update," *Globe and Mail*, November 21, 2018. URL: https://www.theglobeandmail.com/politics/article-media-sector-gets-595-million-package-in-ottawas-fiscal-update/
101. Ibid.
102. Alan Freeman, "Canada plans hefty aid package for its struggling media sector. Not everyone is pleased," *Washington Post*, November 28, 2018. URL: https://www.washingtonpost.com/world/2018/11/28/canada-plans-hefty-aid-package-its-struggling-media-sector-not-everyone-is-pleased/
103. Thomas Walkom, "Ottawa tiptoeing through a minefield with media subsidies," *Hamilton Spectator*, November 27, 2018, p. A11. URL: https://www.thespec.com/opinion/contributors/2018/11/26/ottawa-tiptoeing-through-a-minefield-with-media-subsidies.html
104. John Miller, "Let's boycott THIS," [blog] The Journalism Doctor, May 1, 2019. URL: http://www.thejournalismdoctor.ca/Blog.php/let-s-boycott-this
105. Andrew Coyne, "Liberals' $600M aid package for news media will irrevocably politicize the press," *National Post*, November 23, 2018. URL: https://nationalpost.com/opinion/andrew-coyne-liberals-600m-aid-package-for-news-media-will-irrevocably-politicize-the-press
106. Ibid.
107. Ibid.
108. Stuart Thomson, "Ottawa's $600M in funding for media 'a turning point,'" *National Post*, November 22, 2018, p. A5. URL: https://nationalpost.com/news/politics/600m-in-federal-funding-for-media-a-turning-point-in-the-plight-of-newspapers-in-canada
109. Tim Bousquet, "Postmedia CEO Paul Godfrey was paid $5 million in 2018, but says his company is so broke it needs public subsidies," Halifax Examiner, November 28, 2018. URL: https://www.halifaxexaminer.ca/featured/postmedia-ceo-paul-godfrey-was-paid-5-million-in-2018-but-says-his-

company-is-so-broke-it-needs-public-subsidies/

110. Krashinsky Robertson, "Paul Godfrey steps down as Postmedia CEO."

CHAPTER 5 — A CERTAIN SAMENESS

1. Ian Gill, "Paper Thin: Deathwatch for Alberta's big-city newspapers," Alberta Views, March 1, 2017. URL: https://albertaviews.ca/paper-thin/

2. Margaret Ormrod, personal communication, December 4, 2019.

3. "The path of an E-PETITION," Ourcommons.ca, undated. URL: https://petitions.ourcommons.ca/Documents/poster-e.pdf

4. Marc Edge, "How to solve Canada's biggest media problem in one easy step," J-Source.ca, March 12, 2019. URL: https://j-source.ca/how-to-fix-canadas-biggest-media-problem-in-one-easy-step/

5. Margaret Ormrod, "Petition to the House of Commons in Parliament assembled [petition No. e-2464]," Ourcommons.ca, March 18, 2020. URL: https://petitions.ourcommons.ca/en/Petition/Details?Petition=e-2464

6. Ibid.

7. Ibid.

8. Margaret Ormrod, personal communication, December 5, 2019.

9. MaggieMay, "#MEDIAPETITION Ready for your signature [tweet]," Twitter.com, March 18, 2020. URL: https://twitter.com/CailinasEirinn/status/1240385389031907328

10. Janet Greaves, "Signed [Twitter reply]," Twitter.com, March 18, 2020. URL: https://twitter.com/2jehan/status/1240429626083680256

11. "Ed the Sock," Wikipedia, undated. URL: https://en.wikipedia.org/wiki/Ed_the_Sock

12. Ed the Sock, "You have my unwavering support [Twitter reply]," Twitter.com, March 18, 2020. URL:. https://twitter.com/EdtheSock/status/1240420698943864841

13. Disinfect Democracy - Humanity depends on it, "Signed earlier [Twitter reply]," Twitter.com, March 19, 2020. URL: https://twitter.com/signsaresaying/status/1240544443603746817

14. "Petition On Media E-2464," Hedy Fry.com, June 17, 2020. URL: https://www.hedyfry.com/2020/06/17/petition-on-media-e-2464/

15. "Government Responses to Petitions," Ourcommons.ca, undated. URL: https://petitions.ourcommons.ca/en/Home/AboutContent?guide=PIElectronicGuide

16. Nic Newman, *Journalism, Media, and Technology Trends and Predictions*. Oxford, UK: Reuters Institute for the Study of Journalism, 2022. URL: https://reutersinstitute.politics.ox.ac.uk/sites/default/files/2022-01/Newman%20-%20Trends%20and%20Predictions%202022%20FINAL.pdf

17. "2022 Edelman Trust Barometer: Trust in Canada," Edelman Canada, 2022. URL: https://www.edelman.ca/trust-barometer/2022-edelman-trust-barometer-trust-canada

18. Bruce Anderson and David Coletto, "Millions of Canadians Lack Trust in Government and News Media," Abacus Data, June 8, 2022. URL: https://abacusdata.ca/trust-and-disinformation-in-canada/

19. See Marc Edge, *Asper Nation: Canada's Most Dangerous Media Company*. Vancouver: New Star Books, 2007. URL: http://www.marcedge.com/Asper_Nation_3W.pdf

20. Paula Simons, "And yes. Before you ask, this was a decision made by the owners of the paper," Twitter, October 15, 2015. Available online at https://twitter.com/paulatics/status/655006911117393921

21. Sean Craig, "Postmedia Told Edmonton Journal to Endorse Jim Prentice, Says Edmonton Journal," Canadaland, May 4, 2015. URL: http://canadalandshow.com/article/postmedia-told-edmonton-journal-endorse-jim-prentice-says-edmonton-journal

22. James Bradshaw, "Andrew Coyne exits editor role at National Post over endorsement," *Globe and Mail*, October 20, 2015. URL: https://www.theglobeandmail.com/report-on-business/andrew-coyne-exits-editor-role-at-national-post-will-remain-columnist/article26868832/

23. John Honderich, "Postmedia let down readers by dictating election endorsements," *Toronto Star*, November 9, 2015. URL: https://www.thestar.com/opinion/commentary/2015/11/09/postmedia-let-down-readers-by-dictating-election-endorsements-honderich.html

24. Ibid.

25. Geoff Olson, "Strange days: Playboy gets clean, Postmedia gets dirty, Parliament gets new PM," *Vancouver Courier*, October 20, 2015. URL: http://www.vancourier.com/opinion/strange-days-playboy-gets-clean-postmedia-gets-dirty-parliament-gets-new-pm-1.2091169#sthash.qJErdaCp.dpuf

26. Bradshaw, "Andrew Coyne exits editor role."

27. Ibid.

28. Ethan Cox, "Margaret Atwood vs. the National Post," Ricochet, August 22, 2015. URL: https://ricochet.media/en/557/margaret-atwood-vs-the-national-post

29. Jennifer Pagliaro, "Margaret Atwood's column criticizing Stephen Harper vanishes, then returns to, National Post website," *Toronto Star*, August 21, 2015. URL: https://www.thestar.com/news/gta/2015/08/21/margaret-atwoods-column-criticizing-stephen-harper-vanishes-from-national-post-website.html

30. Sarmishta Subramanian, "The new worry about the next election: your daily news," *Maclean's*, August 6, 2019. URL: https://www.macleans.ca/politics/ottawa/the-new-worry-about-the-next-election-your-daily-news/

31. Ibid.
32. Ibid.
33. Ibid.
34. Ibid.

35. Sean Craig, "You Must Be This Conservative to Ride: The Inside Story of Postmedia's Right Turn," Canadaland, August 12, 2019. URL: https://www.canadalandshow.com/the-conservative-transformation-of-postmedia/

36. Ibid.
37. Ibid.
38. Ibid.
39. Ibid.
40. Ibid.
41. Ibid.

42. "Andrew Potter, outgoing Ottawa Citizen editor in chief, watching industry with 'trepidation,'" CBC News, January 15, 2016. URL: https://www.cbc.ca/news/canada/ottawa/andrew-potter-ottawa-citizen-editor-1.3405131

43. "Postmedia cuts: Edmonton Journal, Sun dismiss top editors," CBC News, January 19, 2016. URL: https://www.cbc.ca/news/canada/edmonton/postmedia-cuts-edmonton-journal-sun-dismiss-top-editors-1.3410452

44. David Climenhaga, "Can one newsroom plus one editor add up to two newspapers? That's Postmedia's story and they're stickin' to it! [blog]," Alberta Politics, January 20, 2016. URL: https://albertapolitics.ca/2016/01/can-one-newsroom-plus-one-editor-add-up-to-two-newspapers-thats-postmedias-story-and-theyre-stickin-to-it/

45. "Message to readers," *Calgary Herald*, August 3, 2019, p. A2. URL: https://www.pressreader.com/canada/calgary-herald/20190803/281573767312122

46. "Calgary Herald Retracts Licia Corbella's Columns Promoting Jason Kenney's 2017 UCP Leadership Bid," PressProgress, August 12, 2019. URL: https://pressprogress.ca/calgary-herald-retracts-licia-corbellas-columns-promoting-jason-kenneys-2017-ucp-leadership-bid/

47. Martin Patriquin, "The 'Prince of Darkness' is back in the Liberal fold," *Maclean's*, April 10, 2009. URL: https://www.macleans.ca/news/canada/the-prince-of-darkness-is-back-in-the-liberal-fold/

48. Warren Kinsella, "Dishonest Trudeau campaign against Scheer must stop," *Toronto Sun*, May 29, 2019. URL: https://torontosun.com/opinion/columnists/kinsella-dishonest-trudeau-campaign-against-scheer-must-stop

49. Warren Kinsella, "Trudeau searching for an enemy to demonize," *Toronto Sun*, June 15, 2019. URL: https://torontosun.com/opinion/columnists/kinsella-trudeau-searching-for-an-enemy-to-demonize

50. Bill Curry and Tom Cardoso, "Kinsella firm hired to 'seek and destroy' Bernier's People's Party, documents show," *Globe and Mail*, October 18, 2019. URL: https://www.theglobeandmail.com/politics/article-kinsella-firm-hired-to-seek-and-destroy-berniers-peoples-party/; Jeff Yates, Kaleigh Rogers, and Andrea Bellemare, "Kinsella consulting firm worked to 'seek and destroy' Bernier's PPC party, documents say," CBC News, October 18, 2019. URL: https://www.cbc.ca/news/politics/project-cactus-maxime-bernier-1.5327555

51. Jonathan Goldsbie, "Kinsella, Postmedia, and the Paid Campaign to 'Seek and Destroy,'" Canadaland, October 21, 2019. URL: https://www.canadaland.com/warren-kinsella-postmedia-seek-and-destroy-ppc/

52. Ibid.

53. Bill Curry, "Maxime Bernier ordered to pay $132,000 in legal costs after failed defamation case over Project Cactus," *Globe and Mail*, March 14, 2022. URL: https://www.theglobeandmail.com/politics/article-maxime-bernier-ordered-to-pay-132000-in-legal-costs-after-failed/

54. Jonathan Goldsbie, "Sun Hires Conservative Operative With No Journalism Experience As New Editor-in-Chief," Canadaland, March 29, 2019. URL: https://www.canadaland.com/mark-towhey-hired-by-sun/

55. James Keller, "Postmedia hires former Kenney chief of staff Nick

Koolsbergen to lobby Alberta for role in 'energy war room,'" *Globe and Mail*, May 17, 2019. URL: https://www.theglobeandmail.com/canada/alberta/article-postmedia-hires-former-kenney-chief-of-staff-nick-koolsbergen-to-lobby/

56. Michelle Bellefontaine, "Postmedia hires former Kenney chief of staff to lobby on 'energy war room,'" CBC News, May 17, 2019. URL: https://www.cbc.ca/news/canada/edmonton/postmedia-hires-lobbyist-alberta-government-war-room-1.5140631

57. Ibid.

58. Keller, "Postmedia hires former Kenney chief of staff."

59. "Introducing Postmedia Content Works," Postmedia, November 4, 2015. URL: https://www.postmedia.com/2015/11/04/introducing-postmedia-content-works/

60. Jill Abramson, *Merchants of Truth: The Business of News and the Fight for Facts*. New York: Simon & Schuster, 2019, p. 71.

61. Jesse Brown, "Leaked memo confirms that Globe and Mail wants journalists to write advertorials," Canadaland, June 10, 2014. URL: https://www.canadaland.com/leaked-memo-confirms-globe-and-mail-wants-journalists-write-advertorials/

62. "Introducing Postmedia Content Works."

63. Ibid.

64. "A Holistic Approach," *Editor & Publisher*, March 2016, p. 11

65. Erin E. Schauster, Patrick Ferrucci, and Marlene S. Neill, "Native advertising is the new journalism: How deception affects social responsibility," *American Behavioral Scientist* 60(12), 2016, p. 1408.

66. Ibid.

67. Hajer Labidi, "Native Advertising: Information or Illusion," Union des Consommateurs, June 2018, p. 6. URL: https://uniondesconsommateurs.ca/wp-content/uploads/2020/12/2018-Publicite_native-Eng.pdf

68. Ibid., p. 7.

69. Ibid., p. 118.

70. Jared Lindzon, "How Canada is cracking down on offshore tax evasion and aggressive tax avoidance," *Ottawa Citizen*, March 3, 2017. URL: https://ottawacitizen.com/news/national/how-canada-is-cracking-down-on-offshore-tax-evasion-and-aggressive-tax-avoidance/wcm/29d8089a-c1b1-4703-9855-d328fa730b8b/amp/

71. Jared Lindzon, "How the CRA's Criminal Investigations Program brings tax cheats to justice," *Calgary Herald*, February 14, 2017. URL: https://calgaryherald.com/news/how-the-cras-criminal-investigations-program-brings-tax-cheats-to-justice/wcm/c255435a-f6ea-48ed-8740-405e81f44c78/amp/

72. Hon. Percy E. Downe, "Online Streaming Bill," Debates of the Senate (Hansard), September 27, 2022. URL: https://sencanada.ca/en/content/sen/chamber/441/debates/063db_2022-09-27-e#61

73. "The Best Media Coverage the Canada Revenue Agency Can Buy [press release]," Senate of Canada, November 9, 2017. URL: http://sen.parl.gc.ca/pdowne/english/Communications/News_Releases/The_Best_Media_Coverage_the_Canada_Revenue_Agency_Can_Buy.htm

74. Senator Percy Downe, "Finally CRA obeys the law," *Hill Times*, March 26, 2018. URL: https://www.hilltimes.com/2018/03/26/finally-cra-obeys-law/138306

75. Vanessa Gordon, "Copy of CAPP - Postmedia Board Presentation – Highlights," Prezi.com, July 10, 2013. URL: https://prezi.com/8zap67vqchv5/copy-of-capp-postmedia-board-presentation-highlights/

76. Jenny Uechi and Matthew Millar, "Presentation suggests intimate relationship between Postmedia and oil industry," Vancouver Observer, February 5, 2014. URL: https://www.vancouverobserver.com/news/postmedia-prezi-reveals-intimate-relationship-oil-industry-lays-de-souza.html

77. Ibid.

78. See Kian Malekanian, "Postmedia's History of Climate Change Denial," North99, January 27, 2020. URL: https://north99.org/2020/01/27/postmedias-history-of-climate-change-denial/; Robert Hackett and Hanna Araza, "The Oil Blotter: Postmedia & Big Oil's symbiosis," *The Monitor*, May 1, 2021. URL: https://monitormag.ca/articles/the-oil-blotter-postmedia-big-oils-symbiosis; Sean Holman, "Will Postmedia Face a Reckoning for Its Climate Coverage?" The Tyee, July 15, 2021. URL: https://thetyee.ca/Analysis/2021/07/15/Will-Postmedia-Face-Reckoning-For-Its-Climate-Coverage/; Sean Holman, "At the Gate of Disaster: A Case Study on the Promotion of Climate Science Rejectionism by Mainstream News Outlets and E-Commerce Companies," *Facts and Frictions* 1(2), 2022. URL: https://factsandfrictions.j-schoolscanada.ca/wp-content/uploads/2022/03/Holman.pdf

79. Rafe Mair, "Canada's biggest newspaper chain sold its soul to oil and gas [blog]," The Common Sense Canadian, October 26, 2015. URL: https://commonsensecanadian.ca/rafe-canadas-biggest-newspaper-chain-sold-soul-oil-gas/

80. Le Blogue Broadbent, "The slippery reach of Big Oil's PR machine [blog]," Broadbent Institute, February 5, 2014. URL: https://www.institut-broadbent.ca/the_slippery_reach_of_big_oil_s_pr_machine

81. "Canada's Oil Sands Innovation Alliance: Collaboration for the environment," *National Post*, March 7, 2014. URL: https://financialpost.com/commodities/energy/a-joint-venture-with-capp-canadas-oil-sands-innovation-alliance-collaboration-for-the-environment?r

82. Carol Linnitt, "Postmedia Gets Away With Running Unmarked Oil Advertorials," The Narwhal, June 20, 2014. URL: https://thenarwhal.ca/postmedia-gets-away-running-unmarked-oil-advertorials/

83. "The way forward for oil and gas," *National Post*, December 17, 2013. URL: https://financialpost.com/commodities/energy/a-joint-venture-with-capp-the-way-forward-for-oil-and-gas

84. Ibid.

85. Linnitt, "Postmedia Gets Away With Running Unmarked Oil Advertorials."

86. Ibid.

87. "Friends of Science," Wikipedia, undated. URL: https://en.wikipedia.org/wiki/Friends_of_Science

88. "Postmedia pulls story sponsored by group that believes climate change is caused by sunshine," PressProgress, April 21, 2016. URL: https://

pressprogress.ca/postmedia_pulls_story_sponsored_by_group_that_claims_climate_change_is_caused_by_sunshine/

89. Ibid.

90. Mike De Souza, "Oil firm kick-started university skeptic fund," *Ottawa Citizen*, September 14, 2011, p. A3. URL: https://mikedesouza.com/2012/12/07/talisman-energy-kick-started-university-of-calgary-climate-skeptic-fund/

91. Ibid.

92. See Regan Boychuk, "Proximity to Power: The oilpatch & Alberta's major dailies," Capital as Power, January 10, 2023. URL: https://capitalaspower.com/2023/01/proximity-to-power-the-oilpatch-albertas-major-dailies/

93. Tamara Baluja, "Postmedia Eliminates Parliamentary Bureau," J-source, February 4, 2014. URL: https://j-source.ca/updated-postmedia-eliminates-parliamentary-bureau/

94. Arik Ligeti, "Mike De Souza joining The Narwhal as managing editor," The Narwhal, May 11, 2021. URL: https://thenarwhal.ca/mike-de-souza-managing-editor/

95. Vivian Krause, "The cash pipeline opposing Canadian oil pipelines," *National Post*, October 3, 2016. URL: https://financialpost.com/opinion/vivian-krause-the-cash-pipeline-opposing-canadian-oil-pipelines?r

96. "Michael De Souza vs National Post," National NewsMedia Council, December 1, 2016. URL: https://mediacouncil.ca/wp-content/uploads/2015/09/2016-68-De-Souza-vs-National-Post-decision-release-1.pdf

97. Linnitt, "Postmedia Gets Away With Running Unmarked Oil Advertorials."

98. "Disguised Advertising Techniques," The Canadian Code of Advertising Standards, undated. URL: https://adstandards.ca/code/the-code-online/

99. Linnitt, "Postmedia Gets Away With Running Unmarked Oil Advertorials."

100. Rafe Mair, *Politically Incorrect: How Canada Lost Its Way and The Simple Path Home*. Comox, BC: Watershed Sentinel Books, 2017, p. 152. URL: https://thetyee.ca/Opinion/2017/11/14/mair-media-unholiest-alliances/

101. Ibid.

102. Ian Austen, "Political Cartoon Taking Aim at Pipeline Company Is Pulled," *New York Times*, June 28, 2012. URL: https://archive.nytimes.com/mediadecoder.blogs.nytimes.com/2012/06/28/political-cartoon-taking-aim-at-pipeline-company-is-pulled/

103. "Cartoonist says Enbridge spoof pulled under pressure," CBC News, June 26, 2012. URL: https://www.cbc.ca/news/canada/british-columbia/cartoonist-says-enbridge-spoof-pulled-under-pressure-1.1267162

104. Bruce Livesey, "The tawdry fall of the Postmedia newspaper empire," National Observer, November 24, 2015. URL: https://www.nationalobserver.com/2015/11/24/news/tawdry-fall-postmedia-newspaper-empire

105. "University Affairs Media Partnership Strategy — Back to School 2020 [memo]," July 29, 2020. URL: https://s3.documentcloud.org/documents/20417852/ubc-postmedia-media-partnership.pdf

106. Ibid.

107. Shannon Kari, "Vancouver Papers Sold News Coverage To UBC, Documents Reveal," Canadaland, November 30, 2020. URL: https://

www.canadaland.com/vancouver-papers-sold-news-coverage-to-ubc-documents-reveal/

108. Charlotte Alden, "Postmedia denies publishing paid UBC op-eds as part of advertising deal," *The Ubyssey*, November 30, 2020. URL: https://www.ubyssey.ca/news/ubc-paid-postmedia-for-coverage/

109. Mark Hecht, "Ethnic diversity harms a country's social trust, economic well-being, argues professor," *Vancouver Sun*, September 6, 2019. URL: https://archive.is/ulGJ4#selection-1525.0-1549.27

110. Ibid.

111. Ibid.

112. "Americans and Social Trust: Who, Where and Why," Pew Research Center, February 22, 2007. URL: https://www.pewresearch.org/social-trends/2007/02/22/americans-and-social-trust-who-where-and-why/

113. "Gatestone Institute," Wikipedia, undated. URL: https://en.wikipedia.org/wiki/Gatestone_Institute

114. Hecht, "Ethnic diversity harms a country's social trust."

115. Ibid.

116. Nick Eagland, "That opinion piece is pathetic [tweet]," Twitter, September 6, 2019. URL: https://twitter.com/nickeagland/status/1170201065607725056

117. Rob Shaw, "What a complete pile of absolute garbage that op-ed is [tweet]," Twitter, September 6, 2019. URL: https://twitter.com/RobShaw_BC/status/1170206961020755968

118. Kim Bolan, "We were all in the newsroom working hard today [tweet]," Twitter, September 6, 2019. URL: https://twitter.com/kbolan/status/1170219267926548480

119. Kasari Govender, "Deeply disturbed to see today's call to hatred [tweet]," Twitter, September 6, 2019. URL: https://twitter.com/KasariGovender/status/1170397419365777408

120. Sarah Rieger, "Advocates condemn xenophobic op-ed by Calgary instructor calling for end to diversity," CBC News, September 7, 2019. URL: https://www.cbc.ca/news/canada/calgary/mark-hecht-vancouver-sun-op-ed-1.5274962

121. Harold Munro, "I agree and apologize to everyone [tweet]," Twitter, September 6, 2019. URL: https://twitter.com/haroldmunro/status/1170211112203079680

122. Harold Munro, "Apology to our readers," *Vancouver Sun*, September 7, 2019. URL: https://vancouversun.com/news/local-news/apology-to-our-readers

123. Ibid.

124. David Beers, "Revolt Grows in Vancouver Sun and Province Newsroom over Op-ed Policies," The Tyee, September 13, 2019. URL: https://thetyee.ca/News/2019/09/13/Vancouver-Sun-Province-Newsroom-Revolt-Grows-Over-Op-Ed-Policies/

125. Ibid.

126. Ibid.

127. Jagdeesh Mann, "Vancouver Sun's Editorial Standards the Real Danger to Social Trust," Canadaland, September 13, 2019. URL: https://www.canadaland.com/vancouver-sun-editorial-standards-the-real-dan-

ger-to-social-trust/

128. See Marc Edge, *Pacific Press: The Unauthorized Story of Vancouver's Newspaper Monopoly.* Vancouver: New Star Books, 2001.

129. Mann, "Vancouver Sun's Editorial Standards."

130. Stephen Smart, "There's a bigger issue behind the disgusting op-ed the Vancouver Sun published," Daily Hive, September 7 2019. URL: https://dailyhive.com/vancouver/vancouver-sun-op-ed-racist

131. Manisha Krishnan, "Vancouver Sun Op-ed Stacks Up Against Actual Nazi Propaganda," Vice, September 12, 2019. URL: https://www.vice.com/en/article/a35kdz/how-that-xenophobic-vancouver-sun-op-ed-stacks-up-against-actual-nazi-propaganda

132. Sarah Beuhler, "Fire the Opinions Editor at Vancouver Sun [petition]," Leadnow.ca. URL: https://you.leadnow.ca/petitions/fire-the-opinions-editor-at-vancouver-sun

133. Sean Holman, "That Sun Column Was No Outlier. Postmedia Has Embraced Dishonest, Dangerous Propaganda," The Tyee, September 9, 2019. URL: https://thetyee.ca/Mediacheck/2019/09/09/Postmedia-Has-Embraced-Dishonest-Dangerous-Propaganda/

134. Charlie Smith, "'Othering' minority communities sometimes helps media companies pay the bills," *Georgia Straight*, September 8, 2019. URL: https://www.straight.com/news/1296901/othering-minority-communities-sometimes-helps-media-companies-pay-bills

135. Fabian Dawson, "Fewer 'Eyes' in Newsrooms Leads to Blind Spots," New Canadian Media, September 9, 2019. URL: https://newcanadianmedia.ca/fewer-eyes-in-newsrooms/

136. Ibid.

137. Gordon Clark, "Cancel culture is doing terrible harm to journalists, journalism and citizenship," Medium, December 8, 2021. URL: https://gordonjclark.medium.com/cancel-culture-is-doing-terrible-harm-to-journalists-journalism-and-citizenship-e3e817db8390

138. Martin Collacott, "Canada replacing its population for no good reason," *Vancouver Sun*, June 5, 2017, p. A10.

139. Ibid.

140. Andrew Kurjata, "Breaking down why that Vancouver Sun op-ed is racist in its first two paragraphs," Medium.com, June 14, 2017. URL: https://medium.com/longer-than-a-tweet/breaking-down-why-that-vancouver-op-ed-is-racist-in-its-first-two-paragraphs-68a3ec95d5ec

141. Charlie Smith, "Postmedia editorial staff in Vancouver disavow published commentary criticizing diversity, tolerance, and inclusion," *Georgia Straight*, September 7, 2019. URL: https://www.straight.com/news/1296656/postmedia-editorial-staff-vancouver-disavow-published-commentary-criticizing-diversity

142. Davide Mastracci, "Postmedia Paper Deletes Article Boosting Great Replacement Theory," Passage.com, May 24, 2022. URL: https://readpassage.com/postmedia-paper-deletes-article-boosting-great-replacement-theory/

143. Collacott, "Canada replacing its population for no good reason." URL: https://web.archive.org/web/20170613004553/http://vancouversun.com/opinion/op-ed/opinion-canada-replacing-its-population-a-case-of-wilful-ignorance-greed-excess-political-correctness; https://www.pressreader

com/canada/vancouver-sun/20170605/281638190171755

144. Rex Murphy, "Canada is not a racist country, despite what the Liberals say," *National Post*, June 1, 2020. URL: https://nationalpost.com/opinion/rex-murphy-canada-is-not-a-racist-country-despite-what-the-liberals-say

145. Vanmala Subramaniam, "Before you declare Canada is not a racist country, do your homework," *National Post*, June 2, 2020. URL: https://nationalpost.com/opinion/vanmala-subramaniam-before-you-declare-canada-is-not-a-racist-country-do-your-homework

146. Murphy, "Canada is not a racist country."

147. Gabe Oatley, "The inside story of how five racialized reporters' anger over a Rex Murphy column led to the unionization of Canada's most conservative national daily newspaper," *Ryerson Review of Journalism*, July 1, 2022. URL: https://reviewofjournalism.ca/post-mortem/

148. Rex Murphy, "If our leaders won't stand against violence, they are unfit to lead," *National Post*, June 16, 2020. URL: https://nationalpost.com/opinion/rex-murphy-if-our-leaders-wont-stand-against-violence-they-are-unfit-to-lead

149. Conrad Black, "Two neighbours, not so much alike," *National Post*, June 20, 2020. URL: https://nationalpost.com/opinion/conrad-black-two-neighbours-not-so-much-alike

150. Oatley, "The inside story of how five racialized reporters' anger."

151. Ibid.

152. Ibid.

153. "Competition Bureau closes investigation of Postmedia and Torstar [press release]," Competition Bureau Canada, January 7, 2021. URL: https://www.canada.ca/en/competition-bureau/news/2021/01/competition-bureau-closes-investigation-of-postmedia-and-torstar.html

154. "Competition Bureau ends probe of Postmedia-Torstar newspaper swap," *National Post*, January 7, 2021. URL: https://financialpost.com/telecom/media/competition-bureau-ends-probe-of-postmedia-torstar-newspaper-swap

155. Bryan Carney, "E-mails Confirm Torstar and Postmedia Knew Both Planned Cuts after Big Swap," The Tyee, March 1, 2021. URL: https://thetyee.ca/News/2021/03/01/E-mails-Confirm-Torstar-Postmedia-Knew-Both-Planned-Cuts/

156. Julie Mouris and Gavin Murphy, "The Canadian Competition Authority Closes Its Investigation Into An Alleged Conspiracy by Large Media Companies," Concurrences, January 7, 2021. URL: https://www.concurrences.com/en/bulletin/news-issues/january-2021/the-canadian-competition-authority-closes-its-investigation-into-an-alleged

157. Julie Dabrusin, "Response by the Minister of Canadian Heritage [petition No. e-2464]," Ourcommons.ca, September 24, 2020. URL: https://petitions.ourcommons.ca/en/Petition/Details?Petition=e-2464#accordion1-collapse-item-21

CHAPTER 6 — SHAKING DOWN BIG TECH

1. "Congratulations to the winners of the 2012 CAJ Awards," CAJ.ca, May 4, 2013. URL: https://caj.ca/congratulations-to-the-winners-of-the-

2012-caj-awards/

2. Tim Bousquet, "Advertorial: An Unnecessary Evil," Tim Bousquet's Next Project, April 23, 2014. URL: https://timbousquethalifax.wordpress.com/2014/04/23/advertorial-an-unnecessary-evil/

3. "Local Business News Website allSaskatchewan.com Launches in Saskatchewan." Business Wire, July 19, 2021. URL: https://www.businesswire.com/news/home/20210719005073/en/Local-Business-News-Website-allSaskatchewan.com-Launches-in-Saskatchewan

4. Tim Bousquet, "'A tale of enormous suffering,'" Halifax Examiner, March 2, 2019. URL: https://www.halifaxexaminer.ca/uncategorized/a-tale-of-enormous-suffering/

5. "Q&A with Filkow Prize Winner Tim Bousquet," PEN Canada, June 11, 2019. URL: https://pencanada.ca/news/qa-with-filkow-prize-winner-tim-bousquet/

6. Tim Bousquet "Canadian Pravda: How the Chronicle Herald fails its readers. A case study," Halifax Examiner, November 4, 2014. URL: https://www.halifaxexaminer.ca/journalism/canadian-pravda-how-the-chronicle-herald-fails-its-readers-a-case-study/

7. "Investing in the Middle Class: Budget 2019," Canada.ca, March 19, 2019. URL: https://www.budget.canada.ca/2019/docs/plan/budget-2019-en.pdf

8. Ibid., p. 373.

9. Tim Bousquet, "The Trudeau government's tax subsidy for journalism puts the Halifax Examiner in an impossible situation," Halifax Examiner, March 22, 2019. URL: https://www.halifaxexaminer.ca/featured/the-trudeau-governments-tax-subsidy-for-journalism-puts-the-halifax-examiner-in-an-impossible-situation/#News

10. Ibid.

11. Ibid.

12. Ibid.

13. Lisa Taylor, "Journalists react to the details – and lack thereof – in Ottawa's news package," J-source, March 25, 2019. URL: https://j-source.ca/journalism-fund-tracker/

14. Erin Millar, "Liberals' journalism funding makes it harder to launch news startups," The Discourse, March 23, 2019. URL: https://thediscourse.ca/communities/journalism-funding-startups

15. Ibid.

16. David Skok, "Letter from the editor: Tilting the playing field," The Logic, March 23, 2019. URL: https://thelogic.co/opinion/letter-from-the-editor-tilting-the-playing-field/?lt=1

17. Ibid.

18. Ibid.

19. Andrew Coyne, "It's when you read details of media bailout that the chill sets in," *National Post*, March 21, 2019. URL: https://nationalpost.com/opinion/andrew-coyne-its-when-you-read-details-of-media-bailout-that-the-chill-sets-in

20. Ibid.

21. Skok, "Letter from the editor."

22. Jesse Brown, "Canada's Subsidy for News Backfires," Nieman-

Lab, undated. URL: https://www.niemanlab.org/2018/12/canadas-subsidy-for-news-backfires/

23. Ibid.

24. Heather Rollwagen and Ivor Shapiro, "As Ottawa helps the news industry, latest research suggests journalists' loyalties are tough to buy," The Conversation, March 20, 2019. URL: https://theconversation.com/as-ottawa-helps-the-news-industry-latest-research-suggests-journalists-loyalties-are-tough-to-buy-108998

25. Kathleen Speckert, "Statement on journalism measures in Budget 2019," Canadian Association of Journalists, March 19, 2019. URL: https://twitter.com/caj/status/1108161357235531778

26. Rachel Aiello, "Minister vows transparency over $600M media fund, defends inclusion of Unifor," CTV News, May 26, 2019. URL: https://www.ctvnews.ca/politics/minister-vows-transparency-over-600m-media-fund-defends-inclusion-of-unifor-1.4436796

27. "News Media Industry," Hansard, 42nd Parliament, 1st Session, May 31, 2019, p. 28345. URL: https://www.ourcommons.ca/DocumentViewer/en/42-1/house/sitting-424/hansard

28. Graeme Gordon, "Media bailout memo to Liberal minister completely redacted by government," The Post Millennial, October 28, 2019. URL: https://www.thepostmillennial.com/media-bailout-memo-to-liberal-minister-completely-redacted-by-government/

29. Chris Selley, "Liberals' media bailout puts foxes in charge of the chickens," *National Post*, May 22, 2019. URL: https://nationalpost.com/opinion/chris-selley-liberals-media-bailout-puts-foxes-in-charge-of-the-chickens

30. Ibid.

31. Tom Parry, "Journalists question Liberal government's $600M media bailout plan," CBC News, May 23, 2019. URL: https://www.cbc.ca/news/politics/journalists-question-media-bailout-1.5147761

32. Andrew Potter, "The government just made its toxic media bailout plan even worse," CBC News, May 24, 2019. URL: https://www.cbc.ca/news/opinion/media-bailout-1.5147053

33. Ibid.

34. "CAJ responds to journalism panel's recommendations," Canadian Association of Journalists, July 18, 2019. URL: https://caj.ca/blog/CAJ_statement_on_Journalism_Panel_recommendations

35. Ibid.

36. "Report of the Journalism and Written Media Independent Panel of Experts," July 16, 2019. URL: https://www.newswire.ca/news-releases/the-canadian-association-of-journalists-responds-to-journalism-panel-s-recommendations-872424032.html

37. Ibid.

38. Ibid.

39. Ibid.

40. "Independent Advisory Board on Eligibility for Journalism Tax Measures," Canada Revenue Agency, undated. URL: https://www.canada.ca/en/revenue-agency/services/tax/businesses/topics/corporations/business-tax-credits/qualified-canadian-journalism-organization/independent-ad-

visory-board-on-eligibility-for-journalism-tax-measures.html

41. Jonathan Goldsbie, "The low bar for accessing government news subsidies," Canadaland, April 4, 2022. URL: https://www.canadaland.com/colette-brin-qcjo-status/

42. "Government kicks off support of Canadian journalism organizations [press release]," Canada Revenue Agency, December 20, 2019. URL: https://www.canada.ca/en/revenue-agency/news/2019/12/government-kicks-off-support-of-canadian-journalism-organizations.html

43. Paul Willcocks, "Postmedia Expects at Least $8 Million in Taxpayer Subsidies," The Tyee, July 11, 2019. URL: https://thetyee.ca/Mediacheck/2019/07/11/Postmedia-Taxpayer-Subsidies/

44. Erin Millar, "How to save the news bailout," The Discourse, July 14, 2019. URL: https://thediscourse.ca/media/how-to-save-the-news-bailout

45. Ibid.

46. For further explanation, see Appendix, Marc Edge, *Greatly Exaggerated: The Myth of the Death of Newspapers.* Vancouver: New Star Books, 2014. URL: http://marcedge.com/Greatly_Exaggerated_5e.pdf

47. "2020 Annual Report," Postmedia Network. URL: https://www.postmedia.com/wp-content/uploads/2020/11/F2020-Corporate-Annual-Report-8.25x10.75-FINAL.pdf

48. Ibid.

49. "Postmedia cuts salaries, shutters 15 community newspapers," *Ottawa Citizen*, April 29, 2020, p. B1. URL: https://financialpost.com/telecom/media/postmedia-cuts-salaries-and-closes-15-community-papers-amid-covid-related-revenue-declines

50. Ibid.

51. Bree Rody, "As media layoffs continue, Canadian government appoints new board," Media in Canada, March 26, 2020. URL: https://mediaincanada.com/2020/03/26/as-media-layoffs-continue-canadian-government-appoints-new-board/

52. Sarah Petz and Peggy Lam, "Postmedia closing several Manitoba, Ontario newspapers due to falling ad sales," CBC News, April 28, 2020. URL: https://www.cbc.ca/news/canada/manitoba/postmedia-manitoba-papers-closing-1.5547793

53. Ben Waldman, "The small publisher who is still standing," *Winnipeg Free Press*, April 30, 2020. p. 8. URL: https://www.winnipegfreepress.com/business/2020/04/29/the-small-publisher-who-is-still-standing

54. Ben Waldman, "Extra! Extra! Carman, Altona have new papers," *Winnipeg Free Press*, May 27, 2020. p. 4. URL: https://www.winnipegfreepress.com/business/2020/05/27/extra-extra-carman-altona-have-new-papers

55. Aleksandra Sagan, "Postmedia to lay off dozens of employees," *Toronto Star*, May 28, 2020, p. B2. URL: https://www.thestar.com/business/2020/05/27/postmedia-to-lay-off-about-40-employees-after-unions-reject-salary-cuts.html

56. "Postmedia tells Unifor local of buyout, layoff plan to cut Vancouver salary expenses," *Medicine Hat News*, November 20, 2020, p. A5. URL: https://www.cochranetoday.ca/national-business/postmedia-tells-unifor-local-of-buyout-layoff-plan-to-cut-vancouver-salary-expenses-2894166

57. Greg Quill, "Who are Friends of Canadian Broadcasting?" *Ottawa*

Citizen, February 22, 1996, p. C10.

58. "Anti-Facebook posters popping up in T.O. in support of Cdn media," *Toronto Sun*, June 12, 2020. URL: https://torontosun.com/news/national/anti-facebook-posters-popping-up-in-t-o-in-support-of-cdn-media

59. Ibid.

60. Ibid.

61. Simon Houpt, "With an election looming, this group sees itself in a battle for Canada's soul – or at least its culture," *Globe and Mail*, August 19, 2019. URL: https://www.theglobeandmail.com/arts/article-foot-soldiers-and-friends-of-canadian-broadcasting/

62. Daniel Bernhard, "Facebook: Wanted for news theft," *Toronto Star*, June 4, 2020. URL: https://www.thestar.com/opinion/contributors/2020/06/04/facebook-wanted-for-news-theft.html

63. Ibid.

64. Richard Stursberg, *The Tangled Garden: A Canadian Cultural Manifesto for the Digital Age*. Toronto: James Lorimer & Co., 2019.

65. Ibid., p. 133.

66. Ibid., p. 161.

67. Ibid., p. 39.

68. Ibid., p. 135.

69. Marc Edge, "Starving Canadian media giants—a case of real fake news [book review]," *The Monitor* (Canadian Centre for Policy Alternatives), September/October 2019, p. 63.

70. John Gapper, "Murdoch will relish a battle over online pay walls," *Financial Times*, November 14, 2009, p. 9.

71. Steven Perlberg and Mark Di Stefano, "Rupert Murdoch is the media's unlikely hero in the war against Facebook and Google," Buzzfeed, October 4, 2017. URL: https://www.buzzfeednews.com/article/stevenperlberg/rupert-murdoch-is-the-medias-unlikely-hero-against-tech

72. Ibid.

73. Bernard Keane, "Media abandons balance in pursuit of Google's billions," Crikey, February 5, 2021. URL: https://www.crikey.com.au/2021/02/05/media-abandons-balance-google/

74. Zoe Samios, "News Corp formalises Google and Facebook deals, announces hiring spree," *Sydney Morning Herald*, May 10, 2021. URL: https://www.smh.com.au/business/companies/news-corp-formalises-google-and-facebook-deals-announces-hiring-spree-20210509-p57q8d.html

75. Bill Grueskin, "Australia pressured Google and Facebook to pay for journalism. Is America next?" *Columbia Journalism Review*, March 9, 2022. URL: https://www.cjr.org/business_of_news/australia-pressured-google-and-facebook-to-pay-for-journalism-is-america-next.php

76. Joanna Chiu, "Why Canada's media industry is in more danger than you think — and what we can do to save it," *Toronto Star*, November 9, 2020. URL: https://www.thestar.com/business/2020/11/09/why-canadas-media-industry-is-in-more-danger-than-you-think-and-what-we-can-do-to-save-it.html

77. Marc Edge, "Torstar...er, Nordstar going all-out for cash [blog entry]," Greatly Exaggerated, November 11, 2020. URL: http://greatlyexagerrated.blogspot.com/2020/11/torstar-er-nordstar-going-all-out-for.html

78. See Marc Edge, *Re-examining the UK Newspaper Industry*. London: Routledge, 2023.

79. Shannon Bond, "New York Times sees boom in online subscribers," *Financial Times*, February 6, 2018. URL: https://www.ft.com/content/bc312102-0cee-11e8-839d-41ca06376bf2

80. Anna Lewis, "Metered pay models comprise bulk of newspaper website pay models," University of Missouri, 2018. URL: https://journalism.missouri.edu/wp-content/uploads/2018/05/summary-paywall-research-anna-lewis-05-2018.pdf

81. Dwayne Winseck, "Growth of the network media economy in Canada, 1984-2017," Canadian Media Concentration Research Project, 2018. URL: http://www.cmcrp.org/wp-content/uploads/2019/01/The-Growth-of-the-Network-Media-Economy-1984-2017-01142019.pdf

82. Steve Ladurantaye, "Postmedia ramps up its paywall push," *Globe and Mail*, October 25, 2012. URL: https://www.theglobeandmail.com/globe-investor/postmedia-ramps-up-its-paywall-push/article4657129/

83. Broadcasting and Telecommunications Legislative Review, "Canada's Communications Future: Time to Act," Innovation, Science and Economic Development Canada, January 2020, p. 157. URL: https://ised-isde.canada.ca/site/broadcasting-telecommunications-legislative-review/sites/default/files/attachments/BTLR_Eng-V3.pdf

84. Ibid., p. 158.

85. Ibid.

86. Timothy Denton, "The BTLR report proposes to destroy what makes the internet free, popular and innovative and to make it resemble the Canadian broadcasting system," *National Post*, February 4, 2020. URL: https://financialpost.com/opinion/broadcasting-report-proposes-to-wreck-the-internet-with-insane-hubris-and-mad-regulatory-overreach

87. Ibid.

88. Chris Hannay, "Amid fears about report, Trudeau says Ottawa will not regulate news content," *Globe and Mail*, February 4, 2020, p. A4. URL: https://www.theglobeandmail.com/politics/article-amid-fears-of-report-trudeau-says-ottawa-will-not-regulate-news/

89. James McLeod, "Minister walks back talk of licensing media," *National Post*, February 4, 2020, p. FP1. URL: https://financialpost.com/telecom/media/minister-walks-back-talk-of-licensing-media-but-crtc-overhaul-plan-still-has-critics-worried

90. Barbara Shecter, "Throne speech gives 'most explicit' statement yet of plan to make tech giants pay their share," *National Post*, September 24, 2020. URL: https://financialpost.com/technology/throne-speech-gives-most-explicit-statement-yet-of-plan-to-make-tech-giants-pay-their-share

91. Bill Curry and Janice Dickson, "Broadcasting bill targets online streaming services," *Globe and Mail*, November 4, 2020, p. B1. URL: https://www.theglobeandmail.com/politics/article-ottawa-says-broadcasting-act-changes-will-raise-over-800-million-from/

92. "Levelling the Digital Playing Field," News Media Canada, October 19 2020, p. 5. URL: https://nmc-mic.ca/wp-content/uploads/2020/10/Levelling-the-Digital-Playing-Field-2020.10.19.pdf

93. Ibid., p. 10.

94. "Canadian Publishers Call for Canadian Government to Tackle Google/Facebook Monopoly [press release]," News Media Canada, October 22, 2020. URL: https://nmc-mic.ca/2020/10/21/canadian-publishers-call-for-canadian-government-to-tackle-google-facebook-monopoly/

95. Bruce Campion-Smith, "Canada's newspaper publishers call for a new regulatory regime to safeguard trusted journalism," *Toronto Star*, October 23, 2020. URL: https://www.thestar.com/opinion/public_editor/2020/10/23/canadas-newspaper-publishers-call-for-a-new-regulatory-regime-to-safeguard-trusted-journalism.html

96. Tony Wong, "How tech giants put squeeze on local news: Critics say tax loopholes leave Canadian media at disadvantage," *Toronto Star*, May 20, 2019, p. A1.

97. Jeff Elgie, "A note to the news media industry and government," LinkedIn, September 13, 2018. URL: https://www.linkedin.com/pulse/note-industry-government-jeff-elgie/

98. Ibid.

99. Ibid.

100. Susan Krashinsky Robertson, "Industry leaders applaud Ottawa's plan to subsidize media," *Globe and Mail*, November 22, 2018. URL: https://www.theglobeandmail.com/business/article-industry-leaders-applaud-ottawas-plan-to-subsidize-media/

101. Bob Cox, "Levelling the playing field for newspapers," *Victoria Times Colonist*, July 7, 2017. URL: https://www.timescolonist.com/opinion/bob-cox-levelling-the-playing-field-for-newspapers-4651504

102. "New Association Aims to Strengthen Independent Journalism in Canada [press release]," Press Forward, December 9, 2020. URL: https://www.newswire.ca/news-releases/new-association-aims-to-strengthen-independent-journalism-in-canada-824080155.html

103. Kayla Zhu, "Press Forward aims to give independent media a seat at the table," J-source.ca, December 18, 2020. URL: https://j-source.ca/press-forward-aims-to-give-independent-media-a-seat-at-the-table/

104. Rachel Gilmore, "A world without news: Papers publish blank front pages to highlight industry struggles," Global News, February 4, 2021. URL: https://globalnews.ca/news/7617779/canada-news-industry-newspapers-blank-struggles-journalism/

105. Josh Kolm, "Newspapers go blank to pressure Google and Facebook," Media in Canada, February 4, 2021. URL: https://mediaincanada.com/2021/02/04/newspapers-go-blank-to-pressure-google-and-facebook/

106. Jamie Irving, "Open Letter to Prime Minister Justin Trudeau," News Media Canada January 29, 2021. URL: https://www.levellingthedigitalplayingfield.ca/open_letter.html

107. Ibid.

108. Ibid.

109. Andrew Coyne, "What self-serving nonsense [tweet]," February 4, 2021. URL: https://twitter.com/acoyne/status/1357322298055929859

110. Andrew Coyne, "And they don't typically sell advertising [tweet]," February 4, 2021. URL: https://twitter.com/acoyne/status/1357323693169512448

111. Andrew Coyne, "Where does Google sell ads off our con-

tent? [tweet]," February 4, 2021. URL: https://twitter.com/acoyne/status/1357332192658087945

112. Andrew Coyne, "Meanwhile, what's the first thing [tweet]," February 4, 2021. URL: https://twitter.com/acoyne/status/1357333183679848450

113. Andrew Coyne, "The publishers' argument is so gaga [tweet]," February 4, 2021. URL: https://twitter.com/acoyne/status/1357333710736150528

114. Andrew Coyne, "Government-led shakedowns of Facebook and Google risk boosting fake news," *Globe and Mail*, September 18, 2020. URL: https://www.theglobeandmail.com/opinion/article-government-led-shakedowns-of-facebook-and-google-risk-boosting-fake/

115. Andrew Coyne, "Slowly but surely, the government is gathering the media into its ghastly embrace," *Globe and Mail*, April 3, 2021. URL: https://www.theglobeandmail.com/opinion/article-slowly-but-surely-the-government-is-gathering-the-media-into-its/

116. "Public Opinion and Experts Agree: The Time to Regulate Social Media Has Arrived [press release]," Public Policy Forum, January 27, 2021. URL: https://ppforum.ca/articles/announcing-the-findings-from-the-canadian-commission-on-democratic-expression-and-the-citizens-assembly-on-democratic-expression/

117. Ibid.

118. Ibid.

119. Bill Curry, "Report calls for powerful new federal body to regulate social media," *Globe and Mail*, January 27, 2021. URL: https://www.theglobeandmail.com/politics/article-report-calls-for-powerful-new-federal-body-to-regulate-social-media/

120. Carl Meyer, "Canada looks at Australia's experience regulating social media," *Toronto Star*, February 2, 2021. URL: https://www.thestar.com/news/canada/2021/02/02/canada-looks-at-australias-experience-regulating-social-media.html

121. Tyler Dawson, "Facebook to pay 14 Canadian media outlets for content, but deal excludes major publishers," *National Post*, May 25, 2021. URL: https://nationalpost.com/news/facebook-to-pay-14-canadian-media-outlets-for-content-but-deal-excludes-major-publishers

122. Anja Karadeglija, "Six more Canadian publishers make deals with Google," *National Post*, June 24, 2021, p. A15. URL: https://nationalpost.com/news/politics/six-more-canadian-publishers-make-deals-with-google-talks-continue-with-others

123. William Turvill, "Google News Shh-owcase: Publishers break silence over secret deals behind $1bn scheme," Press Gazette, September 30, 2021. URL: https://pressgazette.co.uk/news/google-news-showcase/

124. Andrew Willis, "Postmedia pushes for federal, industry-wide legislation on payment for content by tech companies," *Globe and Mail*, July 8, 2021. URL: https://www.theglobeandmail.com/business/article-postmedia-pushes-for-federal-industry-wide-legislation-on-payment-for/

125. Geoffrey Morgan, "Postmedia Network's chief executive renews call for legislation forcing tech giants to pay for content," *National Post*, July 8, 2021. URL: https://financialpost.com/news/postmedia-networks-chief-executive-renews-call-for-legislation-forcing-tech-giants-to-pay-for-content

126. Ibid.

127. Andrew Coyne, "Solidarity for never: News publishers' united front against Big Tech has collapsed," *Globe and Mail*, August 6, 2021. URL: https://www.theglobeandmail.com/opinion/article-solidarity-for-never-news-publishers-united-front-against-big-tech-has/

128. Ibid.

129. Ibid.

130. "Would Abolish Press Subsidy," Blacklock's Reporter, August 17, 2021. URL: https://www.blacklocks.ca/would-abolish-press-subsidy/

131. "Tech firms will pay for news, Liberals vow," *Toronto Star*, September 2, 2021, p. B1. URL: https://www.thestar.com/news/canada/2021/09/01/liberals-election-platform-proposes-that-social-media-companies-pay-for-canadian-journalism.html

132. "2021 Canadian federal election," Wikipedia, undated. URL: https://en.wikipedia.org/wiki/2021_Canadian_federal_election

133. Tim Bousquet, "Lots of COVID news and: the Halifax Examiner will take the government subsidy," Halifax Examiner, January 11, 2021. URL: https://www.halifaxexaminer.ca/uncategorized/lots-of-covid-news-and-the-halifax-examiner-will-take-the-government-subsidy/#Noticed

134. Tim Bousquet, "Here's the Halifax Examiner's tax return," Halifax Examiner, November 18, 2022. URL: https://www.halifaxexaminer.ca/health/covid/heres-the-halifax-examiners-tax-return/#Noticed

CHAPTER 7 — A PERFECT MARRIAGE

1. Dean Jobb, "Rich 100: Inside Irving," *Canadian Business*, December 22, 2008. URL: https://archive.canadianbusiness.com/lifestyle/tech-ceo-ultra-casual-style-gallery/

2. Canada, *The Uncertain Mirror: Report of the Special Senate Committee on Mass Media*, Vol. I. Ottawa: Information Canada, 1970, p. 80.

3. Canada, Standing Senate Committee on Transportations and Communications, Final report on the Canadian news media, Vol. 2, 2006, p. 59. URL: https://publications.gc.ca/collections/collection_2007/sen/YC19-391-1-01-2E.pdf

4. Bruce Livesey, "The Irvings' media monopoly and its consequences," National Observer, July 6, 2016. URL: http://www.nationalobserver.com/2016/07/06/news/irvings-media-monopoly-and-its-consequences

5. Erin Steuter, "He Who Pays the Piper Calls the Tune: Investigation of a Canadian Media Monopoly," *Web Journal of Mass Communication Research* 7(4), 2004. URL: https://wjmcr.info/2004/09/01/he-who-pays-the-piper-calls-the-tune-investigation-of-a-canadian-media-monopoly/

6. Toby D. Couture, "Without Favour: The Concentration of Ownership in New Brunswick's Print Media Industry," *Canadian Journal of Communication* 38(1), 2013, pp. 61-62.

7. Ibid., p. 62.

8. Ibid., p. 72.

9. Jacques Poitras, *Irving vs. Irving: Canada's Feuding Billionaires and The Stories They Won't Tell*. Toronto: Viking, 2014.

10. Russell Hunt and Robert Campbell, *K.C. Irving: The art of the indus-

trialist. Toronto: McClelland & Stewart, 1973, pp. 155-156.
11. Poitras, *Irving vs. Irving*, p. 24.
12. Canada, *The uncertain mirror*, p. 69.
13. Poitras, *Irving vs. Irving*.
14. Ibid.
15. Ibid.
16. Steuter, "He Who Pays the Piper Calls the Tune."
17. Ian Austen, "In Canada, a New Newspaper Faces Off Against a Well-Established Family," *New York Times*, October 29, 2007, p. C4. URL: https://www.nytimes.com/2007/10/29/business/worldbusiness/29irving.html
18. Ian Austen, "A Weekly in New Brunswick Prevails Against Local Family," *New York Times*, November 5, 2007, p. C12. URL: https://www.nytimes.com/2007/11/05/business/media/05irving.html
19. Clara Ho, "Prestigious CAJ awards go to two Canwest writers," *Edmonton Journal*, May 25, 2008, p. A11.
20. Mindelle Jacobs, "Retired prof takes on Irving," *Toronto Sun*, May 27, 2008, p. 22.
21. Chris Morris, "Weekly newspaper files competition complaint," *Fredericton Daily Gleaner*, April 1, 2008, p. A4.
22. Martine Dagenais, Letter to Ken Langdon, July 30, 2008, p. 2.
23. Ibid.
24. Ibid.
25. "Carleton Free Press closing down," CBC News, October 27, 2008. URL: https://www.cbc.ca/news/canada/new-brunswick/carleton-free-press-closing-down-1.731344
26. Jamie Irving, "Google and Facebook's medieval practices," *National Post*, March 29, 2021. URL: https://nationalpost.com/opinion/jamie-irving-google-and-facebooks-medieval-practices
27. Ibid.
28. Quoted in Poitras, *Irving vs. Irving*, p. 122.
29. Quoted in ibid., p. 123.
30. Ibid., p. 117.
31. Ibid., p. 168.
32. Ibid., p. 193.
33. Ibid., p. 197.
34. Ibid.
35. Jacques Poitras, "Monopoly: Newspaper Edition," *CJFE Review*, 2014, p. 28. URL: https://assets.nationbuilder.com/cjfe/legacy_url/974/2014_CJFE_Review-of-free-expression-in-Canada%28web%29.pdf?1414099434
36. Susan Krashinsky, "Brunswick News names Jamie Irving vice-president," *Globe and Mail*, September 10, 2009, p. B10. URL: https://www.theglobeandmail.com/report-on-business/brunswick-news-names-jamie-irving-vice-president/article4287620/
37. Julian H. Walker, "The Once and Future New Brunswick Free Press," *Journal of New Brunswick Studies 1*, 2010. URL: https://journals.lib.unb.ca/index.php/JNBS/article/view/18192/19611
38. Craig Silverman "Three Strikes and You're Fired," *Columbia Journalism Review*, June 26, 2009. URL: https://archives.cjr.org/behind_the_news/three_strikes_and_youre_fired.php

39. "CBC runs baseless story with no regard for facts or truth," *Saint John Telegraph-Journal*, June 6, 2009, p. A3.

40. "Saint John mayor claims Irving demanded city hall changes," CBC News, June 29, 2009. URL: https://www.cbc.ca/news/canada/new-brunswick/saint-john-mayor-claims-irving-demanded-city-hall-changes-1.799186

41. Quoted in Poitras, *Irving vs. Irving*, p. 242.

42. "N.B. paper apologizes for Harper wafer flap," CTV News, July 28, 2009. URL: https://www.ctvnews.ca/n-b-paper-apologizes-for-harper-wafer-flap-1.420569

43. Poitras, *Irving vs. Irving*, p. 249.

44. Ibid., p. 276.

45. Ibid.

46. "Don't rewrite history on LNG tax deal [Editorial]," *Saint John Telegraph-Journal*, December 9, 2015, p. A8.

47. Jamie Irving and Paul Deegan, "Why Canada must fight Big Tech's unregulated monopoly power: The future of journalism depends on it," *National Post*, July 21, 2021. URL: https://nationalpost.com/opinion/opinion-why-canada-must-fight-big-techs-unregulated-monopoly-power

48. Ibid.

49. Ibid.

50. Ibid.

51. Jamie Irving and Paul Deegan, "Time to put a filling in truth decay: Australia leads way with a strong news publishing business," *Ottawa Citizen*, September 7, 2021, p. NP2.

52. Patti Summerfield, "News Media Canada shares the truth delivered by newspapers," Media in Canada, October 5, 2021. URL: https://mediaincanada.com/2021/10/05/news-media-canada-shares-the-truth-delivered-by-newspapers/

53. Tim Kiladze, "Irving family exits media business with sale of Brunswick News to Postmedia," *Globe and Mail*, February 18, 2022. URL: https://www.theglobeandmail.com/business/article-irving-family-exits-media-business-with-sale-of-brunswick-news-to/

54. Mia Urquhart, "Sale of Irving-owned N.B. papers bad news for local content, industry watchers say," CBC News, February 18, 2022. URL: https://www.cbc.ca/news/canada/new-brunswick/irving-sells-newspapers-postmedia-1.6357477

55. James Bradshaw, "Jamie Irving named executive chairman of Postmedia, Paul Godfrey to step down," *Globe and Mail*, July 29, 2022, p. B2. URL: https://www.theglobeandmail.com/business/article-jamie-irving-named-executive-chairman-of-post-media-paul-godfrey-to/

56. Ibid.

57. Edward Greenspon, "Foreword," The Shattered Mirror: 5 Years On. Public Policy Forum, March 3, 2022. URL: https://ppforum.ca/publications/shattered-mirror-5-years-on/

58. Ibid.

59. Ibid.

60. Edward Greenspon, Christopher Dornan, David Moscrop, and Katie Davey, *The Shattered Mirror: 5 Years On*. Public Policy Forum, March 3, 2022. URL: https://ppforum.ca/publications/shattered-mirror-5-years-on/

61. Ibid.
62. Ibid.
63. Ibid.
64. Ibid.
65. "Additional support to strengthen local and diverse journalism," [press release] Newswire.ca, October 20, 2022. URL: https://www.newswire.ca/news-releases/additional-support-to-strengthen-local-and-diverse-journalism-873453699.html
66. "Now The Subsidies Are Secret," Blacklock's Reporter, August 11, 2021. URL: https://www.blacklocks.ca/now-the-subsidies-are-secret/
67. Jonathan Bradley, "Which Media Benefitted From the Trudeau Government's Covid-19 Funds?" Canadaland, September 10, 2021. URL: https://www.canadaland.com/canadian-media-liberals-trudeau-government-funding-covid-cbc-erin-otoole/
68. Jonathan Bradley, "Government subsidies for selected news organizations keep growing," Canadaland, December 1, 2021. URL: https://www.canadaland.com/media-in-trudeaus-10-million-top-up-fund/
69. Question No. 461: Questions on the Order Paper," *Hansard*, May 31st, 2022. URL: https://openparliament.ca/debates/2022/5/31/diane-lebouthillier-1/
70. Ibid.
71. "Question No. 461: Questions on the Order Paper," *Hansard*, May 31st, 2022. URL: https://openparliament.ca/debates/2022/5/31/diane-lebouthillier-1/
72. "Press Bailout Is 'Confidential,'" Blacklock's Reporter, May 25, 2022. URL: https://www.blacklocks.ca/press-bailout-is-confidential/
73. "Bailout Worth $115K A Week," Blacklock's Reporter, August 1, 2019. URL: https://www.blacklocks.ca/bailout-worth-115k-a-week/
74. "'Free' Press Gets $6,204,000," Blacklock's Reporter, May 28, 2021. URL: https://www.blacklocks.ca/free-press-gets-6204000/
75. "$385K Grant For News Lobby," Blacklock's Reporter, December 19, 2018. URL: https://www.blacklocks.ca/385k-grant-for-news-lobby/?fbclid=IwAR2_SaJRMAOkHG-b_euO55K58WTI41opcnMXhf2AHaosxOIB-5GT5hcJVM14
76. Ibid.
77. "Media Gave Selves A Subsidy," Blacklock's Reporter, August 19, 2020. URL: https://www.blacklocks.ca/media-gave-selves-a-subsidy/
78. "Submit Questions In Advance," Blacklock's Reporter, December 1, 2022. URL: https://www.blacklocks.ca/submit-questions-in-advance/
79. "Blacklock's Eviction By Police," Blacklock's Reporter, December 5, 2022. URL: https://www.blacklocks.ca/blacklocks-eviction-by-police/
80. "Lawsuit Names Press Gallery," Blacklock's Reporter, December 22, 2022. URL: https://www.blacklocks.ca/lawsuit-names-press-gallery/
81. Howard Law, "Too Big, Too Postmedia: A not-so-feverish review of federal funding of Canadian journalism [blog]," MediaPolicy.ca, December 13, 2021. URL: https://mediapolicy.ca/2021/12/13/too-big-too-postmedia-a-not-so-feverish-review-of-federal-funding-of-canadian-journalism/
82. Ibid.
83. Howard Law, "Andrew Coyne on the Great Threat to Journal-

ism [blog]," MediaPolicy.ca, March 21, 2019. URL: https://mediapolicy.ca/2019/03/21/andrew-coyne-on-the-great-threat-to-journalism/

84. Howard Law, "Facts About Journalism Panel Lost in the Media Storm [blog]," MediaPolicy.ca, May 28, 2019. URL: https://mediapolicy.ca/2019/05/28/facts-about-journalism-panel-lost-in-the-media-storm/

85. Ibid.

86. Jerry Dias, "Zuckerberg's self-serving push for regulation," *National Post*, November 26, 2020, p. A11. URL: https://nationalpost.com/opinion/jerry-dias-mark-zuckerbergs-self-serving-push-for-regulation; Jerry Dias, "How to save Canadian journalism," *National Post*, October 27, 2020, p. A10. URL: https://nationalpost.com/opinion/jerry-dias-we-need-a-canadian-model-to-save-canadian-journalism

87. Jerry Dias, "Take on Big Tech to save journalism," *National Post*, May 5, 2020, p. A10. URL: https://nationalpost.com/opinion/jerry-dias-why-hasnt-canada-taken-on-facebook-and-google-to-save-journalism

88. Vanmala Subramaniam, "A bag of cash and a bottle of cologne: Inside the alleged undoing of Unifor's Jerry Dias," *Globe and Mail*, March 26, 2022, p. B1. URL: https://www.theglobeandmail.com/business/article-unifor-jerry-dias-national-president-undoing/

89. Michelle Carbert, "Former CRTC leaders say regulator not equipped to oversee Online News Act," *Globe and Mail*, April 12, 2022, p. A4. URL: https://www.theglobeandmail.com/politics/article-former-crtc-leaders-say-regulator-is-not-equipped-to-oversee-the/

90. Ibid.

91. See Marc Edge, "Public benefits or private? The case of the Canadian Media Research Consortium," *Canadian Journal of Communication* 38(1), 2013, pp. 5-34. URL: http://www.marcedge.com/public.pdf

92. Anja Karadeglija, "CRTC chairman Ian Scott defends meeting with Bell CEO at pub," *National Post*, February 9, 2022. URL: https://nationalpost.com/news/politics/crtc-chairman-defends-meeting-with-bell-ceo-at-pub

93. Andrew Coyne, "Trudeau's Tangled Web," *Globe and Mail*, April 16, 2022, p. O1. URL: https://www.theglobeandmail.com/opinion/article-what-a-tangled-web-the-trudeau-government-is-weaving/

94. Ibid.

95. Howard Law, "On the contrary, regulating our Internet is good public policy," [blog] Mediapolicy.ca, April 18, 2022. URL: https://mediapolicy.ca/2022/04/18/on-the-contrary-regulating-our-internet-is-good-public-policy/

96. Anja Karadeglija, "Google pushes for changes to news compensation bill," *National Post*, May 5, 2022, p. A4. URL: https://nationalpost.com/news/politics/google-pushes-for-changes-to-news-compensation-bill

97. Bill Curry, "Google warns Ottawa's Online News Act would 'break' its search engine," *Globe and Mail*, May 16, 2022. URL: https://www.theglobeandmail.com/politics/article-google-warns-ottawas-online-news-act-would-break-its-search-engine/

98. Robert Malcolmson, "Google Canada's position on Bill C-18 does not surprise, but it does mislead," *Globe and Mail*, May 28, 2022, p. B4. URL: https://www.theglobeandmail.com/business/article-google-canadas-position-on-bill-c-18-does-not-surprise-but-it-does/

99. Bill Grueskin, "Great news for Canadian journalism," *National Post*,

April 16, 2022, p. A18. URL: https://nationalpost.com/opinion/bill-grueskin-australias-news-media-bargaining-code-was-a-good-first-step-canadas-approach-looks-to-be-even-better; Hugh Stephens, "Bill C-18 will redress market imbalance," *National Post*, September 13, 2022, p. A11. URL: https://nationalpost.com/opinion/hugh-stephens-bill-c-18%E2%80%AFis-a-necessary-step-to-redressing-a-market-imbalance; Erik Peinert, "Online News Act will be good for journalism," *National Post*, October 18, 2022, p. A11. URL: https://nationalpost.com/opinion/opinion-canadas-online-news-act-is-good-for-journalism

100. Warren Kinsella, "Little-known Bill C-18 could save Canada's free press," *Toronto Sun*, October 23, 2022, p. A7. URL: https://torontosun.com/opinion/columnists/kinsella-little-known-bill-c-18-could-save-canadas-free-press

101. Ibid.

102. Ricard Gil, "Why Ottawa's efforts to get Google and Facebook to pay for news content misses the mark," The Conversation, September 6, 2022. URL: https://theconversation.com/why-ottawas-efforts-to-get-google-and-facebook-to-pay-for-news-content-misses-the-mark-188875

103. Ibid.

104. Ibid.

105. Ibid.

106. A 2018 article I wrote for The Conversation, for example, was picked up by numerous other outlets, including the *Toronto Star* and the *National Post*. See Marc Edge, "Year of reckoning looms for Canada's newspapers," The Conversation, January 1, 2018. URL: https://theconversation.com/year-of-reckoning-looms-for-canadas-newspapers-89066

107. Michael Geist, "Here Comes the Online News Act: Why the Government's Media Shakedown is Bad News For Press Independence and Competition," [blog] MichaelGeist.ca, April 5, 2022. URL: https://www.michaelgeist.ca/2022/04/here-comes-the-online-news-act-why-the-governments-media-shakedown-is-bad-news-for-press-independence-and-competition/

108. Ibid.

109. Michael Geist, "Just How Extreme is Bill C-18?: It Mandates Payments For Merely Facilitating Access to News," [blog] MichaelGeist.ca, April 7, 2022. URL: https://www.michaelgeist.ca/2022/04/just-how-extreme-is-bill-c-18-it-mandates-payments-merely-for-facilitating-access-to-news/

110. Michael Geist, "Spiking Op-Eds: How the Government's Online News Act is Already Leading to Media Self-Censorship," [blog] MichaelGeist.ca, April 14, 2022. URL: https://www.michaelgeist.ca/2022/04/spiking-op-eds-how-the-governments-online-news-act-is-already-leading-to-media-self-censorship/

111. Michael Geist, "Shakedown Complete: The Story Behind Bill C-18's Shameful Legislative Review Process and the Race to Mandate Payment for Links," [blog] MichaelGeist.ca, December 14, 2022. URL: https://www.michaelgeist.ca/2022/12/shakedowncompletec18/

112. Ibid.

113. Dwayne Winseck, "Why Canada should take a critical look at Australia's internet regulations," National Observer, February 17, 2021. URL: https://www.nationalobserver.com/2021/02/17/opinion/why-cana-

da-should-take-critical-look-australia-internet-regulations

114. Dwayne Winseck, "Bad News: Proposed Online News Act Trades on Myths and Misconceptions," [blog] Mediamorphis, April 13, 2022. URL: https://dwmw.wordpress.com/2022/04/13/bad-news-proposed-online-news-act-trades-on-myths-and-misconceptions/

115. Dwayne Winseck, "The rot spreads out from the news publishers [tweet]," April 13, 2022. URL: https://twitter.com/mediamorphis/status/1514260419812237321

116. David Skok, "Letter from the editor: Rebutting critics of the Online News Act," The Logic, April 23, 2022. URL: https://thelogic.co/opinion/letter-from-the-editor-rebutting-critics-of-the-online-news-act/

117. "Postmedia announces strategic investment to bring readers original content from groundbreaking media startup, The Logic [press release]," Postmedia, May 22, 2019. URL: https://www.postmedia.com/2019/05/22/postmedia-announces-strategic-investment-to-bring-readers-original-content-from-groundbreaking-media-startup-the-logic/

118. Raisa Patel, "Are small news publishers being denied big tech money? Canadian legislation lacks transparency, critics say," *Toronto Star*, April 14, 2022, p. B1. URL: https://www.thestar.com/politics/federal/2022/04/13/australias-small-news-publishers-have-been-shut-out-of-deals-for-big-tech-money-could-the-same-thing-happen-in-canada.html

119. Jeanette Ageson, Matthew Dimera, Lela Savic, and Jeff Elgie, "Canada's Online News Act needs to be transparent and equitable," *Globe and Mail*, May 31, 2022. URL: https://www.theglobeandmail.com/opinion/article-canadas-online-news-act-must-be-transparent-and-equitable/

120. Raisa Patel, "Online news bill sparks concerns: Ottawa urged to amend proposed legislation so that smaller publishers are not left in the cold," *Toronto Star*, April 28, 2022, p. A7. URL: https://www.thestar.com/politics/federal/2022/09/27/small-publishers-warn-ottawas-online-news-bill-could-leave-them-out-in-the-cold.html

121. Marie Woolf, "Google tells MPs Bill C-18 will help 'bad actors' and promote propaganda," *Globe and Mail*, October 19, 2022. URL: https://www.theglobeandmail.com/politics/article-google-bill-c-18-online-news/

122. Marie Woolf, "Opposition MPs set to amend online news bill to aid community newspapers," *Globe and Mail*, November 3, 2022, p. A3. URL: https://www.theglobeandmail.com/politics/article-opposition-mps-prepare-to-amend-online-news-bill-to-aid-community/

123. Michael Geist, "Money for Nothing: Government Quietly Expands Bill C-18 Eligibility to Broadcasters That May Not Even Produce News Content," [blog] MichaelGeist.ca, December 2, 2022. URL: https://www.michaelgeist.ca/2022/12/money-for-nothing/

124. Michael Geist, "Why the Online News Act is a Bad Solution to a Real Problem, Part Four: Undermining Canadian Copyright Law and International Copyright Treaty Obligations," [blog] MichaelGeist.ca, September 23, 2022. URL: https://www.michaelgeist.ca/2022/09/why-the-online-news-act-is-a-bad-solution-to-a-real-problem-part-four/

125. Ibid.

126. Michael Geist, "The USMCA cultural poison pill," *Globe and Mail*, March 2, 2020, p. B4. URL: https://www.theglobeandmail.com/business/

commentary/article-the-usmca-cultural-poison-pill-why-the-broadcast-panel-report-could

127. Marie Woolf, "Trade minister admits that online news bill is trade issue with U.S.," *Globe and Mail*, December 3, 2022. URL: https://www.theglobeandmail.com/politics/article-trade-minister-admits-that-online-news-bill-raises-trade-issues-with/

128. "U.S. senators call for trade crackdown on Canada," *Toronto Star*, January 28, 2023, p. A20.

129. Marie Woolf, "U.S. escalates trade concerns over Canada's online news and streaming bills," *Globe and Mail*, February 1, 2023. URL: https://www.theglobeandmail.com/politics/article-us-escalates-trade-concerns-over-canadas-online-news-and-streaming/

130. Michael Geist, "Government Moves to Block Dozens of Potential Witnesses as it Shuts Down Bill C-18 Hearings," [blog] MichaelGeist.ca, October 21, 2022. URL: https://www.michaelgeist.ca/2022/10/shutdownc18/

131. Marie Woolf, "Facebook says it might block Canadians' access to news," *Globe and Mail*, October 22, 2022. URL: https://www.theglobeandmail.com/politics/article-trade-minister-admits-that-online-news-bill-raises-trade-issues-with/

132. Ibid.

133. Marc Dinsdale, "Sharing Our Concerns With Canada's Online News Act," Facebook, October 21, 2022. URL: https://about.fb.com/news/2022/10/metas-concerns-with-canadas-online-news-act/

134. Ibid.

135. Marie Woolf, "Liberals accuse Facebook of 'robber baron tactics' by threatening to block news in Canada," *Globe and Mail*, October 28, 2022. URL: https://www.theglobeandmail.com/politics/article-liberals-accuse-facebook-of-robber-baron-tactics-by-threatening-to/

136. Ibid.

137. Marc Edge, "Meta witnesses get hostile reception from Liberal MPs," *Canadian Dimension*, October 31, 2022. URL: https://canadiandimension.com/articles/view/meta-witnesses-get-hostile-reception-from-liberal-mps

138. Ibid.

139. Michael Geist, "Supreme Court of Canada Stands Up for the Internet: No Liability for Linking," Canlii Connects, June 6, 2014. URL: https://canliiconnects.org/fr/commentaires/27524

140. Woolf, "Facebook says it might block Canadians' access to news."

141. Marie Woolf, "Online news bill would inject $329-million a year into Canadian news, PBO report says," *Globe and Mail*, October 6, 2022. URL: https://www.theglobeandmail.com/politics/article-online-news-bill-would-inject-329-million-a-year-into-canadian-news/

142. Marie Woolf, "Online news bill C-18 would pump most funds into CBC, other broadcasters," *Globe and Mail*, October 20, 2022, p. A8. URL: https://www.theglobeandmail.com/politics/article-bill-c-18-broadcasters-funding/

143. William Turvill, "Canada's news industry expects up to $150m annual windfall from Australia-style big tech crackdown," *Press Gazette*, December 2, 2021. URL: https://pressgazette.co.uk/news/canada-goo-

gle-facebook-regulation-news-industry/

144. Phillip Crawley, "Wording of Bill C-18 needs a rework to protect independent journalism," *Globe and Mail*, November 12, 2022, p. A2. URL: https://www.theglobeandmail.com/canada/article-the-wording-of-bill-c-18-needs-a-rework-to-protect-independent/

145. Ibid.

146. Ibid.

147. Neha Gupta, "How the Globe and Mail has managed to grow revenue, subscriptions – and print," World Association of News Publishers, May 31, 2022. URL: https://wan-ifra.org/2022/05/how-the-globe-and-mail-has-managed-to-grow-revenue-subscriptions-and-print/

148. Ibid.

149. Marie Woolf, "No 'rubber stamp' for online news bill, says Senate," *Globe and Mail*, December 16, 2022. URL: https://www.theglobeandmail.com/politics/article-no-rubber-stamp-for-online-news-bill-says-senate/

CHAPTER 8 — THE TIPPING POINT

1. Sean Craig, "You Must Be This Conservative to Ride: The Inside Story of Postmedia's Right Turn," Canadaland, August 12, 2019. URL: https://www.canadalandshow.com/the-conservative-transformation-of-postmedia/

2. Ibid.

3. Ibid.

4. Ibid.

5. Ibid.

6. Jason Young, "Postmedia's 'transformative journey.' A Q&A with CEO Andrew MacLeod," *National Post*, October 5, 2019, p. FP1. URL: https://financialpost.com/telecom/media/postmedia-on-a-transformative-journey-a-qa-with-ceo-andrew-macleod

7. Ibid.

8. Ibid.

9. Ibid.

10. Victor Ferreira, "Andrew MacLeod named new Postmedia CEO, Paul Godfrey to take on role of executive chairman," *National Post*, January 10, 2019. URL: https://financialpost.com/telecom/media/andrew-macleod-named-new-postmedia-ceo-paul-godfrey-to-take-on-role-of-executive-chairman

11. Susan Krashinsky Robertson, "Postmedia appoints Andrew MacLeod as successor to CEO Paul Godfrey," *Globe and Mail*, October 19, 2017. URL: https://www.theglobeandmail.com/report-on-business/postmedia-reports-profit-as-infomart-sale-boosts-results/article36663722/

12. Stephen Kimber, "One media dinosaur gobbles up another," Halifax Examiner, February 20, 2022. URL: https://www.halifaxexaminer.ca/journalism/one-media-dinosaur-gobbles-up-another/

13. Joe Castaldo, "Clash of the media moguls: Inside the bitter battle to control Torstar," *Globe and Mail*, December 22, 2022, p. A1. URL: https://www.theglobeandmail.com/business/article-torstar-ownership-jordan-bitove-paul-rivett/

14. Mike Connell, "What can Postmedia do for you?" Media in Canada,

May 21, 2021. URL: https://mediaincanada.com/2021/05/21/icymi-what-can-postmedia-do-for-you/

15. "Postmedia launches newest channel – Betting Essentials," *Editor & Publisher*, January 3, 2023. URL: https://www.editorandpublisher.com/stories/postmedia-launches-newest-channel-betting-essentials,241544

16. Joe Castaldo, "Postmedia announces layoffs, will move 12 Alberta newspapers online," *Globe and Mail*, January 19, 2023, p. B2. URL: https://www.theglobeandmail.com/business/article-postmedia-layoffs-newspapers-alberta/

17. "Postmedia shakes up western leadership," *Toronto Star*, January 26, 2023, p. B2. URL: https://www.thestar.com/business/2023/01/25/postmedia-shuffles-editors-day-after-announcing-11-per-cent-of-staff-to-be-laid-off.html

18. Christopher Curtis, "Knives Out at the Montreal Gazette," [blog] The Rover, February 15, 2023. URL: https://rover.substack.com/p/knives-out-at-the-montreal-gazette

19. Ibid.

20. Ibid.

21. Christopher Curtis, "Postmedia Ignored Mitch Garber's Offer to Buy Montreal Gazette," [blog] The Rover, February 16, 2023. URL: https://rover.substack.com/p/postmedia-ignored-mitch-garbers-offer

22. "Postmedia cuts more than 75 printing, inserting jobs in Windsor," *Globe and Mail*, January 30, 2023. URL: https://www.theglobeandmail.com/business/article-postmedia-cuts-more-than-75-printing-inserting-jobs-in-windsor/

BIBLIOGRAPHY

Donald E. Abelson, *Do Think Tanks Matter? Assessing the Impact of Public Policy Institutes*. Montreal: McGill-Queen's University Press, 2002.

Penelope Muse Abernathy, *The rise of a new media baron and the emerging threat of news deserts*. Chapel Hill: University of North Carolina Press, 2016. URL: https://www.usnewsdeserts.com/wp-content/uploads/2016/09/07.UNC_RiseOfNewMediaBaron_SinglePage_01Sep2016-REDUCED.pdf

Penelope Muse Abernathy, *The expanding news desert*. Chapel Hill: University of North Carolina Press, 2018. URL: https://www.cislm.org/wp-content/uploads/2018/10/The-Expanding-News-Desert-10_14-Web.pdf

Jill Abramson, *Merchants of Truth: The Business of News and the Fight for Facts*. New York: Simon & Schuster, 2019.

Nuria Almiron, *Journalism in crisis: Corporate media and financialization*. Cresskill, NJ: Hampton Press, 2010.

Anonymous, "A Holistic Approach," *Editor & Publisher*, March 2016, p. 11

Anonymous, "U.S. Manager Preps Short Credit Fund," *Derivatives Week*, June 28, 2004, p. 1. URL: https://www.globalcapital.com/article/28mwt-9p82de8rfr8pqadc/derivatives/u-s-manager-preps-short-credit-fund

Anonymous, "Who lives where at the Four Seasons Hotel Residences," *Toronto Life*, March 31, 2017. URL: https://torontolife.com/real-estate/lives-four-seasons-hotel-residences/

Anonymous, "Postmedia launches newest channel – Betting Essentials," *Editor & Publisher*, January 3, 2023. URL: https://www.editorandpublisher.com/stories/postmedia-launches-newest-channel-betting-essentials,241544

Ian Austen, "The case against the media giants," *Maclean's*, October 3, 1983, p. 40. URL: https://archive.macleans.ca/article/1983/10/3/the-case-against-the-media-giants

Ian Austen, "An acquittal for the press lords," *Maclean's*, December 19, 1983, p. 34. URL: https://archive.macleans.ca/article/1983/12/19/an-acquittal-for-the-press-lords

Patrick-Yves Badillo and Dominique Bourgeois, "The Swiss press model: Democracy, concentration and digital diversification," *Recherches en communication 44*, 2017, pp. 9-30.

Gerald J. Baldasty, *The Commercialization of News in the Nineteenth Century*. Madison: University of Wisconsin Press, 1992.

M. C. Barrès-Baker, *An Introduction to the Early History of Newspaper Advertising*. Brent Museum and Archive occasional publications No. 2, 2006. URL: https://authorzilla.com/KNd5X/history-of-british-newspapers.html

Conrad Black, *A Life in Progress*. Toronto: Key Porter, 1993.

Walt Bogdanich and Michael Forsythe, *When McKinsey Comes to Town: The Hidden Influence of the World's Most Powerful Consulting Firm*. New York: Doubleday, 2022.

Broadcasting and Telecommunications Legislative Review, "Canada's Communications Future: Time to Act," Innovation, Science and Economic Development Canada, January 2020. URL: https://ised-isde.canada.ca/site/broadcasting-telecommunications-legislative-review/sites/default/files/attachments/BTLR_Eng-V3.pdf

Charles Bruce, *News and the Southams*. Toronto: Macmillan, 1968.

Katherine Burton, Sridhar Natarajan, and Shahien Nasiripour, "National Enquirer Owner Chatham Asset Management Plays Starring Role in Tabloid-Worthy Stories," *Fortune*, March 18, 2019. URL: https://fortune.com/2019/03/18/chatham-asset-management-michael-cohen-ipayment-holidings-lawsuit/

Canada, Competition Act, 1985. URL: https://laws.justice.gc.ca/PDF/C-34.pdf

Canada, *The Uncertain Mirror: Report of the Special Senate Committee on Mass Media*, Vol. I. Ottawa: Information Canada, 1970.

Canada, Standing Senate Committee on Transportations and Communications, *Final report on the Canadian news media*, Vol. 1, 2006. URL: http://www.parl.gc.ca/content/sen/committee/391/tran/rep/repfinjun-06vol1-e.pdf

Canada, Standing Committee on Canadian Heritage, *Disruption: Change and Churning in Canada's Media Landscape*, June 2017. URL: https://www.ourcommons.ca/Content/Committee/421/CHPC/Reports/RP9045583/chpcrp06/chpcrp06-e.pdf

James W. Carey, "Harold Adams Innis and Marshall McLuhan," *The Antioch Review* 27(1), 1967, pp. 5-39.

Alex Carey, *Taking the Risk Out of Democracy: Corporate Propaganda versus Freedom and Liberty*. Sydney: University of New South Wales Press, 1995.

Chris Cobb, *Ego and Ink: The Inside Story of Canada's National Newspaper War*. Toronto: McClelland & Stewart, 2004.

Toby D. Couture, "Without Favour: The Concentration of Ownership in New Brunswick's Print Media Industry," *Canadian Journal of Communication* 38(1), 2013, pp. 57-81

Paul S. Crampton, "The Treatment of Efficiency Gains in Canadian Merger Analysis," pp. 59-72 in Organization for Economic Co-operating and Development, *Competition Policy and Efficiency Claims in Horizontal Agreements*. Paris: OECD, 1995. URL: https://www.oecd.org/competition/mergers/2379526.pdf

Andrew Crisell, *An introductory history of British broadcasting* 2nd ed. London: Routledge, 2003.

Stanley Cunningham, *The Idea of Propaganda*, New York: Praeger, 2002.

Keith Davey, *The Rainmaker: A Passion for Politics*. Toronto: Stoddart, 1986.

Stefano DellaVigna and Ethan Kaplan, "The Fox News Effect: Media Bias and Voting," *Quarterly Journal of Economics 122* (3), 2007, pp. 1187-1234.

Peter J. S. Dunnett, *The World Newspaper Industry*. London: Croom Helm, 1988.

Marc Edge, *Pacific Press: The Unauthorized Story of Vancouver's Newspaper Monopoly*. Vancouver: New Star Books, 2001.

Marc Edge, *Asper Nation: Canada's Most Dangerous Media Company*. Vancouver: New Star Books, 2007.

Marc Edge, *Greatly Exaggerated: The Myth of the Death of Newspapers*. Vancouver: New Star Books, 2014.

Marc Edge, *Re-examining the UK Newspaper Industry*. London: Routledge, 2023.

Marc Edge, "How the camel got in the tent: The 1990s Canadian assault on Australia's foreign media ownership limits," *Media International Australia 132*, August 2009, pp. 42-53.

Marc Edge, "Public benefits or private? The case of the Canadian Media Research Consortium," *Canadian Journal of Communication* 38(1), 2013, pp. 5-34.

Marc Edge, "The never-ending story: Postmedia, press concentration, and the Competition Bureau," *Canadian Journal of Media Studies* 14(1), 2016, pp. 53-81. URL: https://uottawa.scholarsportal.info/ottawa/index.php/CJMS-RCEM/article/view/6474/5222

Marc Edge, "Conspiracy to commit murder? Canadian newspaper trades and closures, 2010-17," *Canadian Journal of Media Studies* 16(1), 2018, pp. 28-45. URL: https://uottawa.scholarsportal.info/ottawa/index.php/CJMS-RCEM/article/view/6454/5211

Marc Edge, "Enabling Postmedia: Economists as the 'rock stars' of Canadian competition law," *Canadian Journal of Communication* 45(2), 2020, pp. 287-303.

Marc Edge, "Starving Canadian media giants — a case of real fake news [book review]," *The Monitor*, September/October 2019, pp. 63-64.

Jacques Ellul, *Propaganda: The formation of men's attitudes*. New York: Vintage Books, 1965.

Rana Foroohar, *Makers and Takers: The Rise of Finance and the Fall of American Business*. New York: Crown Business, 2016.

Hector Garcia-Molina, Manas Joglekar, Adam Marcus, Aditya Parameswaran, and Verroios Vasilis, "Challenges in data crowdsourcing," *IEEE Transactions on Knowledge and Data Engineering* 28(4), 2016, pp. 901-911.

Ian Gill, "Paper Thin: Deathwatch for Alberta's big-city newspapers," *Alberta Views*, March 1, 2017. URL: https://albertaviews.ca/paper-thin/

Ian Gill, *No News is Bad News: Canada's Media Collapse – and What Comes Next*. Vancouver: Greystone Books, 2016.

Margo Goodhand, "Above the Fold," *The Walrus,* February 4, 2016. URL: https://thewalrus.ca/above-the-fold/

Edward Greenspon, Christopher Dornan, David Moscrop, and Katie Davey, *The Shattered Mirror: 5 Years On*. Public Policy Forum, March 3, 2022. URL: https://ppforum.ca/publications/shattered-mirror-5-years-on/

Bill Grueskin, "Australia pressured Google and Facebook to pay for journalism. Is America next?" *Columbia Journalism Review*, March 9, 2022. URL: https://www.cjr.org/business_of_news/australia-pressured-google-and-facebook-to-pay-for-journalism-is-america-next.php

Donald Gutstein, *Not a Conspiracy Theory: How Business Propaganda Hijacks Democracy*. Toronto: Key Porter, 2009.

Jűrgen Habermas, *The Structural Transformation of the Public Sphere: An Inquiry into a category of Bourgeois Society*. Cambridge: MIT Press, 1991.

Robert Hackett and Hanna Araza, "The Oil Blotter: Postmedia & Big Oil's symbiosis," *The Monitor*, May 1, 2021. URL: https://monitormag.ca/articles/the-oil-blotter-postmedia-big-oils-symbiosis

Adolf Hitler, *Mein Kampf*. Munich: Franz Eher, 1925.

Karen K. Ho and Mathew Ingram, "Canada pledges $50 million to local journalism. Will it help?" *Columbia Journalism Review*, February 28, 2018. URL: https://www.cjr.org/business_of_news/canada-journalism-fund-torstar-postmedia.php

C. Ann Hollifield, "Effects of foreign ownership on media content: Thomson papers' coverage of Quebec independence vote," *Newspaper Research Journal* 20(1), 1999, pp. 65-82.

Sean Holman, "At the Gate of Disaster: A Case Study on the Promotion of Climate Science Rejectionism by Mainstream News Outlets and E-Commerce Companies," *Facts and Frictions* 1(2), 2022. URL: https://factsandfrictions.j-schoolscanada.ca/wp-content/uploads/2022/03/Holman.pdf

Russell Hunt and Robert Campbell, *K.C. Irving: The art of the industrialist*. Toronto: McClelland & Stewart, 1973.

Dean Jobb, "Rich 100: Inside Irving," *Canadian Business*, December 22, 2008. URL: https://archive.canadianbusiness.com/lifestyle/tech-ceo-ultra-casual-style-gallery/

Malcolm Johnston, "Q&A: Paul Godfrey, chair of the OLG, is on a mission to bring a Las Vegas–style casino to Toronto," *Toronto Life*, June 4, 2012. URL: https://torontolife.com/city/qa-with-paul-godfrey/

Garth Jowett and Victoria O'Donnell, *Propaganda and Persuasion* 4th ed., Thousand Oaks, CA: Sage, 2006.

Jason Kirby, "Behind closed doors: The 12 most powerful lobbyists in Ottawa," *Maclean's*, November 23, 2014. URL: https://www.macleans.ca/news/canada/behind-closed-doors-the-12-most-powerful-lobbyists-in-ottawa/

Sheldon Kirshner, "A 'general' in Canada's newspaper war," *Canadian Jewish News*, May 25, 2000, p. 11.

Robert Kuttner and Hildy Zenger, "Saving the free press from private equity," *American Prospect* 29(1), December 27, 2017, pp. 22-29. URL: http://prospect.org/article/saving-free-press-private-equity

Hajer Labidi, "Native Advertising: Information or Illusion," Union des Consommateurs, June 2018. URL: https://uniondesconsommateurs.ca/wp-content/uploads/2020/12/2018-Publicite_native-Eng.pdf

John Lester, "Business Subsidies in Canada: Comprehensive Estimates for the Government of Canada and the Four Largest Provinces," University of Calgary School of Public Policy Publications Research Paper 11(1), 2018. URL: https://www.policyschool.ca/wp-content/uploads/2018/01/Business-Subsidies-in-Canada-Lester.pdf

David Lewis, *Louder Voices: The Corporate Welfare Bums*. Toronto: Lorimer, 1972.

Trudy Lieberman, *Slanting the Story: The Forces that Shape the News*. New York: New Press, 2000.

Phil Lind, *Right Hand Man: How Phil Lind Guided the Genius of Ted Rogers, Canada's Foremost Entrepreneur*. Toronto: Barlow Books, 2018.

Lindgren, April, Corbett, Jon, and Hodson, Jaigris, "Mapping change in Canada's local news landscape: An investigation of research impact on public policy," *Digital Journalism* 8(6), 2020, pp. 758–779.

Walter Lippmann, *Public Opinion*. New York: MacMillan, 1922.

Carol J. Loomis, "The Jones Nobody Keeps Up With," *Fortune*, April 1966, pp. 237-242. URL: https://fotst.org/wp-content/uploads/2015/01/Fortune-Magazine-Alfred-Winslow-Jones.pdf

Jason McBride, "Star Wars: Inside the vicious battle for control of the country's largest newspaper," *Toronto Life*, February 8, 2023. URL: https://torontolife.com/city/star-wars-inside-the-vicious-battle-for-control-of-the-countrys-largest-newspaper/

M. T. MacCrimmon, "Controlling Anticompetitive Behavior in Canada: A Contrast to the United States," *Osgoode Hall Law Journal* 21(4), 1983, pp. 569-608.

Duff McDonald, *The Firm: The Story of McKinsey and Its Secret Influence on American Business*. New York, Simon & Shuster, 2013.

James G. McGann, *The Fifth Estate: Think Tanks, Public Policy, and Governance*. Washington, DC: Brookings Institution Press, 2016.

Wendy McLellan, "Study paints journalists as left-wing, biased messengers," *Media* 10(2), Fall/Winter 2003, p. 31.

Rafe Mair, *Politically Incorrect: How Canada Lost Its Way and The Simple Path Home*. Comox, BC: Watershed Sentinel Books, 2017.

Melinda Mattos, "The Scoop on Ed," *Ryerson Review of Journalism*, Summer 2003. URL: https://rrj.ca/the-scoop-on-ed/

Philip Meyer, *The Vanishing Newspaper: Saving journalism in the information age*. Columbia: University of Missouri Press, 2004.

John Morton, "Why Are Newspaper Profits So High?" *American Journalism Review*, October 1994, p. 72. URL: https://ajrarchive.org/Article.asp?id=69

Julie Mouris and Gavin Murphy, "The Canadian Competition Authority Closes Its Investigation Into An Alleged Conspiracy by Large Media Companies," *Concurrences*, January 2021. URL: https://www.concurrences.com/en/bulletin/news-issues/january-2021/the-canadian-competition-authority-closes-its-investigation-into-an-alleged

Ralph Negrine, *Politics and the mass media in Britain* 2nd ed. London: Routledge, 1994.

Nic Newman, *Journalism, Media, and Technology Trends and Predictions*. Oxford, UK: Reuters Institute for the Study of Journalism, 2022. URL: https://reutersinstitute.politics.ox.ac.uk/sites/default/files/2022-01/Newman%20-%20Trends%20and%20Predictions%202022%20FINAL.pdf

Peter C. Newman, "The inexorable spread of the Black Empire," *Maclean's*, February 3, 1992, p. 68.

Linda Nguyen, "Transcontinental will try to sell 34 newspapers for approval in Sun Media deal," *Canadian Business*, May 28, 2014. URL: https://archive.canadianbusiness.com/business-news/coming-soon-cbs-new-website-is-launching-this-week/

Thomas I. Palley, "Financialization: What It Is and Why It Matters," Working Paper No. 525, The Levy Economics Institute, Bard College, Annandale-on-Hudson, NY, December 2007. URL: http://www.levyinstitute.org/pubs/wp_525.pdf

Jacob Parry, "Who is killing the community newspaper?" *B.C. Business*, July 22, 2015. URL: https://www.bcbusiness.ca/who-is-killing-the-community-newspaper

Martin Patriquin, "The 'Prince of Darkness' is back in the Liberal fold," *Maclean's*, April 10, 2009. URL: https://www.macleans.ca/news/canada/the-prince-of-darkness-is-back-in-the-liberal-fold/

Jacques Poitras, *Irving vs. Irving: Canada's Feuding Billionaires and The Stories They Won't Tell*. Toronto: Viking, 2014.

Jacques Poitras, "Monopoly: Newspaper Edition," *CJFE Review 5*, 2014, pp. 28-29. URL: https://assets.nationbuilder.com/cjfe/legacy_url/974/2014_CJFE_Review-of-free-expression-in-Canada%28web%29.pdf?1414099434

Michael E. Porter, *Competitive Strategy: Creating and Sustaining Superior Performance*. New York: Free Press, 1998.

Public Policy Forum, *The Shattered Mirror: News, Democracy and Trust in the Digital Age*. Ottawa: Public Policy Forum, 2017. URL: https://shatteredmirror.ca/download-report

Thomas Ross, "The Evolution of Competition Law in Canada," *Review of Industrial Organization 13*, 1998, pp. 1-23.

Harvey Schachter, "Revolution from within," *Canadian Business* 67(11), November 1994, pp. 30-47.

Erin E. Schauster, Patrick Ferrucci, and Marlene S. Neill, "Native advertising is the new journalism: How deception affects social responsibility," *American Behavioral Scientist* 60(12), 2016, pp. 1408-1424.

Alec Scott, "Searching for Certainty: Inside the New Canadian Mindset [book review]," *Quill and Quire*. URL: https://quillandquire.com/review/searching-for-certainty-inside-the-new-canadian-mindset/

Werner J. Severin and James W. Tankard Jr., *Communication Theories: Origins, Methods and Uses in the Mass Media* 4th ed. New York: Pearson, 1997.

Richard Siklos, *Shades of Black: Conrad Black and the world's fastest growing press empire*. Toronto: McClelland & Stewart, 1996.

Craig Silverman, "Three Strikes and You're Fired," *Columbia Journalism Review*, June 26, 2009. URL: https://archives.cjr.org/behind_the_news/three_strikes_and_youre_fired.php

David Skeel, "Behind the Hedge," *Legal Affairs*, November/December 2005. URL: https://www.legalaffairs.org/issues/November-December-2005/fea-

Will Slauter, "The Rise of the Newspaper," in Richard R. John and Jonathan Silberstein-Loeb, eds., *Making News: The Political Economy of Journalism in Britain and America from the Glorious Revolution to the Internet*. Oxford, UK: Oxford University Press, 2015

Dallas W. Smythe, *Dependency Road*. Norwood, NJ: Ablex, 1981.

Minko Sotiron, *From Politics to Profit: The Commercialization of Canadian Daily Newspapers, 1890-1920*. Montreal: McGill-Queen's University Press, 1992.

Erin Steuter, "He Who Pays the Piper Calls the Tune: Investigation of a Canadian Media Monopoly," *Web Journal of Mass Communication Research* 7(4), 2004. URL: https://wjmcr.info/2004/09/01/he-who-pays-the-piper-calls-the-tune-investigation-of-a-canadian-media-monopoly/

Diane Stone, *Capturing the Public Imagination: Think Tanks and the Policy Process*. Portland, OR: Frank Cass, 1996.

Richard Stursberg, *The Tangled Garden: A Canadian Cultural Manifesto for the Digital Age*. Toronto: James Lorimer & Co., 2019.

Sarmishta Subramanian, "The new worry about the next election: your daily news," *Maclean's*, August 6, 2019. URL: https://www.macleans.ca/politics/ottawa/the-new-worry-about-the-next-election-your-daily-news/

Margaret Sullivan, *Ghosting the News: Local Journalism and the crisis of American democracy*. New York: Columbia Global Reports, 2020.

Miriam van der Burg and Hilde Van den Bulck, "Why are traditional newspaper publishers still surviving in the digital era? The impact of long-term trends on the Flemish newspaper industry's financing, 1990-2014," *Journal of Media Business Studies* 14(2), 2017, pp. 82-115.

Julian H. Walker, "The Once and Future New Brunswick Free Press," *Journal of New Brunswick Studies* 1, 2010, pp. 64-79. URL: https://journals.lib.unb.ca/index.php/JNBS/article/view/18192/19611

Roger Ware and Ralph A. Winter, "Merger efficiencies in Canada: Lessons for the integration of economics into antitrust Law," *The Antitrust Bulletin* 61(3), 2006, pp. 365-375.

Kevin Williams, *Read All About It: A history of the British newspaper*. Abingdon, UK: Routledge, 2010.

Gary Wolf, "The Wisdom of Saint Marshall, the Holy Fool," *Wired*, January 1, 1996. URL: https://www.wired.com/1996/01/saint-marshal/

Daniel Yergin and Joseph Stanislaw, *Commanding Heights: The Battle for the World Economy*. New York: Simon & Schuster, 2002.

Yudian Zhengy, Guoliang Li, Yuanbing Li, Caihua Shany, and Reynold Chengy, "Truth inference in crowdsourcing: Is the problem solved?" *Proceedings of the VLDB Endowment* 10(5), 2017, pp. 541-552.

INDEX

24 Hours 26
Abelson, Donald 71
Abernathy, Penelope Muse 41, 42
Abramson, Jill 120
Adams, Paul 74, 94, 100
Addis, Richard 53, 54
Advertising Standards Canada 126, 127
Alberta Weekly Newspapers Association 193
Alden Global Capital 42, 51
Allan, Robyn 127
allNovaScotia 139
Almiron, Núria 40
American Media Inc. 46, 98
American Prospect 51
AOL-Time Warner 38
Apple 152, 197, 201
Armstrong, Peter 28-9
Armstrong, Stephen 19
Ashfield, Chris 193
Asper family 4, 5, 13, 37, 70, 111, 112
Asper, David 70-1
Asper, Izzy 37-8
Asper, Leonard 71
Atkinson Foundation 56, 102, 179
Atkinson principles 47, 200
Atwood, Margaret 113
bailout (news media) 19-20, 23, 24, 104-6, 108-11, 137, 139, 142-8, 154, 156, 158-60, 166, 179, 181-3, 184, 185-6, 193, 196; campaign 53-77, 94, 98-100, 101, 104, 150, 158-9
Barrie Examiner 24, 25, 81
Barton, Dominic 68
B.C. Business 83
Bell Canada 21, 38, 153, 187, 189
Bell Globemedia 38
Beers, David 131
Benton, Joshua 46
Berne Convention 194
Bernhard, Daniel 150-1
Bernier, Maxime 118-9
Bibic, Mirko 187-8
Black Press 63, 82-3, 99, 155, 164
Blair, Tony 36
BNN Bloomberg 17, 28, 81
Black, Conrad xiii-xiv, 17-18, 33, 36, 37-8, 53, 111, 116, 135
Black Press 63, 82-3, 99, 155, 160, 164
BlackBerry 199, 201
Blacklock's Reporter 101-2, 143, 181, 182-4
Bloomberg 13, 46, 55
Bolan, Kim 130
Boston Globe 183
Bousquet, Tim 106, 139-42, 166
Brandon Sun 163, 182
Brin, Colette 147
Broadbent Institute 11, 118, 124, 126
Broadcasting and Telecommunications Legislative Review 155
Brown, Jesse xv, 143-4
Buzzfeed 120, 153
Calgary Herald 5, 71, 108, 117, 126, 165, 176, 187, 204
Calgary Sun 5, 204
Collacott, Martin 133-4
Camp, Michael 178
Campion-Smith, Bruce 100, 158
Canada-U.S.-Mexico Trade Agreement 194
Canada Revenue Agency 104, 122-3, 141, 147, 182, 184

Canadaland 17, 115, 119, 128-9, 132, 133, 143, 181, 184-5, 199, 200
Canadian Association of Journalists 59, 139, 144, 145-6, 171
Canadian Association of Petroleum Producers 11, 123-5, 126
Canadian Business 67
Canadian Code of Advertising Standards 126
Canadian Community Newspapers Association 20
Canadian Heritage, Department of 2, 23, 56, 57, 102, 137, 144, 157, 162, 181, 185, 191, 193, 195-6; Media and Local Communities hearings 1-3, 8, 21, 55, 102; standing committee 195-6
Canadian International Council 55
Canadian Journalism Foundation 56
Canadian Media Concentration Research Project 27
Canadian Media Fund 22
Canadian Newspaper Association 19
Canadian Periodical Fund 23, 94, 100, 181
Canadian Press, The 33, 55, 58, 94, 190
Canadian Radio-television and Telecommunications Commission 39, 85, 86, 156, 186, 187-8, 192, 194, 197
Canso Investment Counsel 14, 15, 47, 202
Canwest Global Communications 4-5, 7, 37, 38, 39, 70-1
Carey, Alex 72-3
Carleton University 27, 179
Carleton Free Press 170-1
CBC 28, 52, 56, 57, 58, 74, 93, 112, 117, 118-19, 128, 145, 150, 156, 171, 172, 175, 197,
C.D. Howe Institute 71, 72
Chatelaine 177
Chan, Kevin 195-6
Chatham Asset Management 14, 17, 43, 44-6, 98, 204
Chiu, Joanna 154-5
Chretien, Jean 36, 38, 111
Clairvest 56
Clark, Gordon 132-4
Climenhaga, David 117
CN 56
CNN Effect 50
Cobb, Chris 53, 54
Cohen, Michael 98
Collins, Doug 132
Competition Act 21, 24, 27, 85-90, 95-6, 136
Competition Bureau 5, 7, 10, 24, 27, 39, 61, 63, 81-4, 85-8, 89, 90, 91, 92-7, 106, 136, 155, 171
Competition Tribunal 89, 91
Conservative Party 10, 75, 108, 112, 117, 118, 166
convergence 4-5, 38-9, 109
Cooper, Barry 126
Cooper, Michael 110
Corbella, Licia 117-8
Corcoran, Terence 17, 67-9
Covid-19 47, 111, 148, 166, 186
Cox, Bob 59, 75, 93, 100, 146, 158, 183-4
Coyne, Andrew 22-3, 60, 94, 100-1, 105, 113, 143, 161-2, 164, 185, 188
Craig, Sean 115-7, 199
Crawley, Philip 54, 55, 197-8
Crookes v. Newton 196
Cruickshank, John 19
CTVGlobemedia 37
Cunningham, Stanley 74
Curtis, Christopher 204-5
CWA Canada 16, 59-60
Dabrusin, Julie 137
Daily Advertiser 32
Daily Telegraph 33
Davey, Keith 33, 35, 58, 169
Dawson, Fabian 132-3
Denton, Timothy 156-7
De Souza, Mike 126-7
Desmarais family 76
DeSmog 127
Dias, Jerry 26, 75, 165, 186
Digital First Media 42
Discourse, The 160, 163

INDEX

Disruption: Change and Churning in Canada's Media Landscape (Fry report) 21-2
Doctor, Ken 42
Donner Canadian Foundation 70
Dornan, Christopher 179
DoubleClick 151
Downe, Percy 122-3
Dunnett, Peter 36
Eagland, Nick 130
Editor & Publisher 121
Edmonton Journal 5, 107-8, 112
Edmonton Sun 5, 205
Elgie, Jeff 82, 158-9
Ellul, Jacques 73
Enbridge 128
Enron 68
Exeter Times-Advocate 24
Facebook 23, 28, 56, 57, 61, 66, 76, 79, 100, 103, 107, 150-1, 152, 153-4, 157-8, 161-2, 163-5, 166, 171-2, 176, 178, 180, 183, 186, 188, 189, 191, 194, 195-6, 201-2
Fairfax chain 37
Financial Times 53
foreign ownership 2, 3, 6, 8, 9, 13-14, 15, 36-7, 43, 52, 74, 86, 109, 142, 146, 152, 155, 159
Fortune 40, 43, 44, 45
Foroohar, Rana 40
Fox Effect 50
Frank magazine 17
Fraser Institute 69-72, 134
Freeland, Chrystia 53
Friends of Canadian Broadcasting 150-1
Friends of Science 125-6
Fry, Hedy 8, 22, 110-1
Gannett chain 42
Garber, Mitch 205
GateHouse chain 42
Geist, Michael 190-1, 193-4, 195
Gelfand, Phyllise 120
Gill, Ian 16, 108
Glacier Media 14, 63, 82-3, 99, 154-5, 164
Glasbeek, Harry 43
Global Television 5, 37, 127

Globe and Mail 4, 6, 7, 13, 14, 16, 18, 22, 24, 33, 37, 38, 39, 47, 53-5, 59, 60, 71, 74, 75, 80, 83, 85, 95-7, 112, 118, 129, 160, 163, 164, 188, 194, 197-8, 202
Godfrey, Paul 1-8, 10-14, 16-19, 23-5, 27-9, 42-3, 81, 84-5, 93, 101, 105-6, 111-3, 115, 152, 178, 201; bonuses 11-2, 16-17, 19, 43, 105
GoldenTree Asset Management 2-3, 4, 6, 12-13, 14, 15, 42-3
Goldstein, Ken 62
Goodhand, Margo 1, 108, 112, 117
Google 28, 57, 61, 66, 76, 100, 103, 151-4, 157-8, 161-2, 164-5, 166, 171-2, 176, 178, 180, 186, 194, 196, 187, 198, 201-2; News 151, 161, 189, 190-2; News Showcase 164, 192, 194
Gramsci, Antonio 71-2
Greenspon, Edward 20-1, 53-5, 59, 64, 66-7, 68, 75-6, 102-3, 179, 186
Grimstad, Carl 45
Guardian, The 10
Guay, Pierre-Yves 95
Guelph Mercury 3, 63
GuelphToday.com 82
Guelph Tribune 63
Guilbeault, Steven 157, 161, 163
Gutstein, Donald 70-2
Habermas, Jürgen 32
Halifax Chronicle Herald 83, 140, 141
Halifax Examiner 106, 139-41, 166
Hamilton Spectator 97
Hammill, John 79-82, 91, 92, 96
Harbour City Star 63
Harper, Stephen 8, 10, 19, 86, 112, 175
Hayek, Friedrich 69, 70
Hecht, Mark 129-30, 133
hedge funds 1-2, 5, 8-9, 12, 16, 39, 40-45, 48, 50-1, 52, 98, 108-9, 142, 204
Hill Times 53, 101, 123
Hinds, John 92, 102
Hitler, Adolf 73-4

267

Holder, Janet 127
Hollinger chain 33, 36
Holman, Sean 119-20, 125, 132
Honderich, John 98-9, 112
Housefather, Anthony 205
Income Tax Act 36
Independent, The 49
Independent Advisory Board on Eligibility for Journalism Tax Measures 147
Indiegraf 192
Innis, Harold 50
Innovation, Science and Economic Development, Department of 155
Institute for Research on Public Policy 69, 72
Investment Canada Act 36, 37, 182
iPolitics 59, 74
Irving, Arthur 169
Irving family 89, 167-8, 176-8
Irving, Jack 170
Irving, Jamie 160-1, 165, 171-6, 178, 205
Irving, J.D. (Jim) 170, 177-8
Irving, J.K. 170
Irving, K.C. 169-70
Irving Oil 89, 169, 170, 174, 175
Ivanhoé Cambridge 56
Ivison, John 83
Iype, Mark 116
J-source 142, 160
Joly, Mélanie 23, 75, 76-7, 99, 100, 102, 144
Jones, Alfred Winslow 40-1
Journal Register chain 42
Journalism and Written Media Independent Panel of Experts 146
Journalists for Human Rights 160
Jowett, Garth 74
Kenney, Jason 118, 119
Kerzner, Joel 110
Kinsella, Warren 118-9, 189
Koolsbergen, Nick 109
Korski, Tom 184
Kroeger, Arthur 67
La Presse 76, 103
Law, Howard 100, 145, 184-6
Lebouthillier, Diane 182

Lewis, David 52
Libin, Kevin 114-16
Lieberman, Trudy 70
Lind, Phil 7
Lindgren, April 64
Lippmann, Walter 49, 73
Local Journalism Initiative 92, 94, 108, 180-1, 184, 193
Local News Research Project 64
Logic, The 143, 192
London Gazette 31-2
Loomis, Carol J. 40
McDougal, Karen 98
Maclean's 36, 101, 114-5, 118, 144
MacLeod, Andrew 28, 105, 111, 115, 33, 164, 178, 194, 199-201, 203, 205
MacMillan Bloedel 70
Mair, Rafe 60, 124
Malcolmson, Robert 189
Mann, Jagdeesh 132
Martin, Don 22
Max Bell Foundation 56, 70
Max Bell School of Public Policy 162
McClatchy chain 45-6
McConnell Foundation 56, 102, 162, 179
McGann, James 69-70
McKinsey & Company 68
McLuhan, Marshall 50
Mean World Syndrome 50
Meier, Lana 149
Melchiorre, Anthony 44
Menzies, Peter 187
Merrell, Dennis 193
Meta 181, 195
Metcalfe, Isabel 101-2
Metro 26, 47, 140
Metro Marquee 170
Metroland chain 24, 97
Meyer, Philip 48
Mihlar, Fazil 71
Millar, Erin 94, 142, 147, 159, 192
Miller, John 104
Moody's Investor Service 76
Montreal Gazette 126, 165, 176, 204-5
Moriarty, Wayne 128

Morneau, Bill 52, 102, 104
Morton, John 31
Moscrop, David 179
Mulroney, Brian 38, 89
Munro, Harold 129, 131-4
Murdoch, Rupert 49, 113, 153-4, 155
Murphy, Dan 127
Murphy, Rex 134-5
MySpace 154
Nanaimo Daily News 3, 63, 82-3
Nanaimo News Bulletin 63
Narwhal, The 124, 125, 127, 160, 163
National Ethnic Press and Media Council 145
National NewsMedia Council 127
National Post xiii-xiv, 7, 10, 16, 22, 36, 53, 54, 60, 71, 94, 100, 111, 113, 114, 115, 122, 124, 127, 134-6, 143, 145, 155, 160, 165, 171, 176, 186, 189, 191
native advertising 11, 55, 120-2
Netflix 23, 76, 152
New Media Investments 42, 51
New Republic, The 73
New York Post 45, 153
New York Times 12, 15, 120, 128, 155, 170
News Media Canada 19, 20, 23, 59, 64, 65t, 66-7, 74, 75, 92-3, 94, 100, 101-2, 145, 146, 157, 158, 159, 160, 161, 162, 164-5, 172, 176-7, 183, 191
News Media and Digital Platforms Mandatory Bargaining Code (Australia) 154, 180, 186, 191
Newspapers Canada 101
Niagara Falls Review 24
Nordicity 102
NordStar Capital 47, 158, 182, 202
North Shore News 91
Northumberland Today 24
Nott, Gerry 113
O'Donnell, Victoria 74
O'Hanlon, Martin 16, 60, 97, 149, 182
Observer, Vancouver 11, 123
Observer, National 127, 160, 163, 191
Olive, David 8-9
Olson, Geoff 113
Online News Act 186-9, 192, 195, 197, 205
Online Streaming Act 123, 157, 176, 178
Ontario Farmer 181
Ontario Labour Relations Board 16
Ontario Superior Court of Justice 96, 184
Orillia Packet & Times 24, 25, 79-82
Ormrod, Margaret 107-11, 139
O'Toole, Erin 165
Ottawa Citizen 5, 71, 111, 117, 122, 126, 173
Ottawa Journal 26, 35, 112
Ottawa Sun 5
Owen, Taylor 102-3
Pacific Press 90-1
Palley, Thomas 39
Parliamentary Budget Office 196-7
paywalls 49, 155
Pecker, David 98
Pecman, John 88, 91, 95
People's Party of Canada 18
Peterborough Examiner 24
Pew Research Center 130
Phillips, Rod 13
Poilievre, Pierre 104
Policy Options 69, 76
Porter, Michael 51
Postmedia Network 1-19, 21, 23-9, 39, 43, 47, 57, 60-1, 75, 76, 79-82, 83-5, 87, 91, 93-8, 101, 105-6, 108, 111, 137, 142, 147, 152, 160, 163, 164, 198, 201, 202; and bailouts 147-8, 181; and Betting Essentials 203; and Bill C-18 189, 205, 206; and Brunswick News 177-8; closures 149, 204; debt 3-4, 9, 45, 47, 75 , 153; and Facebook/Google 164-5, 172, 176-7, 186, 194-5; foreign ownership 6, 86, 142; layoffs 148-50, 204-5; native advertising 120-9; and oil industry 124-8; Parcel Services 203; partisanship

269

INDEX

111-19, 199-21; paywalls 155; profits 147, 153, 185, 202-3; and racism 129-34; and The Logic 192; and Torstar 8-9, 23-7, 47, 80-1, 82, 91, 95, 97, 136, 202; unionization 134-6
Potter, Andrew 56, 117, 145
Poynter Institute 10
Press Forward 160
PressProgress 11, 118, 126
propaganda ix, 11, 49, 71-4, 123-8, 132, 140, 162
Province, Vancouver 6, 12, 26, 90, 128, 131, 132-3
Public Advertiser 32
Public Policy Forum 20, 28, 53, 55-7, 61-2, 66-9, 72, 74, 94, 99, 102-3, 162-3, 179
Quebecor 7, 12, 38-9
Radler, David 33
RAND Corporation 177
Reader's Digest 36-7
Real Estate Weekly 91
Regina Leader-Post 108, 124, 204
Renzetti, Elizabeth 25
Research in Motion 201
Restrictive Trade Practices Commission 89-90, 169
Ricard, Gil 189-90
Robson, John 71
Rodriguez, Pablo 102, 144, 196
Rogers Communications 5, 18, 21, 39, 153
Royal Commission on Newspapers 35-6
Royal Commission on Publications 26, 35, 36, 38, 90, 109, 167
Royal Commission on the Press (UK) 32
Ryerson Review of Journalism 54, 135
Ryerson University 23, 64
SaltWire Network 149, 141, 149, 163, 164, 202
Saskatchewan Weekly Newspapers Association 193
Saskatchewan Roughriders 103
St. Catharines Standard 24
Scott, Ian 187-8

Selley, Chris 146
Senate report on news media 21, 39, 85-6, 167-8
Shapiro, Steven 12, 42, 43
Shaw Communications 21, 39,
Shaw, Rob 130
Simons, Paula 112, 198
Singh, Jagmeet 165
Skeel, David 41
Skok, David 143, 192
Smart, Stephen 132
Smith, Charlie 132
Smith, Danielle 71
Smythe, Dallas 33
Southam chain xiii-xiv, 4, 10, 34, 35, 36-9, 63, 71, 90-1, 111-2, 116
Special Measures for Journalism 181
Special Senate Committee on Mass Media 33-5, 169
Standard & Poor's 3
StarMetro 47, 140, 142
StarPhoenix, Saskatoon 108, 204
Statistics Canada 65
Sterling Newspapers 33
Stursberg, Richard 18-19, 20-1, 22, 66, 74, 152-3, 186
Subramaniam, Vanmala 135
Sullivan, Margaret 51
Sun Media 1, 2, 5, 7-8, 11, 12, 14, 21, 26, 27, 39, 42, 47, 51, 83, 84-5, 86, 87, 88, 91, 202
Supreme Court of Canada 87, 88, 89, 90, 91, 162, 169, 196
Talisman Energy 126
Taylor-Vaisey, Nick 144
TD bank 56
Tervita Corp. v. Canada 87-8
Tervita Industries 87-8
The Shattered Mirror 58-66, 74-5, 100
The Shattered Mirror Revisited 179, 186
The Tangled Garden 19, 152-3
The Uncertain Mirror 34-5, 58
The Vanishing Newspaper 48
think tanks 8, 20, 53, 55, 69, 73, 130, 17

Think Tanks and Civil Societies Program 69
Thomson, David 33
Thomson family 33, 39, 76, 167
Thomson, Kenneth 33
Thomson Newspapers 32, 34, 35, 90, 112
Thomson Reuters 33
Thomson, Roy 32-3
Times of London 155
Toronto Blue Jays 7
Toronto Life 7, 18
Toronto Sun 5-6, 118-9, 150, 171, 189
Torontoist 6, 10
Towhey, Mark 119
Transcontinental Media 91, 140
Tri-Cities News 154
Tri-Cities Now 154-5
Trinity International chain 37
Trudeau, Justin 1, 22, 67-8, 108, 111, 118-19, 143, 157, 160, 165
Trudeau, Pierre 35, 38
Trump, Donald 61, 98, 135, 194
Twitter 69, 107, 110-1, 112, 130-1, 134, 161, 185-6
Tyee, The 15, 80-2, 131, 160, 163
Ubyssey, The 129
Unifor 19, 26, 74, 75, 94, 100, 102, 115, 135-6, 145, 165, 179, 184, 186, 188
United Conservative Party 108, 117, 118
University of B.C. 128-9
University of Calgary 126
Vancouver Courier 83, 91, 113
Vancouver Foundation 102
Vancouver Sun 6, 12, 71, 90-1, 112, 126, 127, 128-34, 165, 173, 176
Vaughan, Adam 2-3
Vice 120, 132
Village Media 82, 160, 163
VerticalScope 4
von Finckenstein, Konrad 187
Walkom, Thomas 104
Wall Street Journal 153, 155, 173
Warkentin, Chris 181-2
Warner, Mark 136

Waugh, Kevin 193
Washington Post 104, 120
Welland Tribune 24
Westender, The 83
Western Standard 114
Willcocks, Paul 15, 147
Windsor Star 165, 176, 205
Winnipeg Free Press 26, 59, 83, 93, 100, 149, 159, 163, 164, 182, 186
Winnipeg Tribune 26, 35
Winseck, Dwayne 26-7, 65-6, 191-2
World War I 73
Wynne, Kathleen 2
Yale, Janet 156
Zuckerberg, Mark 150, 186